SMASHING
WordPress
2nd Edition

SMASHING
WordPress

BEYOND THE BLOG

2nd Edition

Thord Daniel Hedengren

WILEY

A John Wiley and Sons, Ltd, Publication

ISBN 978-1-119-99596-8

A catalogue record for this book is available from the British Library.

Set in 10/12 Minion Pro by Melanee Habig, Andrea Hornberger

Printed in U.S. by CJK

There are a lot of people involved in writing a book. Friends, family, lovers, pets, and not to mention patient editors — all have had some sort of influence since they have put up with me over this somewhat hectic period. I could dedicate this book to any one of them, or to lost family members that have meant a lot to what I am today.

I won't, though.

This book is dedicated to the wonderful WordPress community. Without them, no WordPress, and without WordPress, no book from yours truly. In fact, if it weren't for WordPress in particular, and open source in general, I probably would be doing something entirely different today.

You've got to love WordPress. I do.

Thord Daniel Hedengren

PUBLISHER'S ACKNOWLEDGMENTS

Some of the people who helped bring this book to market include the following:

Editorial and Production
VP Consumer and Technology Publishing Director: Michelle Leete
Associate Director - Book Content Management: Martin Tribe
Associate Publisher: Chris Webb
Publishing Assistant: Ellie Scott
Senior Project Editor: Sara Shlaer
Technical Editor: Thomas Myer
Editorial Manager: Jodi Jensen
Editorial Assistant: Leslie Saxman

Marketing
Associate Marketing Director: Louise Breinholt
Marketing Executive: Kate Parrett

Composition Services
Compositor: Indianapolis Composition Services
Proofreader: Linda Seifert
Indexer: Potomac Indexing, LLC

About the Author

Thord Daniel Hedengren is addicted to words, which led him to launch his first online newsletter in 1996. It all went downhill from there, with dozens of sites and a career as editor and freelancer in Sweden and abroad.

Going international all started with a blog post, which led to a book deal with Wiley, which in turn resulted in the *Smashing WordPress: Beyond the Blog* book and its follow-up *Smashing WordPress Themes: Making WordPress Beautiful,* and an even stronger voice in the WordPress community. You're holding the second edition of critically acclaimed *Smashing WordPress: Beyond the Blog* in your hands right now. This is really just the beginning since that word obsession keeps Thord spewing out new stuff.

When not obsessed with words, Thord and friends are building cool websites using WordPress at his web design firm Odd Alice. He also edits magazines and writes freelance articles for both print and web publications, in both Swedish and English. You can follow everything Thord on `http://tdh.me`.

Thord lives in the land of kings, Sweden.

Contents

CONTENTS

CONTENTS

Introduction

Writing a book about WordPress isn't the easiest endeavor one could tackle. When my editor and I first started discussing this project, the idea was to create something that not only acts as an introduction to web developers and professionals who want to utilize the power of the WordPress platform, but also to spark the minds to create things beyond the obvious.

Or go *beyond the blog*, as it were, which is also the subtitle of the book.

The whole point is really to prove that WordPress is so much more than a blog-publishing platform. You can build just about anything on it, and you should as well if you like fast deployments and great flexibility. It is not always the perfect choice, but it should definitely be considered at all times. The ease with which you can both build and use this platform is a selling point, just as is the living community that can back you up when you run into problems, and the fact that this is open source at its finest.

While I think that anyone with some knowledge of HTML, CSS and/or PHP can learn Word-Press from this book, it is important to remember that this is not a beginner's book. We start at a pretty high pace to make sure that even professionals get the fundamentals right. It is so easy to stick to familiar territory and do things the way they've always been done, instead of learning to do it right. And while having the basics in here will help anyone get started with WordPress, you really should know some HTML and CSS, and have at least a grasp of what PHP is and does. If those are alien concepts to you, I urge you to read up on them first.

That being said, *Smashing WordPress: Beyond the Blog* is indeed written with the idea that anyone with the suitable background can learn WordPress using this book, as well as take the platform beyond the obvious. When you're done with this book, you're ready to build just about anything using WordPress.

To convey this message, *Smashing WordPress: Beyond the Blog* is divided into four parts.

PART I: GETTING STARTED WITH WORDPRESS

The first part tackles the WordPress essentials, from install to what actually makes the system tick. It gives you everything you need to get started with WordPress, albeit at a slightly quicker pace than traditional beginner books. However, coverage doesn't stop there because there are a lot of things you should be aware of when getting started with WordPress, such as security measures, moving the install, and so on. The idea is to not only help beginners get started, but also enlighten current users to the problems and options available.

PART II: DESIGNING AND DEVELOPING WORDPRESS THEMES

WordPress themes are what the user sees; they are the skin of your site, and control how the content is presented. When you work with a site running on WordPress you'll spend a lot of time altering the theme files to get WordPress to do what you want. This second part not only introduces the technical features of themes, but gives you the required knowledge to start building your own.

PART III: USING PLUGINS WITH WORDPRESS

The third part is all about developing WordPress plugins. The fact that you can extend WordPress with plugins means that there really is no limit to what you can do with the platform. If you can make it work in PHP, you can run it in WordPress, more or less. This also means that this part of the book is highly conceptual, dealing with the basic communication between your plugin (which in fact is your PHP code) and WordPress itself.

PART IV: ADDITIONAL FEATURES AND FUNCTIONALITY

The fourth part is all about using WordPress for purposes other than blogging. Here you look at how WordPress can be used as a CMS to power more traditional websites, and you build a couple of sites from the ground up to prove that the platform can indeed do other things than just run bloggish websites. You also look at plugins that can help you take WordPress one step further. Sometimes you just don't need to develop things from scratch; someone else might have done it for you and released it for free.

This part is all about making you think differently about WordPress. The goal is to do away with all your thoughts about WordPress as only a blogging platform. This is a publishing platform, nothing else.

In this part you'll also find a selection of nifty tricks and techniques that you can use to further enhance your site. A lot of the things you might need in your WordPress projects have been done already, and this part gives you a little peek into that.

START THINKING, GET PUBLISHING!

Smashing WordPress: Beyond the Blog was written with the web developer in mind, but anyone who has fiddled a little bit with (X)HTML, CSS, PHP, and WordPress can benefit from this book. It is truly a breeze to get started in WordPress, and WordPress is all you'll need to begin rolling out your projects. After that you'll have to get your hands dirty, modifying or building themes and creating the necessary plugins to build the site you've envisioned.

In other words, start thinking and get publishing with WordPress, whether you're building the next Engadget or Huffington Post, or something entirely different.

GETTING STARTED WITH WORDPRESS

1

ANATOMY OF A WORDPRESS INSTALL

INSTALLING WORDPRESS IS neither difficult nor time consuming, and the instructions available on `word press.org` are more than adequate to guide you through the basic install. With the extra knowledge that you'll get in this chapter, however, you can supercharge your WordPress setup with themes and plugins. WordPress is the bricks and mortar of the site, but themes and plugins are what make it really tick.

Remember that "WordPress" in this book refers to the stand-alone version of WordPress available for free from wordpress.org. Don't get this mixed up with the multiuser version, called WordPress MU, which is touched upon briefly later, nor with Automattic's hosted version on wordpress.com. This book is all about the main version available from wordpress.org, and more specifically with version 3.1 in mind.

THE BASIC INSTALL

Installing WordPress is a breeze; the PR talk about a "five-minute install" is right on target. In fact, the only reason that the install should take that long is the fact that uploading the files sometimes takes time due to slow Internet connections or sluggish Web hosts. Most likely you'll already have a fair amount of experience with basic WordPress installs, so I'll be brief on this matter.

First, make sure that your system meets the minimum requirements. The most recent set of requirements can be found at http://wordpress.org/about/requirements/. If your host supports PHP 4.3 or higher, and runs MySQL 4.0 or higher, you'll be fine. However, you should make sure your host has mod_rewrite installed since that will be needed for prettier links.

There are two ways to install WordPress: the guided way and the manual way.

A third installation method is the one- click install offered by some Web hosts. One-click installs are briefly described later in this chapter.

THE GUIDED INSTALLATION METHOD

WordPress is one of the easiest open source publishing systems out there to get up and running. Just download the most recent version of WordPress (from http://wordpress.org/download/), extract the archive file (usually you're grabbing a zip file) and then upload the files within the wordpress folder to the place where you want to install WordPress, using FTP. For example, if you want to install WordPress on mysite.com, you just upload the files to the root folder for mysite.com.

Point your Web browser to the install directory (which would be http://mysite.com in our example) and provide the requested information, as shown in Figure 1-1. You'll need your database name, username, and password, and possibly also the address to the database server if you or your host have an external address.

Click Submit to get to the site setup, shown in Figure 1-2. On this screen, fill out the name of the site, the admin account credentials you would like, and so on. Make sure you use a working e-mail address and keep track of your password. After you have entered all the requested information, click the Install WordPress button and you're just about done. Log in and there you have it; WordPress is up and running!

The guided install does not provide options to make WordPress run in any language other than the default, English. If you want your installation to run in a language other than English, consult the manual install procedure detailed in the next section.

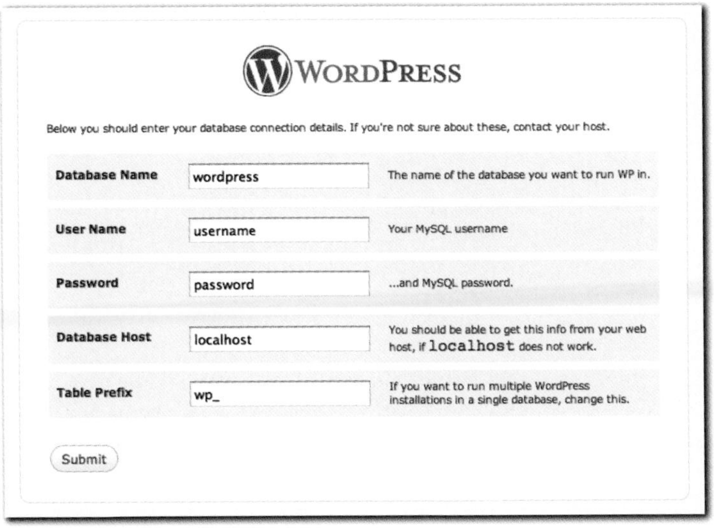

Figure 1-1: The install interface

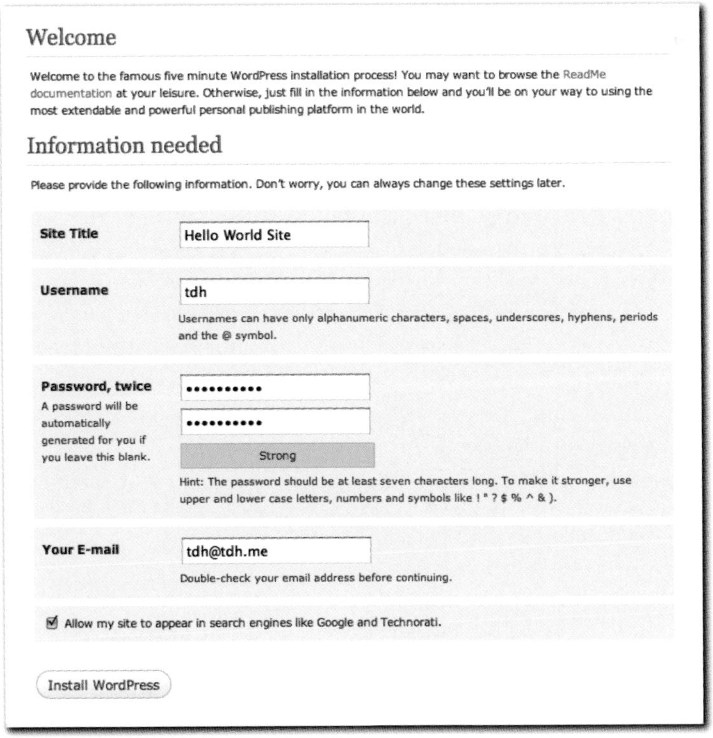

Figure 1-2: Fill out the details

THE MANUAL INSTALLATION METHOD

For a manual install, you'll need the following:

- The most recent version of WordPress (available from `http://wordpress.org/download/`)
- A MySQL database with a user who has write privileges (ask your host if you don't know how to set this up)
- Your favorite FTP program

To install, unzip your WordPress download and upload the contents of the wordpress folder to your destination of choice on your server. Then, open the wp-config-sample.php file and find the database parts where you fill out the database name, and the username and password with write privileges. This is what wp-config-sample.php looks like:

```
define('DB_NAME', 'putyourdbnamehere');     // The name of the  database
define('DB_USER', 'usernamehere');      // Your MySQL username
define('DB_PASSWORD', 'yourpasswordhere'); // ...and password
define('DB_HOST', 'localhost');     // 99% chance you won't need to change this value
```

Next, still in wp-config-sample.php, find the section that deals with Secret Keys. This part will start with commented information text titled "Authentication Unique Keys" followed by four lines (as of this writing) where you'll enter the Secret Keys. This is a security function to make your install more secure and less prone to hacking. You'll only need to add these keys once, and while they can be entered manually and be whatever you like, there is an online generator courtesy of wordpress.org that gives you random strings with each load. Just copy the link (`https://api.wordpress.org/secret-key/1.1/`) to the generator from your wp-config-sample.php file and open it in your favorite Web browser. You'll get a page containing code looking something like this:

```
define('AUTH_KEY',
'PSmO59sFXB*XDwQ!<uj)h=vv#Kle`)dBEOM:0oBzj`V(qd0.nP2|BT~T$a(;6-&!');
define('SECURE_AUTH_KEY',
'o>p3K{TD.tJoM74.Oy5?B@=dF_lcmlB6jm6D|gXnlJ#Z4K,M>E;[ +,22O?Lnarb');
define('LOGGED_IN_KEY',
'c}gR{389F*IG@/V+hg1 45J*H+9i_^HaF;$q(S[5Er[:DVOUjmS@(20E~t0-C*II');
define('NONCE_KEY',
'gz2D:n52|5wRvh)es:80O|O ufZL@C|G.-w/H-E*}K:ygp4wI*.QHO-mUV_PR|6M');
```

Copy the contents from the generator page and replace the following code in wp-config-sample.php with them:

```
define('AUTH_KEY', '');
define('SECURE_AUTH_KEY', '');
define('LOGGED_IN_KEY', '');
define('NONCE_KEY', '');
```

By replacing the code with the lines from the generated page, you've made your install a little bit more secure from those nasty hackers.

The last thing you may want to change in wp-config-sample.php is the language. WordPress is in English (US English to be exact) by default. To change the language, you'll need to upload a language file to your wp-content/language/ folder. The language files are in .mo format; you can find most of them at `http://codex.wordpress.org/WordPress_in_Your_Language`. You also need to alter the following little snippet in wp-config-sample.php to let WordPress know what language you want it to be in:

```
define ('WPLANG', '');
```

You need to add the language code: this is the same as the language file, without the file extension. So if you want your install in Swedish (the language of kings), you'd download the sv_SE.mo file, upload it to wp-content/languages/, and then pass the language to the WPLANG function, like this:

```
define ('WPLANG', 'sv_SE');
```

This won't necessarily make the themes or plugins you use display in your language of choice, but WordPress and its core functionality will, as will any code that supports it. (You'll learn about localization of themes and plugins in Chapter 6.)

And that's it! Rename wp-config-sample.php to wp-config.php, and point your Web browser to your install location. You should see a link that initiates the install procedure, where you'll fill in the blog title, the admin user's e-mail address, and choose whether or not the blog should be open to search engines for indexing (most likely this will be the case, but if you want to fiddle with it first, then disable it; you can enable it in the settings later). After this, you'll get an admin username and a random password (save that!) and hopefully a success message along with a link to the blog.

Not very complicated, right?

USING AN EXTERNAL DATABASE SERVER

One of the most common causes of a failed WordPress install is that the MySQL database is located on a separate server. If you're getting database connection errors, and you're quite sure that both the username and password for the database user are correct, along with the full write capabilities, then this is most likely the problem.

To fix this, just find this code snippet in wp-config.php (or wp-config-sample.php if you haven't renamed it yet) and change localhost to your database server:

```
define('DB_HOST', 'localhost');
```

What the MySQL server may be called depends on your host. It may be `mysql67.thesuper host.com`, or something entirely different. Just swap localhost with this, and try running the install script again.

Naturally, if you can't find your database server address you should contact your Web host and ask them for details.

OTHER DATABASE SETTINGS

You may want to consider some more database options before installing WordPress. (Probably not, but still, they warrant mention.)

First, you may want to change the database character set and collation. These options tell WordPress what character language the database is in, and it should just about always be UTF-8. This is also the default setting in wp-config-sample.php, hence you won't need to fiddle with it unless you have a special need to do so. If you do, however, this is what you're looking for:

```
define('DB_CHARSET', 'utf8');
```

That's the character set, with UTF-8 (obviously spelled out as `utf8` in code) by default. Most likely you won't (nor should you) change this, but there might be situations when you need to so keep this in mind for reference.

The collation, which is basically the sort order of the character set that WordPress will apply to the MySQL database in the install phase, can be changed in this line:

```
define('DB_COLLATE', );
```

It is empty here, which means it will pass the character set in `DB_CHARSET` as the collation. By default, that is UTF-8, but if you need this to be something specific you can add it like this:

```
define('DB_COLLATE', 'character_set_of_choice');
```

A FEW WORDS ON INSTALLERS

Some Web hosts offer installers that will get your WordPress install up and running with just a click from within the Web host admin interface. The most popular of these one-click installers is probably Fantastico. At first, a single-click install sounds like a really good idea, since you won't have to fiddle with config files or anything; it'll just slap the blog up there and you can get started.

However, take a moment to do some research before going down this route. The most important aspect to consider is what version of WordPress the installer is actually setting up. Old versions shouldn't be allowed because they are outdated and, at worst, a security hazard. After all, with every WordPress release a lot of security holes are jammed shut, so it is not just about releasing funky new features for your favorite blogging platform.

Installers like Fantastico are great and can save time if they do install the latest version. If you find one that does use the latest version, you should still do a little investigating to make sure other users haven't reported any serious problems. If the coast is clear and you really don't want to do the five-minute manual install, then by all means go for it.

After having installed WordPress using an installer you should use the built-in upgrade feature, or perform upgrades manually using FTP should your host not support the automatic one. Make sure the installer doesn't do something strange with the install that stops you from doing this: you don't want to be tied to the installer script for updates.

MOVING THE WORDPRESS INSTALL TO A DIFFERENT DIRECTORY

Sometimes you want to put your WordPress install in its own folder. This will help avoid clutter in your Web hosting environment by removing all those WordPress files and folders from the root of your domain, and make it easier to manage your various Web endeavors. Suppose you want to add other Web software installs; you may have a hard time finding the files you need if they're all mixed in together (although it helps that everything WordPress at this level is named wp-something). It just gets messy if you want to do anything other than just use WordPress.

Installing to a subfolder is the same as installing to the root of a domain, so I won't go into that. The idea is to have the WordPress install in a subfolder, but have the blog displaying as if it were in the root folder, while keeping the root folder on the server clean. You can either install WordPress to the subfolder directly, or install it to the root folder and then move the files to a subfolder. How you decide to tackle it is up to you; both ways are easy.

The following instructions assume you have already installed WordPress in your root folder and now want to move it to a subfolder. For this example, suppose you have WordPress installed in the root folder (domain.com), and want it to be in a subfolder called wpsystem instead while keeping the actual site in root. That means that when people visit domain.com they'll see your WordPress site, but when you log in and manage it you'll do that within the wpsystem folder (or `domain.com/wpsystem/wp-admin/`, to be precise).

You should set up permalinks before doing this, since you'll want them to work regardless of whether you use a subfolder or not. The permalink options, shown in Figure 1-3, are found under Settings → Permalinks.

To move your WordPress install to the new directory, first create the wpsystem folder. Then, go to the General Settings page and change the WordPress address URL field to `http://domain.com/wpsystem` to reflect your new folder, and the Blog address URL field to `http://domain.com`, where you want your site to be. Next, click the Update button and move all the WordPress files to their new directory at `http://domain.com/wpsystem`, except for the index.php and .htaccess files, which should be where you want your site to be (`http://domain.com`).

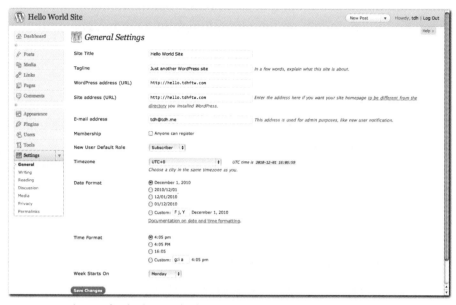

Figure 1-3: General Settings, found under General in the Settings part of the admin interface

When the files have been moved, open index.php and locate this code snippet:

```
require('./wp-blog-header.php');
```

And replace it with this code snippet:

```
require('./wpsystem/wp-blog-header.php');
```

As you can see, the code now points to the wpsystem folder instead, and to the wp-blog-header.php file.

Log in to the WordPress admin interface (which is now on `domain.com/wpsystem/ wp-admin/`) and update the permalinks, and there you have it.

HACKING THE DATABASE

Most of the time you needn't worry about the database; WordPress will take care of it for you. There are database changes between versions sometimes, but program updates will take care of everything, and other than keeping a backup of your content the database can be left to live its own life.

That being said, if something goes wrong you may need to make some edits in the database to fix it. Common issues are password resets, weird URLs as a result of a failed move, domain name changes, and widget-related issues.

A word of caution: Before moving on, you should remember that making alterations in the database is serious stuff. There are no undos here; what is deleted is deleted for good. Even if you know what you're doing you should always make a fresh backup before altering anything at all. If you don't know your way around a MySQL database and PhpMyAdmin, don't mess with the database. You will break things.

LEARNING WHERE EVERYTHING IS

Finding your way in the WordPress database is pretty easy. It consists of eleven tables, which in turn are full of content. Just browsing the database should answer most of your questions, and any edits can be made on the spot if you know what you're after. Naturally, there is a full database description in the documentation (`http://codex.wordpress.org/Database_Description`) and you should consult that whenever you need to find something.

The eleven main tables are

- wp_comment: meta data for comments
- wp_comments: contains all comments
- wp_links: contains added links and links data
- wp_options: the blog options
- wp_postmeta: metadata for the posts
- wp_posts: the actual posts
- wp_terms: categories and tags
- wp_term_relationships: associates categories and tags with posts
- wp_term_taxonomy: descriptions for categories and tags
- wp_usermeta: user metadata
- wp_users: the actual users

All these tables are important, of course, but if you need to fix or change something directly in the database, chances are that it is in wp_options (for blog settings, like URLs and such), wp_posts (for mass editing of your blog posts), or wp_users (for password resets and such).

FIXING ISSUES BY HACKING THE DATABASE

One of the more common issues with WordPress upgrades is the widgets going crazy, sometimes outputting only a blank page on your blog. While this seems to be a lot less common in later versions of WordPress, the upgrade instructions still state that you should disable all plugins and revert to the default theme. If you follow this advice, most likely you'll never get that blank page.

However, should you get a blank page, it is probably a widget issue. A possible solution is to clean out the widgets in the database; they are hiding in the wp_options table. Exactly what you need to do and what the various widgets are called depends on what plugins you have, so tread carefully. Most likely the data is named in a way that seems logical compared to the plugins you use, and with that in mind you should be able to find what you're looking for. It may sound a bit hazardous, but it is worth giving it a go should you encounter a blank screen on your blog after an upgrade. If need help, the support forums on wordpress.org are a good resource.

Another issue you may want to resolve in the database is changing or resetting a password for a user. You can't actually retrieve the password from the database since it is encrypted and all you'll see is gibberish, but you can change it to something else. Just remember that passwords need the MD5 treatment, which can be done through PhpMyAdmin or just about any MySQL managing tool you may use. Basically, what you do is type the new password in plain text, and choose MD5 for that particular field. You'll end up with a new line of gibberish, which actually says what you typed in the first place. Again, if this sounds scary to you, don't do it without learning more first!

Finally, you may want to mass edit your posts. Maybe you've got a new domain and want to change the source for all images you've used over the years, from `olddomain.com/wp-content/image.jpg` to `newdomain.com/wp-content/image.jpg`, for example. There are plugins that will help you with this, so you should probably check those out first. If you're comfortable with the database though, you can run a SQL query to search for all these elements and replace them with the new ones. It could be something like this:

```
UPDATE wp_posts SET post_content = REPLACE (
  post_content,
  'olddomain.com/wp-content/',
  'newdomain.com/wp-content/');
```

That code would search the wp_posts table for any mention of `olddomain.com/wp-content/` and replace it with `newdomain.com/wp-content/`. That in turn would fix all the image links in the example. Nifty little SQL queries for batch editing can come in handy, but remember: there are no undos here and what's done is done, so make sure you've made a backup of the database before even considering doing these things.

BACKING UP

Anyone who has lost data in a hard drive crash or similar event knows the importance of backing up, and it goes without saying that this applies to your online content as well. Backing up WordPress is actually a two-step process, since your blog consists of both a database (with all the content) and static files (image uploads and other attachments). Then you have your theme, your plugins, and so on, that you may or may not have altered but still don't want to lose since doing so would mean that you would have to collate them all over again. In fact, with the inclusion of automatic updates within the admin interface in WordPress (a great feature in itself), backing up these things has become even more important.

The only elements you can lose without causing too much trouble is the core WordPress files. These you can always download again, although you may want to keep a copy of wp-config. php somewhere safe.

Several options are available for your database backup needs. The most obvious one would be to use a Web interface like PhpMyAdmin and just download a compressed archive containing the data. However, you need to remember to do this on a regular basis, and that may be a problem. Also, PhpMyAdmin and similar database management interfaces aren't exactly the most user-friendly solutions out there, and most of us would rather not mess around with the database more than we truly have to.

Enter the wonderful world of WordPress plugins, specifically one called wp-db-backup. This plugin, which is featured in Chapter 9 in full, will let you set up various rules for database backups, and have your plugins stored on a server, e-mailed to you, or otherwise backed up, at regular intervals.

That's the database content; now for the static files. This part is very simple: just keep backing up the wp-content folder. This folder contains all your uploads (images, videos, and other files that are attachments to your blog posts) along with your themes and plugins. In fact, it is the only part in the WordPress install that you should have been fiddling with, not counting the wp-config.php file, the .htaccess file, and possibly the index.php file in the root folder. Backing up wp-content will save all your static files, themes, plugins, and so on, as long as you haven't set up any custom settings that store data outside it.

So how can you back up wp-content? Unfortunately, the simplest backup method, which of course is downloading it using an FTP program, relies on you remembering to do so. Some Web hosts have nifty little built-in scripts that can send backups to external storage places, such as Amazon S3 or any FTP server, really. This is a cheap way to make sure your static data is safe, so you should really look into it and not just rely on remembering to make an FTP download yourself. In fact, these built-in solutions often manage databases as well, so you can set up a backup of that as well. Better safe than sorry, after all.

The last stand, and final resort should the worst happen to your install, is the Web host's own backup solution. There is no way anyone can convince me to trust that my Web host, no matter how good they may be, will solve any matter concerning data loss. Some are truly doing what they claim, which may be hourly backups, RAID disks, and other fancy stuff, but even the most well thought out solution can malfunction or backfire. Most hosts have some automatic backup solution in place, but what happens if the whole datacenter is out for some reason, or there's a power outage? You may not think that this could happen today, but if Google can go offline, so can your Web host.

In other words, make sure you have your very own backup solution in place. Hopefully you'll never have to use it, but if you do, you'll be happy you thought it through from the start.

SWITCHING HOSTS

Sometimes you need to switch Web hosts. Maybe you've outgrown the host and need more power for your site (congratulations!), or perhaps the quality of service has declined. Whatever the reason, it is not very uncommon that you want to move your site from one host to another. This involves everything from pointing domains to actually moving the files for your site, not to mention the database. I just cover the WordPress parts of the move here, so if you need help moving your domain, e-mail, and stuff like that, by all means contact your new host, who should be able to give you the help you need.

There are several ways of moving to a new server. My preferred method is using the Export/ Import functionality found under Tools in WordPress admin.

USING THE EXPORT AND IMPORT TOOLS

Previously there were a few exporters and importers there, but these have been moved to plugins so you might be prompted to download and install a plugin. Go ahead and do that if necessary. Also, before moving, make sure your WordPress install is up to date. Then, go to Tools and choose to export the content, as shown in Figure 1-4. You'll get a file containing the data.

Figure 1-4: Exporting data

Next, install WordPress on your new server. Any decent Web host will have alternate URLs to access your content on the server online, without actually having to have your domain pointing to it. When you've got a running WordPress install, delete the automatic pages and posts since these won't be overwritten. You want the install to be clean.

Next, download the wp-content folder from your old server, and upload it to your new one. Now you've got all your images, plugins, themes, and so forth in place. There is a built-in option in the post importer that will try and download the images from your posts to your new server, but it fails more often than not, so it is better to manage the static files in wp-content manually using your favorite FTP program.

Finally, you're ready to import the exported file from your old server. Go to Tools (see Figure 1-5) and go through the import wizard, taking care that your exported file from the old server is up to date. Import it, let the script chew through the content, and then you're all done! Verify that everything is working properly, give yourself a pat on the back, and then redirect your domain to your new server. You may have to edit your new blog's settings, since it may have taken URLs from the Web host's internal system, so change them to correspond with your blog's domain name. While waiting for the domain to be pointed to your new server the blog will break, of course, but then again your old one is still working. You may want to close comments on it though, since those will be "lost" when the visitor is suddenly pointed to the new server with your new WordPress install, which is based on the content of your old one at the point when you exported the file.

Figure 1-5: WordPress can import from a number of systems, but you want WordPress this time since that's what you exported from

WHEN EXPORT/IMPORT WON'T WORK

Unfortunately, there are times when the Export/Import way won't work — usually because there is just too much content for PHP to parse in the import. This is possibly due to your host's server settings, and is only a problem if you have a big blog.

If this is the case, you'll have to do things a little bit differently. Ideally, you can re-create your environment identically on your new server, with the same database name, and the same username and password to manage it. If you can do this, moving will be a breeze. All you have to do is get a dump from the MySQL database using your favorite MySQL admin tool, and then import it into the new one. This probably means using PhpMyAdmin and the backup instructions from the WordPress Codex (found at `http://codex.wordpress.org/Backing_Up_Your_Database`). Here's how you do it:

1. Log in to PhpMyAdmin and select the database you want to back up.
2. Click the Export tab (shown in Figure 1-6) in the top menu.

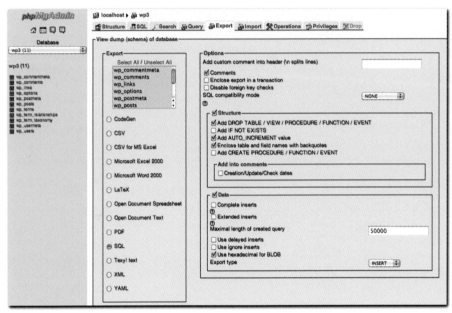

Figure 1-6: PhpMyAdmin is a lot more daunting than WordPress, but it gets the job done

3. On the left side, make sure all the necessary tables are marked (the Select All link will help). This would be all of them, unless you have other stuff in the same database as well.
4. On the right side, tick the Structure checkbox, then select Add DROP TABLE, Add AUTO_INCREMENT value, and Enclose table and field names with backquotes. Also tick the Data checkbox, but leave the choices within unchecked.
5. Scroll down and tick Save as file and pick the kind of file you want to download, probably a zipped one.
6. Click the Go button. This will download the database, which you will import on your new server.
7. Importing a dump in PhpMyAdmin is even easier. Make sure you have created a database with the same name and username as well as password as you had on your previous server. This means you won't have to alter the wp-config.php file.

8. Import the dump to the new database by logging in with your favorite MySQL manager. If this is PhpMyAdmin, just select the database and choose the Import tab (sits next to the Export one) at the top. Use the importer to find your downloaded dump, and import it.

9. Finally, download your full WordPress install from your old server, and upload it in an identical manner to your new one. Again, give it a spin using your Web host's temporary addresses and make sure that everything seems to be working. Point the domain to the new server, and when it resolves everything should be running smoothly.

However, you may not be able to re-create the environment in exactly the same way. If this is the case, just alter wp-config.php accordingly; most likely it is the database name, username and password, as well as possibly the need for an external database server, that you'll have to edit.

Moving WordPress from one server to another may seem scary at first, but it isn't as bad as it once was. Sure, if you've got a big blog and aren't comfortable doing stuff in database admin interfaces like PhpMyAdmin, then this may be a bit much. Get help, or give it a go yourself. Just make sure that you have all the backups you could possibly need, and don't mess things up on your old (current) server, but rather on the new one. After all, you can always just create a new database and WordPress install there and give it another go.

HOW TO MAKE YOUR WORDPRESS INSTALL MORE SECURE

There are a few simple things you can do to make your WordPress install more secure, and a few that are pretty much hardcore. The first and foremost task, however, is to keep WordPress up to date. Each new version removes a bunch of security holes, bugs, and other possible exploits that can make your install vulnerable, and not updating regularly means you won't get these fixes.

> *You should also make sure that you've got your Secret Keys set in the wp-config.php file. Those make the install more secure. See the installation process earlier in this chapter for more on this. Usually they're set, but if you used an installer they might not be, so it doesn't hurt to check in wp-config.php and add them if needed.*

This brings us to the first tip. Check your theme's header.php file to see if the following code is there (it almost always is):

```php
<?php add_action('wp_head', 'wp_generator'); ?>
```

Then remove it! This line outputs the version of WordPress you're using, and while that may be a nice thing for bots and spiders looking for statistics, it's not worth the additional risk it brings. After all, if a certain version is known to have an open security hole, and people are looking for installs of that version to exploit, why make it easier on them and tell them outright?

USERS AND PASSWORDS

The first thing I do after having installed WordPress is to create a new user with admin privileges, and log in with that user instead of the default "admin" user. Why? Because everyone knows that if there is a user named admin, then that account has full admin capabilities. So if you wanted to hack your way into a WordPress install, you'd start by looking for the admin user to try to brute force a login. Once you're in via this method, you can do anything you want. So it's worth getting rid of the admin user, after you have logged in for the first time and created a proper account, because it has fulfilled its purpose.

That being said, deleting the admin user won't guarantee that hackers won't find another user to build their attempts on. If you have user archives on your blog, those will give you away. One solution would be to not display these, nor any links to an author page (other than ones you've created outside of WordPress's own functionality), but what do you do if you feel you need them?

The solution is to be sparse with account credentials. There is no need to have an administrator account for writing or editing posts and pages; an editor's credentials are more than enough. Granted, should an account with editor status be hacked then it will be bad for your site since the editor can do a lot of things, but at least it is not an administrator account and that will keep the worst things at bay. And besides, you keep backups, right?

Passwords are another obvious security risk. You've probably been told to use a strong password, to make it long and to use letters, numbers, special characters, and so on. Do that: the more complicated the password is, the harder will it be to crack.

SERVER-SIDE SECURITY STEPS

The MySQL user for your WordPress database, which incidentally shouldn't be shared with any other system, doesn't actually need all write privileges. In fact, you don't need to be able to lock tables, index, create temporary tables, references, or create routines. In other words, you can limit the capabilities somewhat to make the system more secure.

Some people will also recommend that you add extra logins using Apache's .htaccess. I don't do that myself since these login forms are annoying. Besides, there are plugins that can do the job better (see Chapter 9 for more).

One step you may want to take is make sure that there is an empty index.php or index.html file in every folder that doesn't have an index file. This is usually the case by default in WordPress, but it doesn't hurt to check. What this does is make it impossible to browse the folders directly, something that some Web hosts support.

Another server-side issue is forcing SSL encryption when logging in to the WordPress admin. This means that the traffic sent when you're doing your thing in the admin interface will be a lot harder to sniff out for potential bad guys. It's pretty easy to force SSL; just add this code snippet to your wp-config.php file, above the "That's all, stop editing! Happy blogging" comment:

```
define('FORCE_SSL_ADMIN', true);
```

SSL won't work without support from your host. Some Web hosts give you all you need to start this service from within their admin interface, but others will have to activate it for you, and may even charge you for it.

LOOKING AHEAD

It doesn't matter if this is your first foray into the wonderful world of WordPress, or if you're an experienced user and developer. The important thing is that you have the basic installation figured out, have made it secure, and understand the publishing beast that is WordPress. From here on, you'll start building sites and creating plugins to achieve your goals.

Next up is diving into what makes WordPress tick. That means you'll get to play with the loop, start looking at themes and plugins, and activate that idea machine in the back of the head that comes up with all those cool adaptations. The brilliance of WordPress is that it is so flexible and that you can build so many things with it; just thinking about the possibilities will undoubtedly inspire you.

If you have a WordPress install to play with (preferably something that isn't too public, since you may break something), get your sandbox set up and get ready to dive into the WordPress syntax.

2

THE WORDPRESS SYNTAX

NOW THAT YOU'VE got your Word-Press install set up, it's time to do something with it. This chapter is all about getting to know more about WordPress. It doesn't go into depth on every file in the system, but rather serves an introduction to how WordPress outputs content. You learn about the important template tags as well as conditional tags, and how you can control their output and actions by passing parameters. You also take a look at themes and what they consist of, to help you further grasp how WordPress sites are built.

Let's get started.

WORDPRESS AND PHP

From here on, it will help if you know a little bit about PHP, as well as (X)HTML and CSS. If these are alien concepts to you, be sure to read up on them at least a bit. A good place to start is W3Schools (`http://www.w3schools.com/`) and Zend's PHP 101 course (`http://devzone.zend.com/article/627`). You don't need to be an expert, but a little knowledge is definitely needed.

WordPress is written in PHP, a popular scripting language offering developers the possibility to build just about anything. If you're even the least bit knowledgeable in PHP you'll quickly find your way around WordPress and the various functions it offers on the plugin and theme development end of things. That being said, you don't need any prior PHP experience to do funky stuff with WordPress. Granted, you won't be able to create WordPress plugins without knowing PHP, but you can certainly make things happen with the built-in template tags used in themes, and that will get you a long way. These template and conditional tags help the developer do things with WordPress, without having to write brand new functions for everything.

Does this sound like Greek to you? Don't worry, even if you've never written a *Hello World!* PHP script you'll be able to build just about anything content-driven with WordPress before you're done with this book.

THE WORDPRESS CODEX

The WordPress Codex (see Figure 2-1), which is the manual in wiki form found on `http://codex.wordpress.org`, will be very helpful when you start working with the code. You should become familiar with it and add a bookmark to the main page. Whenever you branch out from the examples in the coming chapters, or when you want to know more about a concept, the Codex is where you'll find the information needed to keep moving. While the Codex contains basic information and tutorials, you'll often find yourself returning to a few reference listings, such as the template tags (`http://codex.wordpress.org/Template_Tags/`), which are explained shortly, and the function reference (`http://codex.wordpress.org/Function_Reference`) for your more advanced needs.

ABOUT THE WORDPRESS CORE

Any good content management system (CMS) will keep its core files separate from other files so that you don't ruin the code that makes the system work, and WordPress is no exception. For WordPress, the core refers to the internal files that make WordPress work. These are the parts of WordPress that you should never touch, as any update to the platform will overwrite your changes. Messing around with WordPress core files can also break theme and plugin functionality, as well as open up your install for malicious use from outsiders. In short, don't touch the WordPress core. The only core file you should ever touch is wp-config.php (see Chapter 1), which contains the necessary details for your install.

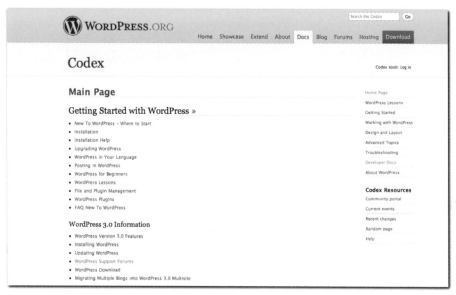

Figure 2-1: You'd better get used to browsing the WordPress Codex

Outside of the core is the wp-content folder, where you'll drop themes as well as plugins and uploaded files. All these things work on top of WordPress, so there's no risk of actually ruining the actual system files (unless you've installed malicious code, but that's a completely different matter) when you develop a site. In fact, the whole idea is that the only time you're editing or even doing anything outside of the wp-content folder is when you're installing the system, and possibly when moving the install files to a different folder. Naturally, there is some cool stuff that requires editing the .htaccess file, and you'll come across plugins that want you to do things outside of wp-content. That's fine of course, although you should be a bit cautious. In short, whenever you're told to edit a file outside of wp-content, you should beware. Creating new files is one thing, editing existing files is a no-no, wp-config.php and .htaccess excluded.

The whole point, however, is that the WordPress core is untouchable. Don't mess with it unless you really need to, and if you do, you should rethink and rethink again since the chances are there's a better solution. Hacking the core is bad, and that's why the *wp-content*-based theme and plugin structure is so good.

THEMES AND TEMPLATE FILES

To put it simply, a *theme* is a skin for your blog. You can choose from among different themes to have WordPress display your content in different designs, as shown by Figures 2-2 and 2-3, which display the same post using two different themes.

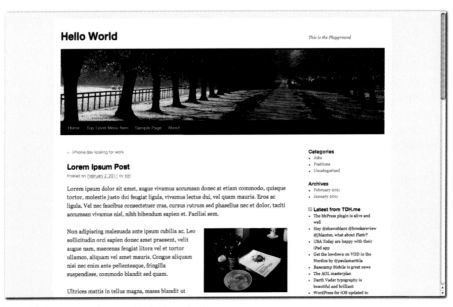

Figure 2-2: This screenshot shows a dummy post using the Twenty Ten theme

Figure 2-3: The same post, but viewed in the Notes Blog theme

You can use a really basic theme that simply outputs the content in the default presentation scheme, or you can completely alter the way your site's content is displayed, giving it whatever presentation you like.

A theme must always contain a stylesheet file called style.css. This file holds your basic style, the theme name, and data. In addition to the stylesheet, you'll have a bunch of PHP files, some absolutely necessary and some just good practice to make life easier on you or to make interesting stuff happen. These PHP files are called *template files*. You'll find index.php, which will be the main file for listings and search results, and is the fallback file for situations where there is no other template file available. Other common template files include sidebar.php, which holds the sidebar content, comments.php for comment functionality, and header.php and footer.php files for your site's header and footer, respectively. You may also have a single.php for single post view, and a page.php for static WordPress pages, and maybe a dedicated template file for search results (search.php), along with your category listings in category.php, and so on. Add any number of page templates that you can apply to WordPress pages, and you get a tiny little glimpse of how versatile WordPress is.

With your template files, and the WordPress functions as well as plugins and traditional PHP code, you can make your site behave in just about any way imaginable. Don't want the commenting capability enabled? Just remove the code! Maybe you want a specific product page to look completely different? Then create a page template and style it any way you like. It goes on and on, and later in the book you'll see how to build sites that are nothing at all like the common blog.

Just to make things a little more complicated, you can have even more functionality in your themes. The functions.php file can provide plugin-like features to your theme, and just about any template file can contain PHP code that does things beyond WordPress. We haven't even gotten started on widgets yet, which are areas where you can drop elements from within the admin interface. There is also the option to keep the loop, which is the code that outputs the main content in your theme, separate from your other template files using loop.php and similar. The loop is covered in-depth in Chapter 3.

Figure 2-4 shows the Manage Themes page in the WordPress admin interface. From this page, you can change your theme with a single click, or get new themes from the wordpress.org theme repository.

The best way to learn about themes is to use them. Install a theme on a test blog, play around, and then take a look at the files it consists of. Don't bother with images, and forget about the stylesheet as well (it is just a design), but do take a look at index.php and both header.php and footer.php to understand the way themes are built. It's not very complicated: first you load header.php, then whatever main template file is used (like index.php, single.php, or something else), possibly a sidebar.php file, and then footer.php.

Figure 2-4: The WordPress admin interface makes theme management easy

You'll play with themes later, but for now all you need to know is that it's in the theme's template files that the magic happens. There you'll find the code that outputs the content you've posted using WordPress, and while various themes may look and behave differently, they are just displaying the same thing in different ways thanks to the template files.

USING THE TEMPLATE TAGS

Although WordPress is written in PHP, it is in fact a framework in itself. You can use PHP to do stuff with your WordPress theme or plugin, but most of the functionality is managed with template tags. If you open a theme file (just about any file with the extension .php, like index. php or single.php) you'll find a lot of PHP-like functions, such as this one, for example:

```
<?php bloginfo('name'); ?>
```

That is a template tag, and it outputs the blog's name. The PHP part, which consists of `<?php` at first, and `; ?>` at the end, tells WordPress to process whatever's inside it, and in this case it is the template tag `bloginfo()`. Inside the parentheses you'll find the parameter, passed inside the quotation marks. In other words, `'name'` is the parameter above (which would output your blog's name).

You'll be using `bloginfo()` a lot in your themes, for example for finding the theme's directory. For example, the following code outputs an image called smashing.gif in a theme file,:

```
<img src="<?php bloginfo('template_directory'); ?>/smashing.gif" />
```

You'll recognize the img HTML tag. The bloginfo() template tag has another parameter here, template_directory. This outputs the path to the theme's folder, called template_directory instead of theme directory just to make things a little more complicated. And then you just add the smashing.gif file name to complete the path, and you've got a potentially working image path in your theme. Of course, you would need the image in the theme folder as well.

So template tags are basically PHP functions that can handle parameters to do different things. Some have default values, others don't, and some have more settings for you to play with than others. Most of them will work anywhere in your WordPress theme files, but some need to be within the loop. (The loop is basically the code that outputs the content, like posts or pages. Loops are examined in the next chapter.)

You'll find a complete listing of template tags in the Codex at http://codex.wordpress.org/Template_Tags/. Consult it whenever you need to do something out of the ordinary within your themes, or when you want to alter things in an existing theme. Each template tag is described, along with usage and sample code to help you understand it. This is the beauty of WordPress: you can actually copy and paste your way to a different result without knowing any PHP at all.

The Include TagsThere are a couple of template tags that you'll find in just about any theme template file. The *include tags* are basically PHP include functions used to output the content of the necessary files within your theme. In other words, it is just a way to make it a bit easier to grab that header, footer, and sidebar:

```php
<?php get_header(); ?>
<?php get_footer(); ?>
<?php get_sidebar(); ?>
```

The include tags differ from other template tags in that what you're doing is including other files, rather than adding a specific type of functionality or element. In other words, the include tags include the template files which contain the template tags.

You'll find them in your theme's index.php file, for instance, and they automatically include header.php, footer.php, and sidebar.php, respectively, where the tags are placed. The first two won't take any parameters, but get_sidebar() actually supports alternate sidebars by adding a string to the tag, like this:

```php
<?php get_sidebar('left'); ?>
```

This would include sidebar-left.php rather than the default sidebar.php, so you'd need to create that file of course.

You might also find the get_template_part() include tag, fetching the loop from its own template file, like so:

```php
<?php get_template_part('loop', 'index'); ?>
```

27

The first parameter, `loop`, tells WordPress that it is supposed to get a loop template. The second parameter tells WordPress to look for a loop template called loop-index.php. If the second parameter had been `page` instead of `index`, WordPress would have looked for loop-page.php instead. Should loop-index.php not be found, WordPress will default to loop. php. We'll dig into this in Chapter 3.

Should you want to include other files such as an alternate header, for example, you can use this nifty little PHP snippet:

```
<?php include (TEMPLATEPATH . '/altheader.php'); ?>
```

That is a traditional PHP include with `TEMPLATEPATH` that shows PHP where to look for the file, which is your theme folder. This is what the other include template tags do as well: they look in the theme folder for their respective files. This example tells WordPress to include altheader.php wherever the PHP code snippet is put. You can just as easily include something else this way, so it is very handy.

Finally, there's an include tag for the comments, which any good theme has in comments.php. Should there be no comments.php file, WordPress will include one from wp-includes/ theme-compat/comments.php instead, which is a fallback file that the system provides. Just put the `comments_template()` tag where you want comment functionality, and remove it where you don't think you need it:

```
<?php comments_template(); ?>
```

Note that you can't pass parameters to `comments_template()`.

PASSING MULTIPLE PARAMETERS TO A TEMPLATE TAG

Outputting content with template tags is easy enough. Some won't take parameters at all, and others, like `bloginfo()`, will just take one. Others, however, will take several parameters.

Two really useful template tags for bloggers are `edit_post_link()` and `edit_comment_link()`. They basically do the same thing, which is to add an edit link to posts or comments so that you (when logged in as a user having the necessary credentials) can fix errors quickly by clicking the edit link: this will take you to the admin interface where you can correct your error or censor that particularly nasty (but most likely valid) comment.

To use these tags, put them in your theme's file along with the posts/comments. Both tags work the same way. The tags need to be within the loop, which is discussed in the next chapter, but for now all you need to know that `edit_post_link()` goes with the code that outputs the posts, and similarly `edit_comment_link()` goes with the code that outputs the comments.

For example, this is how `edit_post_link()` looks when passing its default parameters:

```php
<?php edit_post_link(); ?>
```

If you put that code in your theme, you'll get a link that says "Edit This" wherever you put the code, and that's it. Suppose you want this link to show up on its own row, say "Admin" before the actual link, and say "Edit this post" rather than the "Edit This" default. Simple — just use this instead:

```php
<?php edit_post_link('Edit this post', '<p>Admin: ','</p>'); ?>
```

As you can see, `edit_post_link()` supports three parameters. The first one is the link text, `'Edit this post'` in this case, and the second is what goes before the link. Remember, you wanted a separate paragraph for the edit link, and we wanted it to say "Admin" in front, so here's `'<p>Admin:  '`. (Note the blank space after the text to make some room in front of the link.) Finally, the third parameter is what goes after the link, which is just `'</p>'` since you need to close the <p> tag.

In other words, `edit_post_link()` can handle three parameters, and they are passed, in this sense, to speak a little PHP:

```php
<?php edit_post_link( $link, $before, $after ); ?>
```

Remember, parameters are usually passed within quotation marks, and separated with commas and a space to make them more readable.

Not all that complicated, right? All you need to know is which parameters there are to pass, and in what order they need to be. The order is important: without the correct order, you might get the wrong text linked and would definitely break your design, or at least the validation of the site.

Now look at something a bit more complicated:

```php
<?php wp_tag_cloud(); ?>
```

This template tag will output a tag cloud displaying at most 45 tags, with the smallest one at the font size of 8 pt (points), and the largest at 22 pt. They are displayed in a flat listing and sorted by name, in ascending order. You know this because these are the default values, and there are a lot of them as you can see in Table 2-1. In fact, `wp_tag_cloud()` can pass 13 parameters.

Table 2-1 Default tag-cloud Parameters

Parameter	Description	Default Value
smallest	Smallest tag size	8
largest	Largest tag size	22
unit	What font size unit is used	pt
number	How many tags to display at most	45
format	How to display the tags	flat separated with white space
separator	What goes between the tags	white space
orderby	How to order the tags	name
order	How to sort the tags	ascending
exclude	What tags to exclude	none
include	What tags to include	all
link	Should links be edit or view	view
taxonomy	The basis for the tag cloud	post_tag
echo	Whether to show the tag cloud or not	true

If you compare these values to the description of the default output of `wp_tag_cloud()`, you'll see that they are are passed without you needing to pass any parameters manually.

Now try altering the tag by changing some parameters. Be aware, however, that `wp_tag_cloud()` reads its parameters in what is commonly referred to as *query style*. That's a good thing, because having to type in all the 13 possible parameters when you really just want to change the font size unit from pt to px wouldn't be very user-friendly. Instead, you can just write it in plain text:

```
<?php wp_tag_cloud('unit=px'); ?>
```

I didn't know that `px` was valid for the unit option; I found that on the description of the template tag (`http://codex.wordpress.org/Template_Tags/wp_tag_cloud`). Other possible font size units are em, %, and of course pt, which is the default.

If you want to pass more parameters, just add an ampersand (&) between them, within the parameter, with no spaces. Change the tag order to `count` rather than `name`:

```
<?php wp_tag_cloud('unit=px&orderby=count'); ?>
```

You can add even more just by separating the various parameters for the template tag with ampersands. Now randomize the order, changing the smallest tag to 10 px (since the default 8 is a bit small when you're using pixels rather than points) and the largest to 24 px:

```php
<?php wp_tag_cloud('smallest=10&largest=24unit=px&orderby=count&order=RAND'); ?>
```

The order value, RAND, is in capitals. That is intentional; it is just how you pass data to order (the other options are ASC for ascending and DESC for descending). Also, you probably noticed that both smallest and largest were placed before the unit option. It is good form to put the various parameters in the order they are described, as you'll be able to find them more easily whenever you need to edit the code or look something up.

MORE ON PARAMETERS

Since you'll be doing a lot of stuff with the template tags, the understanding of parameters is crucial. There are three types of template tags, which have been touched on already. The first kind takes no parameters at all, the second will take one or several parameters within quotation marks, and the third type is the one called *query style*, separating the various options with ampersands.

Naturally, not passing a parameter at all means that you just put the template tag wherever you need it; this is also true for the other template tags since there is a default output. The problems come when you need to change that default output, and hence the parameters.

In the preceding examples, you have done all this. Remember, you passed just one piece of information in a parameter to the bloginfo() template tag:

```php
<?php bloginfo('name'); ?>
```

Then you passed a parameter in PHP function style, with the edit_post_link() template tag. Here, you told the template tag what the link text should be, and what should come before and after it, separating each instruction with a comma and putting the data within quotation marks:

```php
<?php edit_post_link('Edit this post', '<p>Admin: ', '</p>'); ?>
```

Finally, you passed a lot of options within a query style parameter to output a tag cloud with wp_tag_cloud(). This method splits parameters with ampersands, and lets you change just the settings you want:

```php
<?php wp_tag_cloud('smallest=10&largest=24unit=px&orderby=count&order=RAND'); ?>
```

UNDERSTANDING DATA TYPES

There are three types of data you can pass to template tags: strings, integers, and Booleans. Although the template tag's definition (as stated in the WordPress Codex wiki) will tell you exactly how to pass data to that particular template tag, it's important to know what's behind it so you can select the correct type.

The first data type is *strings*, which are lines of text. The bloginfo('name') example is a string, since you tell it that 'name' is the parameter. Strings are found within single or double quotation marks (they do the same thing), although the single version is a lot more common and the one used in the examples in this book.

The second data type is *integers*. Integers are whole numbers, such as 55900 or -3. You can pass them inside quotation marks if you want, but you don't need to. They are commonly used when you need to fetch something that has an ID, which is a lot of things. You'll stumble onto template tags as well as conditional tags that do this later on.

Finally, there are the *Boolean* parameters, which are used when the value can be only true or false. You can pass this information with all capitals (TRUE or FALSE), all lowercase letters (true or false), or using numbers (1 being true and 0 being false). You cannot put Boolean values within quotation marks; they always stand by their own. For example, the get_calendar() template tag only takes one instruction, and that is whether to display the full day, or just a one-letter abbreviation. True is the default value and displays the first letter in the name of the day (for example, M for Monday), so if you want to output Monday instead of M, you need to set get_calendar() to false:

```
<?php get_calendar(FALSE); ?>
```

Another example of Boolean instructions is the the_date() template tag, usually used to output the date of a post. You may, for example, want to use that information in your own PHP script instead, and display nothing from the_date() tag. You can change the output format of the date (the first string in the parameter), what goes before the outputted date (the second string), and what comes after it (the third string). The fourth instruction you can pass, however, is a Boolean that tells the system whether to output or not (true by default). Say you want to output a year-month-day date (Y-m-d according to the PHP manual for date functions; WordPress can take them all) within a paragraph. The code would look like this:

```
<?php the_date('Y-m-d', '<p>', '</p>'); ?>
```

However, if you want to use this with PHP outside of the WordPress functions for some reason, outputting nothing, you can set it to false with the echo option that this template tag has. This goes last and is a Boolean value, and hence you won't put it within quotation marks:

```
<?php the_date('Y-m-d', '<p>', '</p>', FALSE); ?>
```

This would give you the same result, being year-month-day within a <p> tag, but it would output nothing, so if you want to use it with your own PHP code, this is the way to go about it.

Remember that strings are text within quotation marks, integers are whole numbers, and Boolean parameters are true or false without any quotation marks. With this in mind, it'll be a lot easier to understand the template tags you'll use to build really cool WordPress sites later on.

CONDITIONAL TAGS

Conditional tags are very handy. You use them in your theme's template files, and as the name implies they are for setting various conditions. In other words, you can use them to display different things depending on the situation. A very good example is the conditional tag is_home(), which checks whether the page you're on is the home page. Use it to output a greeting, since that is the polite thing to do:

```php
<?php if (is_home())
{
    echo '<p class="welcome">Hey you, welcome to the site. I love new
    visitors!</p>';
} ?>
```

This would output a paragraph with the class welcome, and the text within. So You have a simple test to determine if the page is_home(), and then an echo with the paragraph if it is in fact the home page. That's very straightforward, so let's try something else. Suppose you've got a specific category that should have a different sidebar than the rest of the site. You can check for that with the conditional tag is_category(), and then output another sidebar if appropriate. Whenever it is another page within the site, use the traditional get_sidebar() include tag.

This code will replace the get_sidebar() PHP snippet in the theme's template files wherever it matters, which probably means files like index.php, category.php, single.php, and so on:

```php
<?php if (is_category('very-special')) {
    get_sidebar('special');
} else {
    get_sidebar();
} ?>
```

Here you're asking if the category is very-special, which is the category slug (used in permalinks and such) in this case. You could have asked for the category ID or the category name as well, and while an ID is pretty foolproof, the code is a lot easier to read if you use the slug since it is nicenamed, meaning it can't contain nasty special characters and such. If the category is in fact the one with the very-special slug, then use the include tag get_sidebar('special'), where 'special' is a parameter indicating that you want sidebar-special.php. If you wanted to, you could have done a traditional PHP include, using the TEMPLATEPATH option to find the theme folder (see the section "The Include Tags" earlier in this chapter), but get_sidebar() does the work for you, so go with that.

Should the category not be the one with the very-special slug, the code will move on to the else clause and tell WordPress to use the normal get_sidebar() include tag, which means you'll include sidebar.php.

This is all very simple stuff, but it clearly shows how conditional tags can be used to create dynamic pages. You'll do fun stuff with it later.

NEXT UP: THE LOOP

Now that you know that WordPress sites are built on themes, which in turn consist of template files containing different kinds of tags that do funky stuff, it's time to start manipulating the content. This is done with the *loop*, a bit of PHP snippet that is the heart and soul of WordPress. While you can do a lot with WordPress without knowing about the loop, you certainly have to understand it if you want to truly bend the platform to your will. You can use the loop to make posts show up in a different order and generally display things the way you want.

A lot of the things you'll want to do with WordPress are only possible within the loop. And that in turn means that you sometimes need multiple loops with custom outputs. Or, at the very least, you need to figure out where the loop begins and ends so that you can add the cool template tags and plugin features you no doubt will find or create on your own.

There's no way of getting around it, the loop is important. Better hop to it, then.

3

THE LOOP

NOW THAT YOU have WordPress installed and the theme concept under control, it's time to look at what really makes the system run. This chapter will teach you about the *loop*, which basically is a PHP query that talks to WordPress and makes it output the content requested. The chapter starts with some basic loop usage, and then branches out to multiple loops and some nice little trickery used within to achieve various effects.

You need to understand the loop to create really cool WordPress sites. While you won't need to be an expert, you should grasp what it does. That way, you can research the many functions and features available when you run into a solution that requires custom content output.

UNDERSTANDING THE WORDPRESS LOOP

The loop is the heart of WordPress, and it resides in your theme's template files. While you can in fact have a theme without the loop, it would make the fluidness of the content handling, like displaying the latest posts and browsing backward, quite difficult to pull off. Some template files, for example 404 error pages, don't have the loop at all, but most do.

Some template tags only work within the loop, so you need to be able to identify it. This is easy, as you will see in the next section.

THE BASIC LOOP

If you want to create sites using WordPress, you need to understand the loop. Luckily, the basic one is pretty easy. It starts with this:

```php
<?php if ( have_posts() ) : while ( have_posts() ) : the_post(); ?>
```

And ends with this:

```php
<?php endwhile; else: ?>
    <p>Some error message or similar.</p>
<?php endif; ?>
```

Actually, you don't need that error message part other than in template files that are used to output errors, but since a lot of themes do have it, it is included here. It can be a "404 page not found" error, or a search result message telling the visitor that that particular query didn't return any hits.

What follows is a fully functional loop, with the common template tags for outputting post content. You'll find it, or something pretty similar to it, in the index.php file of most themes:

```php
<?php if ( have_posts() ) : while ( have_posts() ) : the_post(); ?>
    <div id="post-<?php the_ID(); ?>" <?php post_class(); ?>>
        <h2><a href="<?php the_permalink(); ?>" title="<?php the_title(); ?>">
            <?php the_title(); ?>
        </a></h2>
        <?php the_content(); ?>
        <?php get_comments(); ?>
    </div>
<?php endwhile; else: ?>
    <div class="post">
        <h2>Error!</h2>
        <p>Something went wrong! Please try again.</p>
    </div>
<?php endif; ?>
```

Naturally, you'd want a more comprehensive error message than the one in this code, but that's not the point right now.

The basic loop checks whether there are any posts to return, and in turn the loop is controlled by the global blog settings (how many posts to display and such), and whereabouts on the blog you are. A single post would return just one post (the one you want, presumably), while a category listing would return the number of posts specified in the WordPress settings, but only the ones that belong to that particular category.

If there are posts, a `while` loop is started, and as long as there are posts to return, as controlled by the situation and settings, posts will be returned and displayed. When the `while` loop is done (all posts that should be returned have been output), it ends with `endwhile`, and then the loop ends with `endif`.

Should there be no posts that match the criteria of the particular situation, the `else` clause is called, and that's when the error message (or similar) will be output (or nothing at all, if there is nothing defined). After that, the loop ends.

So the loop actually loops content from the database, based on the WordPress settings and any criteria that the page you're on may bring. Makes sense, doesn't it?

SEPARATING THE LOOP USING THE LOOP.PHP TEMPLATE FILE

There was a time when the loop would always be in theme's index.php template file, and possibly several other template files as well. These days not all themes include the loop in index.php. In fact, I recommend that you not include the loop in your index.php file, but instead use the `get_template_part()` include tag (mentioned in Chapter 2) along with a separate loop template file. In fact, while some template files will contain the loop itself and not rely on `get_template_part()` for loop inclusion, others will use loop.php but render the content differently depending on what part of the site that is being displayed. A category archive often looks different from a single post, but both of these could be generated by the same loop.php template file (albeit not exactly the same code within said loop.php template), or from completely different files altogether. It is all a matter of where on the site you are, and how many template files you've got in your theme.

Recall from Chapter 2 that `get_template_part()` will include the loop.php template file, and that is obviously where you would put the loop.

So the example loop code in the previous section wouldn't be found in index.php at all. Instead, you would have this:

```php
<?php get_template_part('loop', 'index'); ?>
```

This will look for loop-index.php first, and failing that, it'll revert to loop.php. You'd put your loop code in either of those files. The purpose of using loop-index.php (in this case) would be to enable you to control the loop on a specific page (index.php in this case), while keeping the general loop (found in loop.php, the one WordPress reverts back to) free of custom stuff for specific pages. So if you want a completely different loop for your category archives, for example, you'd use the following line in category.php, the template file used in our example:

```php
<?php get_template_part('loop', 'category'); ?>
```

This would look for loop-category.php first, where you'll put your custom loop, hence making loop.php clean and slim. You'll put this to good use with child themes in Chapter 5. For now you can be content knowing that this is a great way to separate the loop code, which can be quite extensive, from the various template files.

A FEW WORDS ABOUT WP_QUERY

WP_Query is the heart of the loop, even though you don't see it spelled out in the most basic code. It is really a class that handles all the loop magic, and you'll find it in wp-includes/query.php if you want to dig deep within the WordPress core files. Refer to the Codex page (http://codex.wordpress.org/Function_Reference/WP_Query) for an explanation of all the properties and methods that go with WP_Query.

The basic loop uses WP_Query, or rather it uses the default $wp_query object. This means that when you use necessities such as have_posts() and the_post() you'll in fact use $wp_query->have_posts() and $wp_query->the_post(). In other words, have_posts() and its friends take it for granted that you want to be using $wp_query. Whenever you go outside $wp_query by creating your own queries, as you'll do in the multiple loops section as well as in examples and adaptations further in the book, you'll have to create an object for it, like this:

```php
<?php $brand_new_query = new WP_Query(); ?>
```

Here, you're loading everything into $brand_new_query instead of the default $wp_query, and that means that you can do stuff outside of the main loop.

Most parts of WordPress will connect to the WP_Query class, including templates and conditional tags. You can tap into and alter things within the WP_Query class, but you should refrain from it if there is an available solution already. As you master WordPress, there may come a time when you want to do things that are truly out of the box, but that's a whole other matter.

USING THE LOOP

Now that you've established where you need the loop (in post listings, no matter if it is one or several), and that you can run several l at once, the question becomes how to use the loop most effectively. For one thing, maybe you don't want to display the full post in your category listings — maybe you just want an excerpt? This brings you back to the template tags, and the ones that control the output of the loop.

This section takes a quick look at the most frequently used tags. Chances are, you'll want to display and link the title of the various posts. This little code snippet is present in just about every theme's template files that list several posts, and sometimes in the ones that just display the one as well:

```
<h2>
    <a href="<?php the_permalink(); ?>" title="<?php the_title(); ?>">
        <?php the_title(); ?>
    </a>
</h2>
```

It's really simple: using the tags for outputting the post title, you display just that (and also use it for the title attribute in the link). Around the title is a traditional hyperlink, getting its `href` value from `<?php the_permalink(); ?>`, which of course is the permalink to the post in question. Nothing weird or anything there, so let's output some content. Here you have two options, using either one of these two template tags:

```
<?php the_content() ;?>
<?php the_excerpt() ;?>
```

The first tag outputs the full post content, unless you're on a page listing several blog posts. In that case, it outputs the content until the point where the `<!--more-->` tag is inserted; if that tag is not used then the full post is displayed (see Figure 3-1). If you're a WordPress user you know all about that one; it is the More button in the HTML editor, inserting a Read More link. Incidentally, you can make that appear in any way you like. For example:

```
<?php the_content('Read more here, mate!') ;?>
```

This would change the default read more link text to "Read more here, mate!" There are more options for this, and you can even put HTML code in it (or perhaps a graphic instead of text). The important thing is that the template tag `the_content()` outputs the post content, and if it is a blog listing it breaks it with a read more link if the `<!--more-->` tag is inserted.

Naturally, when you're on a single-post page, and `the_content()` is used (whether a custom read more text is defined or not), it won't output a read more link. You'll see the full post.

The second content template tag available is `the_excerpt()`. As the name implies, it only outputs an excerpt of the actual content, by default the first 55 words. All HTML, whether it is images or paragraph breaks or YouTube videos, is stripped from this excerpt, so it should really be used with caution. Neither are there any parameters, which is a bit weird; you would think that you'd be able to control the length of the actual excerpt, but there is no such setting.

However, `the_excerpt()` does fulfill a purpose. You know that excerpt box on the Write Post screen in WordPress? (See Figure 3-2; depending on your setup you might have to enable it using the Screen Options settings in the top right, also shown in Figure 3-2.) If you put something there, `the_excerpt()` will output that instead of the first 55 words. So if you put a simple "Hi, this is my post!" in the excerpt field for a post, the usage of `the_excerpt()`, will result in a mere "Hi, this is my post!" output, despite it being a lot shorter than 55 words.

Figure 3-1: All these posts are outputted with the loop

What good is `the_excerpt()`, then? It may be useful for lists where you don't want the blog posts to take up so much space, such as in search results or perhaps some kind of archive page. However, the most obvious usage would be as an alternative way of promoting a post. You can have a separate loop that would feature posts with a specific tag, and display their title as usual, but then just output `the_excerpt()` rather than the content. In fact, I'll show you how in the upcoming example.

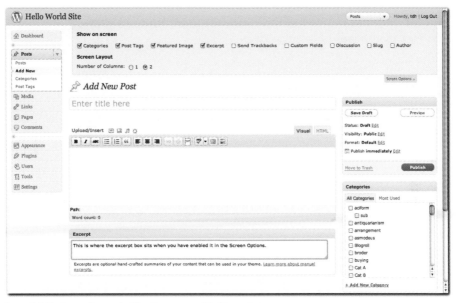

Figure 3-2: The Excerpt box on the Write Post screen in WordPress admin

For clarity's sake, this is the default usage of `the_excerpt()`:

```php
<?php the_excerpt(); ?>
```

Remember not to use `the_excerpt()` on templates displaying just one post, like single.
php, for example. You need `the_content()` to display the full content! And, yes, should
you want to, you can use them together.

The following example shows you how to use `the_excerpt()` to create a catchy intro to
your posts in the Twenty Ten theme (but just on single posts, of course).

1. Open the Twenty Ten folder (found at `wp-content/themes/twentyten/`) and find
   the single.php template file. This is the one used to display single posts, so take a look at
   it. As you can see it uses `get_template_part()` to fetch loop-single.php.

```php
<?php
/**
 * The Template for displaying all single posts.
 *
 * @package WordPress
 * @subpackage Twenty_Ten
 * @since Twenty Ten 1.0
 */
```

```
get_header(); ?>

        <div id="container">
                <div id="content" role="main">

                <?php
                /* Run the loop to output the post.
                 * If you want to overload this in a child theme then
                 * include a file
                 * called loop-single.php and that will be used instead.
                 */
                get_template_part( 'loop', 'single' );
                ?>

                </div><!-- #content -->
        </div><!-- #container -->

<?php get_sidebar(); ?>
<?php get_footer(); ?>
```

2. Now forget about single.php and open loop-single.php instead. Add `the_excerpt()` just above `the_content()` in loop-single.php, around line 33. You'll see that it sits in a div with the class `entry-content`:

```
<div class="entry-content">
    <?php the_content(); ?>
    <?php wp_link_pages( array( 'before' => '<div class="page-link">' . __(
        'Pages:', 'twentyten' ), 'after' => '</div>' ) ); ?>
</div><!-- .entry-content -->
```

3. Add `the_excerpt()` just above, with a div of its own around it so that you can style it the way you want:

```
<div class="entry-content">
    <div class="entry-intro">
            <?php the_excerpt(); ?>
    </div>
    <?php the_content(); ?>
    <?php wp_link_pages( array( 'before' => '<div class="page-link">' . __(
        'Pages:', 'twentyten' ), 'after' => '</div>' ) ); ?>
</div><!-- .entry-content -->
```

4. Save and upload loop-single.php. Now you'll see the default excerpt (the first 55 characters from the post) above the content on single posts. But hang on, there's a weird "Continue reading" link there (see Figure 3-3). That won't do!

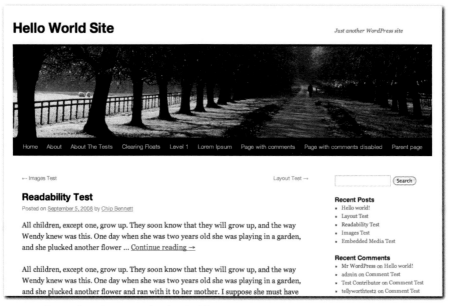

Figure 3-3: This post shows the excerpt rather than the full post. Note the ellipses at the end.

That link is due to a function in Twenty Ten that adds the link to the `excerpt_more` filter (we'll get to hooks and filters later). You can remove that with two simple lines of code before `the_excerpt()`. You need two lines because there are two conditions where the link shows (if you filled out an excerpt or if it is automatically generated). Figure 3-4 shows the new output:

```
<div class="entry-content">
    <div class="entry-intro">
            <?php
                    // Remove the excerpt_more filters by Twenty Ten
                    remove_filter( 'excerpt_more',
                    'twentyten_auto_excerpt_more' );
                    remove_filter( 'get_the_excerpt',
                    'twentyten_custom_excerpt_more' );
                    // Now the_excerpt outputs per default
                    the_excerpt();
            ?>
    </div>
    <?php the_content(); ?>
    <?php wp_link_pages( array( 'before' => '<div class="page-link">' . __(
        'Pages:', 'twentyten' ), 'after' => '</div>' ) ); ?>
</div><!-- .entry-content -->
```

Figure 3-4: The link is gone and there's a default [...] treatment instead

5. If you fill out a custom excerpt in the appointed box found on the Write Post screen in WordPress admin (see Figure 3-5), the excerpt of your choice will display instead, as shown in Figure 3-6. No more nasty [...] stuff!

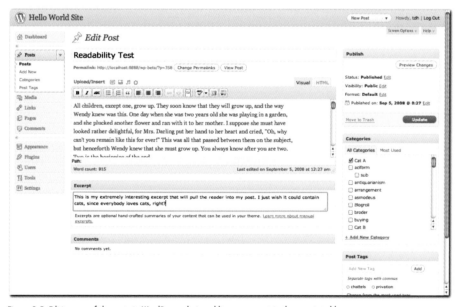

Figure 3-5: Editing one of the posts in WordPress admin, adding an excerpt in the appointed box

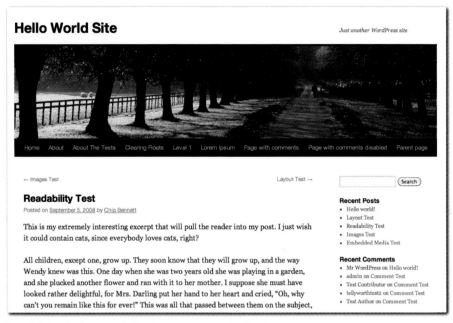

Figure 3-6: The edited post now displays the custom excerpt rather than the automatic one

6. Almost done! Now you need to style it accordingly, so open up style.css and add something like this to it (at the end, or where it makes sense for you). This will make the text in the `div.entry-intro` larger, but you could style it any way you'd like of course. You can see the result of this particular code in Figure 3-7.

```
div.entry-intro {
        font-size: 130%;
        line-height: 130%;
        font-variant: small-caps;
}
```

USING STICKY POSTS

WordPress added something called *sticky posts* back in version 2.7. People familiar with online discussion forums will recognize the lingo; it is basically something that sticks to the top of the post listing at all times. No matter how many new posts are added, the sticky post remains the first item at the top of the listing of posts. In the Edit Post screen, you can set a blog post to sticky, hence making it stay on top at all times (see Figure 3-8). If two or more posts are sticky they will all appear at the top of the list, in chronological order. When you remove the sticky setting from the Edit post screen, the post will automatically sort itself into place with the others.

There is a `sticky_class()` template tag to output the sticky post class, but with the addition of `post_class()` it really isn't very useful.

```
<div id="post-<?php the_ID(); ?>" <?php post_class(); ?>>
```

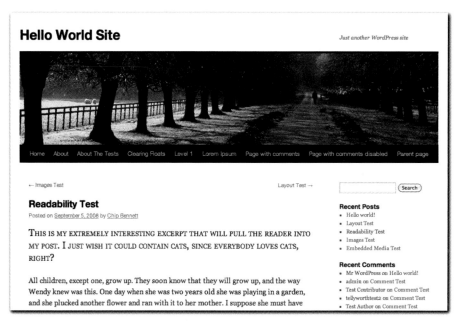

Figure 3-7: Uppercase intro text added

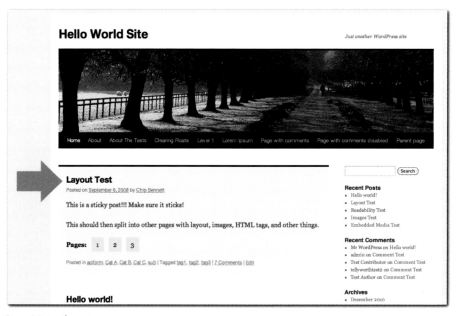

Figure 3-8: A sticky post

The lovely `post_class()` template tag will add a number of classes to the post, depending on the details of the post. This is very useful for a designer, so this book covers `post_class()` in more depth in Chapter 6.

If the post is marked as sticky, `post_class()` will add a CSS `.sticky` class. That way you can alter it in any way you want. Maybe you want it to have a light grey background, larger type, or something else? Just add the necessary styles to your stylesheet, applying them to the `.sticky` class as in the following example:

```
.sticky { padding: 15px; background: #eee; border: 1px solid #bbb; color: #444;
  font-size: 18px; }
```

That CSS code would put the sticky post in a light grey box with a slightly darker frame, and 18-pixel-sized default font size. Here it is in action, within a basic loop:

```
<?php if ( have_posts() ) : while ( have_posts() ) : the_post(); ?>
    <div id="post-<?php the_ID(); ?>" <?php post_class(); ?>>
        <h2><a href="<?php the_permalink(); ?>" title="<?php the_title(); ?>">
            <?php the_title(); ?>
        </a></h2>
        <?php the_content(); ?>
    </div>
<?php endwhile; else: ?>
    <p>Some error message or similar.</p>
<?php endif; ?>
```

In plain HTML you'd get the following containing `div`. Notice the classes applied by `post_class()` in particular.

```
<div id="post-1" class="post-1 post type-post status-publish format-standard sticky
  hentry category-uncategorized">
    <!--POST CONTENT GOES HERE -->
</div>
```

Want to do more with sticky posts? The conditional tag `is_sticky()` will help you do some funky stuff. Maybe you really want to rub in the importance of this post above all others? Then why not say so:

```
<?php if (is_sticky()) echo 'Super important post! Read it! Now!'; ?>
```

A bit over the top, of course, but there may indeed be times when it is a good idea to output or change things if there is a sticky post involved. Say you sell e-books on your blog; you could use sticky posts to promote your latest one:

```
<?php if (is_sticky()) echo 'The latest e-book release by yours truly'; ?>
```

Not all themes support sticky posts and the functionality is a bit hidden in the admin interface, so keep that in mind when building around the sticky post feature.

47

WORKING WITH POST FORMATS

Post formats were introduced in WordPress 3.1 and join sticky posts as a separate way to add a bit of control over the content. There are nine different post formats:

- **aside** for short updates, usually without a title
- **audio** for use with audio files
- **chat** used to publish chat transcripts
- **gallery** for gallery posts
- **image** for displaying a single image
- **link** to link the reader onwards
- **quote** used to show quotes
- **status** for short status updates
- **video** for displaying a single video

Obviously you can use these for anything you want, but there is some built in functionality as to how they work. For the image post format, for example, the first image found in the post content will be considered the single image, which you then can work with.

Just as with sticky posts, you pick the format in the top right box. Figure 3-9 shows the box for the Twenty Ten theme, which obviously only supports the aside and gallery post formats.

Figure 3-9: Pick the post format

A post published in accordance with the options selected in Figure 3-9 will show up as a title-less post when using Twenty Ten.

So what's the purpose of using post formats? Well, for starters they add new CSS classes for you to play with. The aside post format will add the `format-aside` class, for example (see Figure 3-10), an alternative to using a dedicated asides category. This can be very handy. You'll also get added classes from `body_class()` which should sit in your body tag, giving you further control.

Figure 3-10: CSS classes added to the aside post, styled using the format-aside class

The real power comes into play when you use conditional tags within the loop. You can check whether a post is a certain post format or not, and act on it, like so:

```
if ( has_post_format( 'aside' ) ) {
    echo 'This is an aside post so expect it to be short!';
}
```

To add this functionality to your theme you'll have to use `add_theme_support()` in your functions.php file, telling WordPress which post formats your theme supports by passing an array. If you want to support the aside, gallery, and video post formats, for example, you would add this line to functions.php:

```
add_theme_support( 'post-formats', array( 'aside', 'gallery', 'video' ) );
```

More details on post formats are available in the Codex at `http://codex.wordpress.org/Post_Formats`.

PUTTING QUERY_POSTS() TO GOOD USE

Every WordPress loop hacker and ambitious theme designer should know about the nifty `query_posts()` tool. In essence, `query_posts()` represents a way to take the loop WordPress wants to output (most frequently, the latest posts) and do something else with it. Perhaps you want to limit the number of posts, exclude a set number of categories, or change the order of things.

> *A few words of caution: the idea is to apply the `query_posts()` template tag on the main loop, not to use it to build multiple loops. That is possible, but things can get weird if you do, so it's best not to use it that way. See the "Multiple Loops" section later in this chapter to see how to create as many loops as you like.*

To use `query_posts()`, apply it before your main loop, like this:

```
<?php query_posts();
if ( have_posts() ) : while ( have_posts() ) : the_post(); ?>
    <!-- Doing stuff here, styling the posts and so on. -->
<?php endwhile; else: ?>
    <p>Some error message or similar.</p>
<?php endif; ?>
```

You can tighten that code a bit; there is no need for separate PHP tags for `query_posts()` and the `have_posts()` part.

So what does this do to the loop? Nothing really, since you haven't passed any parameters to `query_posts()` yet. There are no default values; this would just return the standard loop according to your WordPress settings. What `query_posts()` does is alert the SQL query from the loop to fit your needs.

Now that you're acquainted with `query_posts()`, you can execute a few examples to get used to it. There are tons of things you can do with this template tag when it comes to controlling the content flow. It really has a lot of settings, and combining it with conditional tags is the route to hundreds of possible combinations.

Start by removing all posts from a category from the listings; try that Asides category where you push out your short, nonsensical posts. The first thing you need to do is figure out what ID it has, which is easily done by logging in to the WordPress admin interface and finding your way to the Edit category page. There you'll find the ID hidden at the end of the URL of the Edit page:

```
http://notesblog.com/wp-admin/categories.php?action=edit&cat_ID=130
```

As you'll probably have gathered, `cat_ID=130` tells you that the ID is 130. Remember, category IDs (or any IDs really) don't relate to the each other in any other way than they are all numerical values. Posts, categories, tags, and everything else are mixed, so you may have one category with ID 3 and the next with ID 749. This is because they are assigned by the database when you create the post or category.

Back to the example: you don't want to display posts from the Asides category, which has the ID 130. The `query_posts()` page in the Codex (`http://codex.wordpress.org/Template_Tags/query_posts`) says that you can use a number of ways to pass category information to `query_posts()`, but for this example, use the `cat` parameter, which takes IDs:

```php
<?php query_posts('cat=-130'); ?>
```

This, in front of the loop shown previously, will exclude posts belonging to the category with the ID 130. Notice the minus sign in front of the ID: you really need that. If you forget about it, you would get the exact opposite result, which would be to show posts *only* from the category with ID 130.

Next, display posts tagged with `blue`, `green`, or `yellow` by applying this before the loop:

```php
<?php query_posts('tag=blue+green+yellow'); ?>
```

Here, you obviously use that particular tag parameter. There's a bunch of parameters as well, just as with categories. Other things you can do with `query_posts()` are fetch posts from a specific author, do time-based queries, and order whatever data you choose any way you like. You can even grab the custom fields data and use it for sorting, for example, which means that posts suddenly can get even more parameters to be sorted with. You'll do a lot of these things later on when you're building cool WordPress-powered sites.

One snag you may run into when working with `query_posts()` is the number of posts being returned. This is still controlled by the main WordPress settings related to how many blog posts to display per page. Luckily, you can control that as well. Say you want your front page to display just five posts, but all other listings should display ten. You can tackle this problem in two ways. You can either create a home.php template, and do the `query_post()` magic there, or use a conditional tag for your index.php template. Start with the home.php variant since it is the cleanest and easiest one. Using `query_posts()` and the `posts_per_page` parameter, you can control these things:

```php
<?php query_posts('posts_per_page=5'); ?>
```

By placing that before the loop on your home.php template, you'll display five posts per page. Simple, huh? Now, put those conditional tags to use and add this functionality to the index.php page instead, since you really don't need a separate home.php for this. All you need to do is use the conditional tag `is_home()` in an `if` clause to check if you're on the home page. If not, nothing will happen, but if you are, the `query_posts()` statement will go through. By adding this before the loop in index.php you achieve the same thing as you did with the home.php template:

```php
<?php
    if (is_home()) {
        query_posts('posts_per_page=5');
    }
?>
```

Now, since you can limit the number of posts, naturally you can remove the limit as well. Just set the `posts_per_page` parameter to `-1` and you'll show all posts that fit the loop criteria. Beware of putting that on a blog with thousands of posts, since if you do that on the front page it will show all your posts, and that's not a fun SQL query to pass to the database at all. That being said, why not show all posts written by the author with the name TDH, published in 2009?

```php
<?php query_posts('author_name=TDH&year=2009&posts_per_page=-1'); ?>
```

As you can see, `query_posts()` takes its parameters in query string style. That means you can cram a lot of things into it without it being too complicated. You'll be using `query_posts()` a lot from now on, so get some practice with it.

ALTERNATIVES TO THE LOOP

You may be tempted to create multiple loops or advanced loop queries in your theme's template files when you've figured out how those work. However, while that may be the solution to what you want to do in some cases, you should consider alternative methods as well. Doing a lot of funky stuff with the loop, often utilizing `query_posts()`, is sometimes completely unnecessary. Here's why.

First, ask yourself if it really is another loop you need. Often there are template tags that can do what you need, and that is almost always a better solution. Custom loop magic should be saved for actions that truly deserve and need it. At other times a conditional tag might be the solution to the problem, which usually is a better approach than another loop.

Second, are there any plugins that can do the work for you? The WordPress community is full of brilliant solutions to common problems, and while it may be a lot cleaner to sort these things from within your own theme, a plugin may in fact enhance the functionality and be easier for you to manage. A lot of the plugins that work with post listings are in fact doing stuff with the loop that you could do yourself, from within your theme. Normally I would recommend the latter solution, but what if you're not the one responsible for maintaining the theme in the long run, as is common when doing theme design work and then leaving it to the client to nurture? If the client is reluctant to pay more for customizations, or if the client thinks that their in-house HTML skills are enough, then you're probably better off finding a plugin solution than one that will break when they do something with their template files. Granted, plugins come with their own issues, like suddenly not being developed anymore, or relying on WordPress functionality that isn't favored, but still, it is something to consider as an alternative to more loops.

Chapter 8 dives deeper into the question of when to rely on plugins to replace built-in functionality.

Finally, there is the possible strain on the server and database. Doing loop after loop means a lot of PHP and SQL queries and that will slow down the site. Simple is not always best, but keeping things as simple as possible while managing to get the required result is always a good idea. Both Web hosts and WordPress have come a long way since the early days, but that doesn't mean that you should make things more clunky or complicated than they need to be.

My point is this: always question the need for that extra loop. It may save you some headaches in the future.

MULTIPLE LOOPS

Sometimes you want several loops on a page. Perhaps you have a category for your extremely important posts, and want to run those by themselves on the front page, or maybe you just want the latest posts in the sidebar. Either way, whenever you need to fetch posts a second time, you'll want another loop. This is often essential when you want to break from the traditional blog mold, so you may as well master it.

Start with the most basic multiple loop solution, which is to just get another loop on the page. This is done with `rewind_posts()`, which just resets the loop's counter and lets you run it again:

```php
<?php
    rewind_posts();
    while (have_posts()) : the_post();
?>
    <!-- And then the basic loop continues... -->
```

Naturally, this would just output the exact same thing as your first loop, which would neither look good nor be particularly useful, so to actually do something with `rewind_posts()` you need to change something. Say you want a box at the bottom of the page showing the last five posts from the News category; this can be achieved by using `query_posts`, which was touched upon earlier:

```php
<?php
    rewind_posts();
    query_posts('category_name=news&showposts=5');
    while (have_posts()) : the_post();
?>
    <!-- And then the basic loop continues... -->
```

This would then output the five latest posts from the News category, which you would put in the box mentioned in the previous paragraph.

FEATURED POSTS WITH MULTIPLE LOOPS

Another common usage for multiple loops is to display a featured post at the top of the page. This allows the WordPress theme to break from the traditional blog layout, and has become quite popular, especially with the so-called magazine themes that mimic their print counterparts.

To do this, you first need a loop that fetches a single post — the latest one, naturally — from the Featured category. Then, you need a second loop that does the regular thing, listing the latest posts from all categories. To pull this off, you need to store the first loop query inside its own query object. Do that by calling the `WP_Query` object and storing it in a new query. `WP_Query` is the big huge thing that makes the loop tick. While you don't see it in the basic loop you actually use it with `have_posts()`, for example, which in essence is `$wp_query->have_posts()`; you just don't have to write it all out all the time. `WP_Query` is huge and somewhat complicated, so messing with it requires some decent coding skills or a lot of trial and error. As any experienced PHP coder will tell you, a little of both usually does the trick. Often, however, you'll interact with `WP_Query` by using the various template and conditional tags.

Recall the `query_posts()` template tag. The usage description says that it is intended to modify the main loop only, so you won't be using that for your new loop. Instead, pass the same variables to `WP_Query`. Here is the code:

```php
<?php
    $featured_query = new WP_Query('category_name=featured&showposts=1');
    while ($featured_query->have_posts()) : $featured_query->the_post();
    $do_not_duplicate = $post->ID;
?>
    <!-- Styling for your featured post -->
<?php endwhile; ?>
    <!-- Put whatever you want between the featured post
        and the normal post listing -->
<?php
    if (have_posts()) : while (have_posts()) : the_post();
    if( $post->ID == $do_not_duplicate ) continue; update_post_caches($posts);
?>
    <!-- Your normal loop post styling goes here -->
<?php endwhile; else: ?>
    <p>Some error message or similar.</p>
<?php endif; ?>
```

Let's break down this code, starting with the first loop that kicks off with the first line, where you load `$featured_query` with a new `WP_Query` loop query. This query is served `query_post()`-like parameters, which means you're limiting it to the category Featured, and showing just one post:

```php
$featured_query = new WP_Query('category_name=featured&showposts=1');
```

Then, you move into a `while` loop (which will only contain one turnaround; you said just one post after all) looking somewhat like the basic loop:

```
while ($featured_query->have_posts())  :  $featured_query->the_post();
```

Remember that `have_posts()` in the basic loop was actually `$wp_query->have_posts();` this is the same, but instead of the default `$wp_query` you're using the brand-new `$featured_query`. This means that you're doing the exact same thing as in the basic loop, but not in the default `$wp_query` object but rather in the new one, hence not affecting `$wp_query` at all.

The third line is simple. You're loading the post ID into the `$do_not_duplicate` object. The idea here is to make sure that a featured post won't turn up both in the featured post section, and in the post listing below it. If you've ever looked at an example of multiple loops doing this, you recognize this code snippet; it is featured in the Codex as well. You'll use it in your main loop, but for now the post ID is sorted in `$do_not_duplicate`. Of course, this would only work if you only have one featured post. If you had several, you would need to store them in an array instead.

```
    $do_not_duplicate = $post->ID;
?>
    <!-- Styling for your featured post -->
<?php endwhile; ?>
```

After that you've got the typical post output section, usually an *h2* heading with a linked title for the post, and then the content or an excerpt of the content. You may want to make it fancy with images and so forth. For now, though, you can be satisfied that this will contain your output of the featured post.

Moving on, you have a typical basic loop with an addition. Line eight is an if clause checking if the post ID is the same as the ID stored in the `$do_not_duplicate` object. If it is, you continue and update the post cache, otherwise you output it as normal. In other words, when you get to the featured post in your main loop, you'll skip it and move on:

```
<?php
    if (have_posts())  :  while (have_posts())  :  the_post();
    if( $post->ID == $do_not_duplicate ) continue; update_post_caches($posts);
?>
```

After that it is the basic loop all the way, with post output and all:

```
<!-- Your normal loop post styling goes here -->
<?php endwhile; else: ?>
    <p>Some error message or similar.</p>
<?php endif; ?>
```

So, in other words, first you output the featured post in a loop of its own. Then you do the regular loop, checking the post ID to make sure that our featured post won't show up again.

THREE'S A CHARM, BUT FOUR LOOPS ARE WAY COOLER

Using the knowledge you've gained thus far, in this section you'll put the multiple loop concept to the test. In this example you'll have three featured posts in one loop, then you'll imagine three columns underneath consisting of the latest posts from one category each. The idea is to mimic the front page of a non-bloggish site. In terms of template files, this would ideally be in the home.php template, which means that it would only be loaded when on the front page. Consider the following code:

```php
<?php
    // The featured query
    $featured_query = new WP_Query('category_name=featured&showposts=3');
    while ($featured_query->have_posts()) : $featured_query->the_post();
    $do_not_duplicate[] = $post->ID ?>
    <!-- Styling for your featured posts -->
<?php endwhile; ?>
    <!-- Now begins the first column loop -->
<?php
    // First column
    query_posts('category_name=apples&showposts=10');
    while (have_posts()) : the_post();
    if (in_array($post->ID, $do_not_duplicate)) continue;
    update_post_caches($posts);
?>
    <!-- Category Apples post -->
<?php endwhile; ?>
    <!-- Now begins the second column loop -->
<?php rewind_posts();
    // Second column
    query_posts('category_name=oranges&showposts=10');
    while (have_posts()) : the_post(); ?>
    if (in_array($post->ID, $do_not_duplicate)) continue;
    update_post_caches($posts);
?>
    <!-- Category Oranges post -->
<?php endwhile; ?>
    <!-- Now begins the third column loop -->
<?php rewind_posts();
    // Third column
    query_posts('category_name=lemons&showposts=10');
    while (have_posts()) : the_post();
    if (in_array($post->ID, $do_not_duplicate)) continue;
    update_post_caches($posts);
?>
    <!-- Category Lemons post -->
<?php endwhile; ?>
```

What happened here? Start with the three featured posts. This is pretty much similar to the previous featured post loop example, but since you have three posts here and you don't want them to show up more than once, you need to store their IDs in an array. (An *array* is a series of stored information; in this case, three post IDs.) PHP-savvy readers will recognize the square brackets on $do_not_duplicate, which indicates that it is an array. You check for these in every loop that follows.

Moving on, every one of the three column loops, one per category, is the basic (main) loop using the query_posts() template tag to limit the output. You should recognize the category sorting and the number of posts they'll show from previous examples.

Since you don't want to output any of the featured posts in the three category loops, you need to check the $do_not_duplicate array. Notice that the if clause for this has changed a bit to reflect that it is an array.

Finally, after the first column loop, which is the main one, you need to use rewind_posts() to be able to use it again, but with different sorting thanks to query_posts(). Repeat as needed.

An optional solution for this would have been to create four different loops of your own, just like you did with the featured post example, thus sidestepping $wp_query. However, there really isn't any need here.

The following listing is the actual post code output stripped of everything that would go in the CSS file, but with the necessary IDs and classes.

```php
<div id="featured">
    <?php $featured_query = new WP_Query('category_name=featured&showposts=3');
    while ($featured_query->have_posts()) : $featured_query->the_post();
    $do_not_duplicate[] = $post->ID ?>
        <div id="post-<?php the_ID(); ?>" <?php post_class(); ?>>
            <h2>
                <a href="<?php the_permalink(); ?>" title="<?php the_title(); ?>">
                    <?php the_title(); ?>
                </a>
            </h2>
            <?php the_excerpt(); ?>
        </div>
    <?php endwhile; ?>
</div>
<div class="column left">
    <h2>Latest from <span>Apples</span></h2>
    <ul>
    <!-- Now begins the first column loop -->
    <?php query_posts('category_name=apples&showposts=10'); ?>
    <?php while (have_posts()) : the_post();
        if (in_array($post->ID, $do_not_duplicate)) continue;
            update_post_caches($posts); ?>
        <li>
```

```html
            <h3>
                <a href="<?php the_permalink(); ?>" title="<?php the_title(); ?>">
                    <?php the_title(); ?>
                </a>
            </h3>
            <?php the_excerpt(); ?>
        </li>
    <?php endwhile; ?>
    </ul>
</div><div class="column left">
    <h2>Latest from <span>Oranges</span></h2>
    <ul>
    <!-- Now begins the second column loop -->
    <?php rewind_posts(); ?>
 <?php query_posts('category_name=oranges&showposts=10'); ?>
    <?php while (have_posts()) : the_post();
        if (in_array($post->ID, $do_not_duplicate)) continue;
        update_post_caches($posts); ?>
        <li>
            <h3>
                <a href="<?php the_permalink(); ?>" title="<?php the_title(); ?>">
                    <?php the_title(); ?>
                </a>
            </h3>
            <?php the_excerpt(); ?>
        </li>
    <?php endwhile; ?>
    </ul>
</div><div class="column right">
    <h2>Latest from <span>Lemons</span></h2>
    <ul>
    <!-- Now begins the third column loop -->
    <?php rewind_posts(); ?>
    <?php query_posts('category_name=lemons&showposts=10'); ?>
    <?php while (have_posts()) : the_post();
        if (in_array($post->ID, $do_not_duplicate)) continue;
        update_post_caches($posts); ?>
        <li>
            <h3>
                <a href="<?php the_permalink(); ?>" title="<?php the_title(); ?>">
                    <?php the_title(); ?>
                </a>
            </h3>
            <?php the_excerpt(); ?>
        </li>
    <?php endwhile; ?>
    </ul>
</div>
```

There you have it: four loops starting with one for featured posts, and then three more to display the latest from three different categories. This code can easily be implemented in just about any WordPress theme, but you would need to alter it to fit your category setup to make it work properly.

USING CUSTOM FIELDS

Custom fields are database fields with content defined entirely by the user, and are always used within the loop. You'll find the Custom Fields box in your Add New Post screen within the WordPress admin, however you might have to enable it using the Screen Options feature in the top right, and then ticking the box for Custom Fields. The Custom Fields box lets you add one or several custom fields, and a value for each (see Figure 3-11).

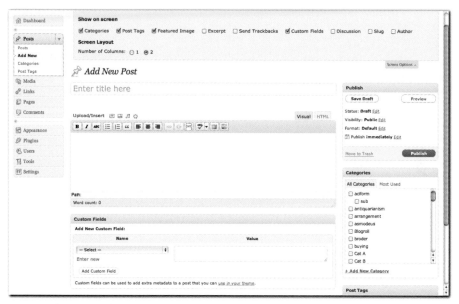

Figure 3-11: The Custom Fields box resides on the Add New Post screen, underneath the regular post-writing box — don't forget to enable it if needed!

Custom fields always belong to posts, and consist of two things: a key and a value. You can add new keys whenever you want, and after you've used them once they show up in a drop-down box, which is nice since you may misspell or forget about them otherwise.

CUSTOM FIELDS BASICS

Getting started with custom fields is easy; just write a post and add something in the key field, and then something in the value field, and click the Add Custom Field button to save. You've now stored your custom field data, although it won't show up anywhere unless you call it within the loop. The idea is to reuse the key across posts, in a way like a categorization of the kind of data you're storing, and just alter the value.

The template tag you use to make things happen with custom fields is the_meta(). By default it outputs an unlimited list (or a ul tag with list items; li's, in HTML speak) displaying the post's custom fields. That works great if you just store things such as how happy you are and what you're reading right now, or perhaps a grade for a review or something. The ul will have the class post-meta and then there's a li for each custom field, and within this li there is a span with the class="post-meta-key" that wraps around the key for that particular custom field. After that is the value in plain text.

Suppose you have a custom field with a key called Actor with the value Harrison Ford. Then you have another custom field called Director with the value Stephen Spielberg. Finally, you have a custom field called Movie Title with the value Indiana Jones and the Raiders of the Lost Ark. All these custom fields and their values belong to a specific post, and if you put the template tag the_meta() somewhere within the loop, and this post shows, it will output this code:

```
<ul class='post-meta'>
    <li><span class='post-meta-key'>Actor</span> Harrison Ford</li>
    <li><span class='post-meta-key'>Director</span> Steven Spielberg</li>
    <li><span class='post-meta-key'>Movie</span> Indiana Jones and the Raiders of
    the Lost Ark</li>
</ul>
```

As long as you just want to display simple stuff, that is enough and you can style it with CSS. Naturally, you'll want to do more, so let's move on.

POSTING HEADER IMAGES

One of the easiest and most popular uses of custom fields is attaching additional images to a post. First, you need to decide what to call your custom field key. Go with post-image, which will be easy to remember. When you see it in your code you'll instantly understand what it is, which is a good thing.

Next, you need some data to experiment with. Upload an image to your post using the WordPress image uploader, and then copy the image URL. It will be something like this:

```
http://notesblog.com/wp-content/2009/05/splashimage.jpg
```

Now, add that to the post-image key using the Custom Fields box on the Write Post screen. If you haven't used the post-image key before, you just type it in the key field; otherwise, you can choose it from the drop-down menu. Then, paste the image URL in the value field, and save. Now you have attached the URL with the post-image key for this particular post, which means that you can use it.

Find a place in your theme where you want this image to show, perhaps along with your posts on the home page. It all depends on how you shape the image: it can be anything from a thumbnail that goes to the right of your post's title, to a huge magazine-style photograph that sits behind it. This example shows you how to output the content in the custom field.

Here's a simple example of putting the custom fields image above the h2 title tag, something a lot of magazine themes like to do, accomplished with just a few additions to the basic loop you've become accustomed to by now:

```php
<?php if ( have_posts() ) : while ( have_posts() ) : the_post(); ?>
    <div id="post-<?php the_ID(); ?>" <?php post_class(); ?>>
    <?php
        // Image time
        $splashimg = get_post_meta($post->ID, 'post-image', $single = true);
        if($splashimg !== '') {
    ?>
        <img src="<?php echo 0; ?>" alt="<?php { echo the_title(); } ?>"
          class="splashimg" />
    <?php } else { echo ''; } ?>
    <h2>
        <a href="<?php the_permalink(); ?>" title="<?php the_title(); ?>">
            <?php the_title(); ?>
        </a>
    </h2>
    <?php the_content(); ?>
</div>
<?php endwhile; else: ?>
    <p>Some error message or similar.</p>
<?php endif; ?>
```

The third line is a PHP function where you store the variable $splashimg, created by you for this example, with the data from the get_post_meta() function. This is similar to the the_meta() template tag touched on previously, and you're getting three parameters from it. First, there is the post ID, which is needed for WordPress to figure out where to collect the custom field data from. Second, you need to request a custom field key and get the value of it, which in this case is post-image. Remember, you named the key just that, so now you'll get the value of the particular post's post-image key, which in turn is the image URL you saved. Finally, the third and last parameter you're passing is setting $single to true. You're doing this to tell get_post_meta() to pass the data as a string. If you set it to false, you would get an array of custom fields data, which can come in handy too, but not in this case. All this is stored in $splashimg.

Arriving at the fourth line, you're checking whether there is anything in the $splashimg function, and if there is, you're outputting an image with the source fetched from within the $splashimg.

That is of course the data you got from get_post_meta(); in other words, the custom field data for post-image. Should there not be anything in $splashimg, which would mean that you haven't saved any custom field data for the key post-image, then you echo nothing at all. Maybe you want a default image there instead, in which case you would echo that.

After that it is the same standard loop, outputting the linked post title and the content, and so on.

GETTING MORE COMFORTABLE WITH THE LOOP

The loop can certainly feel tricky to work with at first. The basic loop isn't too hard to identify, and that is really all you need to get started with WordPress. With a little practice, you will find it easier to understand the loop's mechanics, and when you start to build your own themes to power your WordPress site, you'll soon find yourself fiddling with it. The fact that a lot of plugins and template tags that you will want to use have to reside inside the loop makes it important, but the custom stuff, such as using multiple loops or specific content outputs, becomes more important when you begin pushing WordPress.

If you're having a hard time understanding the loop fully after reading this chapter, don't worry. The more examples you read and the more you play with it, the easier it will become to alter the loop to your needs. And that's what you're going to do next: actually start to build stuff. First up are themes, which you'll work with for the next few chapters. That means that you'll see a lot of the loop from now on, but you'll also delve deeper into template tags and other tools supplied by WordPress to control the content.

II

DESIGNING AND DEVELOPING WORDPRESS THEMES

4

WORDPRESS THEME ESSENTIALS

IF YOU WANT to do more advanced stuff with WordPress, you need to understand theme essentials. You could just start hacking the default theme, or download Notes Blog and go from there, but there are some things that won't be obvious from just using and tinkering with the code. This chapter helps you dive into the WordPress theme concept to get acquainted with themes and how they work. You'll learn how to alter them to fit your needs. After doing that, you'll be able to put your knowledge to good use in the coming chapters.

In this chapter, you will examine the Notes Blog theme to become better acquainted with the template files, so you'll know how to build your own. Those files include the stylesheet and the fairly extensive functions.php file, so you can learn how to work with all those elements you encountered in the previous chapters.

THEME BASICS

You may already be somewhat familiar with WordPress themes and the premises under which they operate. In theory, themes are a way to separate the design from the code, but in reality there is still a lot of coding happening in the more advanced themes out there.

A theme consists of a folder with template files and any other files that may be needed. The only two absolutely necessary template files are style.css and index.php. The former contains the header that identifies your theme (and generally some styling code), while the latter is the basic layout. In fact, even if you don't put in the sidebar.php template file, or the comments.php comments template, you'll get both sidebar and comment functionality served by WordPress automatically. If you're looking for a challenge, try to create a WordPress theme consisting of just the two necessary files, and see what you can do with it. It is an interesting exercise, but is not a very good idea for more advanced sites, of course.

ELEMENTS OF THE BASIC THEME

Figure 4-1 is a common blog layout. At the top, spanning the full width, is the blog header, which in fact is the header.php file. Underneath is the actual blog area, with the content to the left (index.php) and the sidebar to the right (sidebar.php). Finally, there is a footer to wrap it up, using the footer.php template file.

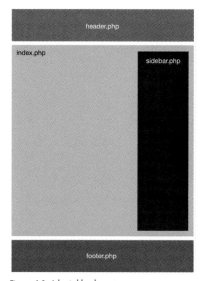

Figure 4-1: A basic blog layout

This setup is not mandatory; you can change it, exclude parts of it, or expand it further. It is, however, a very common setup, one that the default WordPress theme as well as the Notes Blog theme adheres to (see Figure 4-2 for comparison). You can find a lot of themes using template files in this manner, but it is in no way the only way to do things.

While you can get by with just style.css and index.php in your theme, it is generally not such a good idea to be so minimalist. At the very least, you should also have a header.php and a footer.php for your theme. These are called from within index.php, with the template tags `get_header()` and `get_footer()`. You'll also want a comments.php for commenting functionality, and you call that with `get_comments()`, also from within index.php. The same goes for the sidebar; you should have a template file for that too, and call it with `get_sidebar()`.

Figure 4-2: The Notes Blog theme layout looks a lot like the one shown in Figure 4-1

The header.php file consists of the doctype heading and everything related. You'll get a closer look at that in the following example section. The header.php file also generally does basic tasks like getting the right favicon, generating proper title tags, and having the necessary keywords so that search engines can find the pages more easily. However, one thing it must have is a link to the stylesheet, and the `wp_head()` is also needed to start the whole WordPress shebang.

Moving on, footer.php should include `wp_footer()` to stop WordPress and, of course, all the necessary closing tags. Make sure to close the `body` and `html` tags, and anything else you may have opened in header.php.

Finally, comments.php needs the code for outputting comments, as well as the necessary forms so that people can actually post new comments. This is done with simple template tags these days, so comments.php files aren't as messy to work with as they once were. The simplest file of all is sidebar.php, which is just the stuff you want in the sidebar.

As you may have gathered, everything revolves around index.php. However, there are other template files that can replace index.php, depending on the situation. If you're on the front page, for example, home.php takes the top slot, and index.php will only be used if there isn't a home.php. The same goes for single post view, where single.php takes precedence above index.php, and for WordPress pages page.php goes before index.php. Actually, if you utilize every one of the possible template files, your index.php file will never load. The concept is the same though, so leave things like that for a little while.

A FEW WORDS ABOUT THE CODE

There's a lot of code ahead. Most of it is pretty simple, and I'll keep things as conceptual and straightforward as possible. That way, the actual usage of the various template tags and functions is in focus, rather than the various sidetracks that really don't matter when it comes to learning the WordPress basics.

That being said, you should be aware that the following examples include localization tags and both template and conditional tags that you may not be entirely familiar with. Most of the latter two categories speak for themselves, but localization may be a bit harder to grasp. You'll get to the details of that in Chapter 6, but for now you only need to know that when you localize, you either wrap the text/code within _e() or __(). You use __() within PHP code, while _e() is used pretty much anywhere. Add a textdomain and you've got the basics, like this:

```
<?php _e('This text can be localized, mate!', 'the-textdomain'); ?>
```

Both _e() and __() rely on the premise that the text or code you can localize gets passed first, and then the textdomain that should be used. In the Notes Blog examples, the textdomain is called 'notesblog', so it would look like this:

```
<?php _e('This text can be localized, mate!', 'notesblog'); ?>
```

Then, thanks to language files, users can fully localize the theme. The purpose of the textdomain, by the way, is to identify where this particular string belongs. In the case of Notes Blog, it's all the strings the theme needs to have translated, whereas a plugin would have its own textdomain. You load the textdomain in the functions.php file (if it's a theme), or in your plugin.

Now that the basics are out of the way, it's time to get our hands dirty!

WALKING THROUGH THE NOTES BLOG THEME

A few words about the Notes Blog theme are in order here. This theme is free to download from http://notesblog.com and is designed and maintained by yours truly. It is actually meant to be a host for child themes, which are covered later on, but like any good theme it works perfectly well by itself.

We'll be touching on the Notes Blog theme frequently from now on, so this section walks you through the basic theme, cutting it down a bit to illustrate what a minimal WordPress theme can look like. Download the full thing from `http://notesblog.com` to get the complete picture.

Remember, all your document heading stuff is in header.php, the footer stuff in footer.php, and the sidebar content is in sidebar.php. Comment functionality is in comments.php, and finally, the theme information is in the style.css file, along with any basic styling you may have. This will be a lot of code, even though I'll stick to the most important parts.

THE STYLESHEET: STYLE.CSS

The first thing any theme needs is the stylesheet. Not only does it have the actual theme information header at the very top, it is also where as much of the design as possible should be managed. If you can do something with CSS, you should put it in style.css.

First is the theme's header, at the very top of the stylesheet:

```
/*
Theme Name: Notes Blog
Theme URI: http://notesblog.com/
Description: The Notes Blog theme is a clean blog theme created for your enjoyment.
  <a href="http://tdh.me/">Made by TDH</a> and maintained at <a href="http://notes
  blog.com/">notesblog.com</a>. Requires WordPress 3.1 or higher.
Version: 0.2.8
Tags: light, two-columns, right-sidebar, fixed-width, threaded-comments,
  sticky-post,
translation-ready, custom-background, custom-menus
Author: Thord Daniel Hedengren
Author URI: http://tdh.me/
License: GNU General Public License
License URI: license.txt


        Get support and services for the Notes Blog theme:
        http://notesblog.com


        Created and managed by Thord Daniel Hedengren:
        http://tdh.me


*/
```

Nothing weird or fancy there. Theme designers will be pleased to note that the description field supports some basic HTML code.

Moving on, I have a reset segment. I'm generally opposed to the popular practice of applying a margin and padding reset to everything, since many elements lack these settings. That being said, some resets are helpful, such as the fairly extensive one that follows:

```
/* =====
   RESET */

html, body, div, span, applet, object, iframe,
h1, h2, h3, h4, h5, h6, p, blockquote, pre,
abbr, acronym, address, big, cite, code,
del, dfn, em, font, img, ins, kbd, q, s, samp,
small, strike, strong, sub, sup, tt, var,
b, u, i, center,
dl, dt, dd, ol, ul, li,
fieldset, form, label, legend,
table, caption, tbody, tfoot, thead, tr, th, td {
    border: 0;
    margin: 0;
    padding: 0;
    vertical-align: baseline;
}

ol, ul {
    list-style: none;
}

table {
    border-collapse: collapse;
    border-spacing: 0;
}
```

Note that I've omitted most of the type and link styling, detailing which fonts and colors are used where from the code examples in the book to save space. Most of it is just simple stuff. I encourage you to dive deeper into it by nabbing the full version from `http://notesblog.com`. Just open style.css for a more complete look, and note the differences.

The layout section is fairly extensive, controlling every main element, but not so much how content within the elements should look. The full section is not presented here due to its length, but you should scan through it and become familiar with the general structure. You'll note some generic classes at first, for alignment and typical column widths, but after that is the code consists mainly of the key building blocks of the theme. While most of this file speaks for itself, take a deeper look at the comments section:

```
ol.commentlist { margin: 20px 0 20px 20px; padding: 20px 20px 1px 20px;
    background: #e9e9e9; }
    li.comment {}
        div.comment-author {}
            div.comment-author img { float: left; margin-right: 10px; }
            div.comment-author cite { font-weight: bold; font-style: normal; }
        div.comment-meta { margin-bottom: 10px; }
        div.comment-body {}
            div.comment-body p { margin-left: 16px; padding: 5px 0 5px 20px;
                border-left: 1px dotted #fff;   }
```

```
        div.reply { margin-top: 0; padding-bottom: 10px;
          border-bottom: 1px dotted #fff; text-align: right; }
          li.comment ul.children { margin: 20px 0 0 20px; }
    li.depth-1 { margin-bottom: 20px; }
    li.byuser {}
    li.bypostauthor {}
    li.pingback { padding: 10px 10px 1px 10px; background:#efefef; }
          li.pingback p, li.pingback div.reply { display:none; }
```

This should be pretty self-explanatory. Comments are outputted within the
`ol.commentlist` element, with each comment a list item in itself. After that is the
`div#respond` area with the necessary forms for posting a comment.

There are just two more things I want to highlight from style.css. The first is what I've labeled
Elements & Design in the file. It is basically some image handling, text alignments, and other
stuff that WordPress needs for the default output.

```
/* =================
   ELEMENTS & DESIGN */

p.right { text-align:right; }
p.center { text-align:center; }
p.admin { color: #aaa; font-size: 12px; }
p.nocomments { padding: 0 20px; font-style: italic; color: #777; }

div#content embed, .embedded { text-align:center; margin: 0 0 14px 0;
  padding-left:0; border:0; } /* for movies */

blockquote { margin: 0 0 16px 20px; padding: 0 20px; border: 1px solid
      #e9e9e9;
  border-width: 0 0 0 1px; }
    blockquote.pullquote { width: 220px; padding: 5px 0; border: 0;
  font-size: 18px; line-height: 150%; }
        blockquote.pullquote p { margin-bottom: 0; }
ol.commentlist li blockquote { border: 0; padding:0; }

/* Images and aligns */
.alignleft, blockquote.alignleft { margin: 0 20px 20px 0; }
.alignright, blockquote.alignright { margin: 0 0 20px 20px; }
img.aligncenter, .aligncenter { margin: 0 auto 16px auto; text-align:center; }
.frame { padding: 1px; border: 1px solid #e9e9e9; }
.wp-caption { padding: 20px 18px; border: 1px solid #e9e9e9; color: #888;
  font-style: italic; text-align:center; }
p.wp-caption-text { margin: 10px 0 0 0 !important; padding:0; font-size: 12px;
  line-height: 14px !important; }

div.gallery { margin-bottom: 14px; }
    dl.gallery-item {}
        dt.gallery-icon {}
```

```
        img.attachment-thumbnail { border:0; }
    dd.gallery-caption { margin-top: 8px; font-size: 12px; color: #777;
        font-style: italic; }

/* Quick color fixes */
div.postmeta { color: #777; }
span.alert { color: red; }
div#content strong { color: #333; }
```

One element to note in the preceding code is the image classes (img.frame is my own addition; I put it in just about every theme to add classy borders to images) as well as the wp-caption classes for image captions.

Another element worth drawing attention to is some styling that Notes Blog has for post formats. Post formats must be enabled to be used, but they are quite handy. Tasks that used to be handled with categories or custom fields can now be managed by post formats, either by using conditional tags to manage the content differently, or by styling it, as I have in this case:

```
/* ============
    POST FORMATS */

.format-aside { margin-left: 25px; margin-right: 25px; padding: 0 10px 0 20px;
border-left: 1px solid #efefef; }
    .format-aside h2.entry-title { margin-bottom: 6px; font-size: 16px; line-
height: 16px; }
    .format-aside div.entry-meta { display:none; }
    .format-aside div.entry-content {}
        .format-aside div.entry-content p { color: #666; font-size: 14px; margin-
  bottom: 14px; }
```

As you can see it is only the one post format, called aside, in this example. The class format-aside is automatically outputted by post_class(), which you'll see later in this chapter.

That wasn't too complicated, right? Remember, Notes Blog is meant to be a simple theme to build upon, so a lot of the bling you may add normally is completely left out, as are images.

THEME TOP: HEADER.PHP

When the active theme is loaded, it starts with the header.php file. This is where you put all the metadata, fire up WordPress with wp_head(), and usually put the top of your page:

```
<!DOCTYPE html>
<html <?php language_attributes(); ?>>
<head>
<meta charset="<?php bloginfo( 'charset' ); ?>" />
<title>
    <?php
        // Print the right title
```

```php
        if (is_home () ) {
            bloginfo('name');
        } elseif (is_category() || is_tag()) {
            single_cat_title(); echo ' &bull; ' ; bloginfo('name');
        } elseif (is_single() || is_page()) {
            single_post_title(); } else { wp_title('',true);
        }
    ?>
</title>
<link rel="profile" href="http://gmpg.org/xfn/11" />
<link rel="stylesheet" type="text/css" media="all" href="<?php
  bloginfo( 'stylesheet_url' ); ?>" />
<link rel="pingback" href="<?php bloginfo( 'pingback_url' ); ?>" />
<?php
    // Comment javascript
    if ( is_singular() ) wp_enqueue_script( 'comment-reply' );

    //  Use this hook to insert things into HEAD
    notesblog_inside_head();

    // Kick off WordPress
    wp_head();
?>
</head>

<body <?php body_class(); ?>>
<div id="site">

    <?php
        // Use this hook to insert things before the wrap
        notesblog_above_site();
    ?>

    <div id="wrap">
        <div id="header">
            <div class="header-widgetarea">
                <ul id="header-widgets">
                <?php
                    // Adding the Beside the logo widget area, empty by
                        default
                    dynamic_sidebar('beside-the-logo');
                ?>
                </ul>
            </div>
            <?php if (is_home() || is_front_page()) { ?>
                <h1 id="site-header">
                    <a href="<?php echo home_url(); ?>" title="<?php
                      bloginfo('name'); ?>">
                        <?php bloginfo('name'); ?>
                    </a>
                </h1>
```

```php
<?php } else { ?>
    <div id="site-header">
        <a href="<?php echo home_url(); ?>" title="<?php
          bloginfo('name'); ?>">
            <?php bloginfo('name'); ?>
        </a>
    </div>
<?php } ?>
</div>
<div id="blog">
    <div id="top-navigation">
      <?php wp_nav_menu('top-navigation'); ?>
    </div>
    <?php
        // Use this hook to do things between the menu and the main
        // content
        notesblog_below_menu();
    ?>
```

The first WordPressy thing here is the title tag. Here I use conditional tags to output a slightly different title depending on where on the site the visitor is. If you're on a Page you get the Page title, a tag archive gives you the tag in the title, and so on. It is possible to write pretty elaborate stuff here, but I've kept it simple for this version. Moving on, the `Comment javascript` might raise an eyebrow. I want to load the necessary JavaScript for replies when using threaded comments, but only on single posts and Pages (hence the `is_singular()` conditional tag, which checks for just that). I use `wp_enqueue_script()` to make sure it gets loaded properly with WordPress, from the wp-include/js/ folder.

In the same section you'll also find `notesblog_inside_head()`, which is a hook that lets developers insert code where it is located, in this case within the head section of the site. You'll learn more about this later, but for now it's enough to know that the presence of this little line, along with the declaration of its existence in functions.php (which we'll get to) makes it possible to insert code there from the outside, so to speak. Further down in index.php you'll find two other hooks: `notesblog_above_site()` and `notesblog_below_menu()`.

It is a good idea to put `wp_head()` just before you close the head tag; this is what initializes WordPress. Also note `body_class()` in the body tag, which more or less does what `post_class()` does for posts, which is to say it adds various CSS classes depending on where on the site the visitor is. Very handy for theme designers.

You may notice the absence of this row:

```html
<meta name="generator" content="WordPress <?php bloginfo('version'); ?>" />
  <!-- leave this for stats -->
```

That's because you don't want the wrong people to find out what version of WordPress you're running. Why make it any easier for hackers than it already is, eh?

The `dynamic_sidebar()` line is a widget area, situated beside the logo. Incidentally, while I use `bloginfo()` to output the site title, the URL pointing to the home page is an echo of `home_url()`, which is recommended these days. You'll also note that depending on if you're on the front page (checking with `is_home()` and `is_front_page()` respectively), the title will be wrapped in an `h1`, otherwise in a `div#site-header`, but both will look the same. (Consult style.css to confirm that!) The reason for this is merely to please search engines. On the front page, the title of the site is the highest header, but on a post, for example, the site title isn't as important as the title of the post, so in that case I'll encase the site title in a `div` instead, and let the post title be `h1`.

Finally comes `wp_nav_menu()`, which is a menu area, much like `dynamic_sidebar()` is a widget area. We'll cover all these cool things in more depth as we proceed. Widgets and menus are both declared and defined in functions.php, and then populated in WordPress admin using the appropriate interface. Theme files use `dynamic_sidebar()` for widgets and `wp_nav_menu()` for menus, as placeholders to which the content you've put them in will be outputted.

THE MAIN TEMPLATE: INDEX.PHP

There was a time when index.php contained every fallback you needed, since it is the template that will be used if no more fitting ones are present. However these days you can extract the loop, which is what powers WordPress, from the template files into their own files. That's why index.php in Notes Blog is a short and sweet affair:

```php
<?php get_header(); ?>

    <div id="content" class="widecolumn">
        <?php
            // Look for loop-index.php, fallback to loop.php
            get_template_part( 'loop', 'index' );
        ?>
    </div>

<?php get_sidebar(); ?>
<?php get_footer(); ?>
```

It's really simple, as you can see. First, you load the header.php template with `get_header()`, then the content div starts. In this file you find a `get_template_part()`, which includes the loop, first looking for loop-index.php and failing that reverting to loop.php. In Notes Blog, there is no loop-index.php so it'll load loop.php (which you'll learn about in just a little while).

The index.php template ends with calling first the sidebar.php template with `get_sidebar()`, and then the footer.php template with `get_footer()`.

LOOPING IT: LOOP.PHP

You tackled the loop in the previous chapter, but let's go through it quickly here as a refresher. The fallback loop in Notes Blog is obviously loop.php, but there are some loops used for the front page, as well as single, Page, and attachment view. Take a look at loop.php, where everything's covered:

```php
<?php
    // When possible, display navigation at the top
    if ( $wp_query->max_num_pages > 1 ) : ?>
    <div id="nav-above" class="navigation">
        <div class="nav-previous">
            <?php next_posts_link( __( '<span class="meta-nav">&larr;</span>
                Older posts', 'notesblog' ) ); ?>
        </div>
        <div class="nav-next">
            <?php previous_posts_link( __( 'Newer posts <span
                class="meta-nav">&rarr;</span>', 'notesblog' ) ); ?>
        </div>
    </div>
<?php endif; ?>


<?php
    // 404 Page Not Found or empty archives etc.
    if ( !have_posts() ) : ?>
    <div id="post-0" class="post error404 not-found">
        <h1 class="entry-title">
            <?php _e( 'Not Found', 'notesblog' ); ?>
        </h1>
        <div class="entry-content">
            <p>
                <?php _e( 'Sorry, there is nothing here. You might want to try
                    and search for whatever it was you were looking for?',
                    'notesblog' ); ?>
            </p>
            <?php get_search_form(); ?>
        </div>
    </div>
<?php endif; ?>


<?php
    // The basic loop
    while ( have_posts() ) : the_post(); ?>

    <div id="post-<?php the_ID(); ?>" <?php post_class(); ?>>
        <?php
            // Use this hook to do things between above the post title
            notesblog_above_post_title_listing();
        ?>
        <h2 class="entry-title">
```

```php
        <a href="<?php the_permalink(); ?>" title="<?php
          the_title_attribute(); ?>" rel="bookmark">
            <?php the_title(); ?>
        </a>
    </h2>
    <?php
        // Use this hook to do things between below the post title
        notesblog_below_post_title_listing();
    ?>
<?php
    // For archives and search results, use the_excerpt()
    if ( is_archive() || is_search() ) : ?>
        <div class="entry-summary">
            <?php the_excerpt(); ?>
        </div>
<?php
    // For everything else
    else : ?>
        <div class="entry-content">
            <?php the_content(); ?>
            <?php wp_link_pages( array( 'before' => '<div
              class="page-link">' . __( 'Pages:', 'notesblog' ),
              'after' => '</div>' ) ); ?>
        </div>
<?php endif; ?>
</div>

<?php comments_template( '', true ); ?>

<?php
    // End the loop
    endwhile; ?>

<?php
    // When possible, display navigation at the bottom
    if ( $wp_query->max_num_pages > 1 ) : ?>
    <div id="nav-below" class="navigation">
        <div class="nav-previous">
            <?php next_posts_link( __( '<span class="meta-nav">&larr;</span>
              Older posts', 'notesblog' ) ); ?>
        </div>
        <div class="nav-next">
            <?php previous_posts_link( __( 'Newer posts <span
              class="meta-nav">&rarr;</span>', 'notesblog' ) ); ?>
        </div>
    </div>
<?php endif; ?>
```

The code is pretty documented with comments, I think, but I'll walk through it anyway.

If you feel a bit lost, go back to the Chapter 3 and read up on the loop again.

First is a block for displaying navigation should you need to. That would cover jumping to previous and next pages on a category archive, for example.

```php
<?php
    // When possible, display navigation at the top
    if ( $wp_query->max_num_pages > 1 ) : ?>
    <div id="nav-above" class="navigation">
        <div class="nav-previous">
            <?php next_posts_link( __( '<span class="meta-nav">&larr;</span>
                Older posts', 'notesblog' ) ); ?>
        </div>
        <div class="nav-next">
            <?php previous_posts_link( __( 'Newer posts <span
                class="meta-nav">&rarr;</span>', 'notesblog' ) ); ?>
        </div>
    </div>
<?php endif; ?>
```

You'll find a similar block at the end of loop.php, since you want the navigation both on the top and the bottom when it's needed.

Moving on, you come to the 404 page not found error handling. This is what will show if WordPress can't find the post or page the user was looking for, usually due to faulty links. It would be overrun by a 404.php template file of course, which Notes Blog doesn't include.

```php
<?php
    // 404 Page Not Found or empty archives etc.
    if ( !have_posts() ) : ?>
    <div id="post-0" class="post error404 not-found">
        <h1 class="entry-title">
            <?php _e( 'Not Found', 'notesblog' ); ?>
        </h1>
        <div class="entry-content">
            <p>
                <?php _e( 'Sorry, there is nothing here. You might want to try
                    and search for whatever it was you were looking for?',
                    'notesblog' ); ?>
            </p>
            <?php get_search_form(); ?>
        </div>
    </div>
<?php endif; ?>
```

As you've probably noticed by now, Notes Blog is fully localized, meaning that every string that the user might want to translate into another language is either wrapped in __ () or in _e (). The latter is an automatic echo of the content of the string. Next, we move on to the actual loop for content:

```php
<?php
    // The basic loop
    while ( have_posts() ) : the_post(); ?>

    <div id="post-<?php the_ID(); ?>" <?php post_class(); ?>>
        <?php
            // Use this hook to do things between above the post title
            notesblog_above_post_title_listing();
        ?>
        <h2 class="entry-title">
            <a href="<?php the_permalink(); ?>" title="<?php
              the_title_attribute(); ?>" rel="bookmark">
                <?php the_title(); ?>
            </a>
        </h2>
        <?php
            // Use this hook to do things between below the post title
            notesblog_below_post_title_listing();
        ?>
    <?php
        // For archives and search results, use the_excerpt()
        if ( is_archive() || is_search() ) : ?>
            <div class="entry-summary">
                <?php the_excerpt(); ?>
            </div>
    <?php
        // For everything else
        else : ?>
            <div class="entry-content">
                <?php the_content(); ?>
                <?php wp_link_pages( array( 'before' => '<div class="page-
                    link">'
                    . __( 'Pages:', 'notesblog' ), 'after' => '</div>' ) ); ?>
            </div>
    <?php endif; ?>
    </div>

    <?php comments_template( '', true ); ?>

<?php
    // End the loop
    endwhile; ?>
```

You'll notice another bunch of those hooks mentioned in the header.php section earlier. They are `notesblog_above_post_title_listing()` for inclusion of stuff above the title, and `notesblog_below_post_title_listing()` for the same but under the title. Both are declared in functions.php and covered later.

Other than that it is a pretty typical loop, outputting the (linked) title and so on. If you're looking at an archive page (category or date archive, for example) or a search result, you just get excerpts of the posts, using `the_excerpt()`, but otherwise you get the full content using `the_content()`.

That's about it for loop.php; it's pretty straightforward but covers the bases should any page revert to it. Since Notes Blog has dedicated loop files for single pages (for example), there aren't any particular handling of those in loop.php. Otherwise that could have been done with a conditional tag, `is_singular()`, preferably to manage both single posts and Pages.

You should have the gist of it now. If you want the complete overview I suggest you take a closer look at the other loop files in the theme (loop-single.php, loop-attachment.php, and so on) and see how they tackle their respective tasks.

SIDE ORDER: SIDEBAR.PHP

Moving on, you come to sidebar.php, which is loaded to the right in the Notes Blog theme, as you've probably already gathered from the style.css file:

```php
<div id="sidebar-container" class="column">
    <ul id="sidebar">
        <?php
            // Global right sidebar (always on)
            dynamic_sidebar('global-right-column');

            // Front page
            if ( is_home() || is_front_page() ) {
                dynamic_sidebar('front-page-right-column');
            }
            // Single post
            elseif ( is_single() ) {
                dynamic_sidebar('posts-right-column');
            }
            // Page
            elseif ( is_page() ) {
                dynamic_sidebar('pages-right-column');
            }
            // Archive listings
            elseif ( is_archive() ) {
                dynamic_sidebar('archives-right-column');
            }
            // Fallback widget area
            else {
                dynamic_sidebar('fallback-right-column');
            }
        ?>
    </ul>
</div>
```

This is really simple. The sidebar sits in `ul#sidebar` (which in turn is positioned with `div#sidebar-container`), where you have a bunch of conditional checks to see what widget area you should output where. The top one, `dynamic_sidebar('global-right-column')`, is always loaded, whereas the others only show their faces on the appropriate page. Notice that there is no default content in any widget area, so leave them empty if you don't want to use them. You could just stick to using the global widget area if you prefer to keep it simple. More on widgets when we get to functions.php, where you'll find that all of these are declared.

SOAPBOXING: COMMENTS.PHP

The comment functionality is controlled by comments.php. You don't actually need to include it, because if WordPress fails to find comments.php in your theme it will load the file from wp-includes, which sometimes is a good idea. Notes Blog has its own comments.php file, based on said file from wp-includes. The file (fully localized, of course) is broken down in the following segments.

The top part isn't something you usually need to fiddle with; it just stops the comments from being shown if a password is required:

```php
<div id="comments">
<?php
    // Password protected?
    if ( post_password_required() ) : ?>
        <p class="nopassword">
            <?php _e( 'This post is password protected. Enter the password to
                view any comments.', 'notesblog' ); ?>
        </p>
</div>
<?php
        // Stop comments.php from being processed
        return;
    endif;
?>
```

Moving on, you have a comment loop that checks if there are any comments, and then outputs them. Thanks to `wp_list_comments()`, the comments.php template isn't as much of a hassle to work with as it was once upon a time:

```php
<?php
    // There are comments
    if ( have_comments() ) : ?>
        <h3 id="comments-title">
            <?php printf( _n( 'One response to %2$s', '%1$s responses to
                %2$s',
                get_comments_number(), 'notesblog' ),
                number_format_i18n( get_comments_number() ), '<em>'
                . get_the_title() . '</em>' ); ?>
        </h3>
```

```php
<?php
    // Do we need pagination?
    if ( get_comment_pages_count() > 1 && get_option( 'page_comments' ) ) : ?>
        <div class="navigation">
            <div class="nav-previous">
                <?php previous_comments_link( __( '<span
                 class="meta-nav">&larr;</span> Older comments', 'notesblog' )
                    ); ?>
            </div>
            <div class="nav-next">
                <?php next_comments_link( __( 'Newer comments <span
                    class="meta-nav">&rarr;</span>', 'notesblog' ) ); ?>
            </div>
        </div>
<?php endif; ?>


        <ol class="commentlist">
            <?php
                // Loop comments, dictated by notesblog_comment() from
                // functions.php
                wp_list_comments('callback=notesblog_comment');
            ?>
        </ol>

<?php
    // Do we need pagination?
    if ( get_comment_pages_count() > 1 && get_option( 'page_comments' ) ) : ?>
        <div class="navigation">
            <div class="nav-previous">
                <?php previous_comments_link( __( '<span
                 class="meta-nav">&larr;</span> Older Comments', 'notesblog' )
                    ); ?>
            </div>
            <div class="nav-next">
                <?php next_comments_link( __( 'Newer Comments <span
                    class="meta-nav">&rarr;</span>', 'notesblog' ) ); ?>
            </div>
        </div>
<?php endif; ?>
```

Notice that `wp_list_comments()` is asking for something called `notesblog_comment`. This is declared in functions.php, and contains the actual comment output. We'll get to it later.

What if there are no comments?

```php
<?php
    // There were no comments
    else :

        // Comments were closed
```

```php
        if ( ! comments_open() ) : ?>
            <p class="nocomments">
                <?php _e( 'Sorry, comments are closed.', 'notesblog' ); ?>
            </p>
        <?php endif;

    // Wrap up have_comments()
    endif;
?>
```

The code just outputs a message if comments were closed, and says nothing if there just aren't any.

Finally, you come to the response section. There used to be a fully fledged form right here, but today you can just use `comment_form()` to handle it all:

```php
<?php
    // The comment form
    comment_form( array(
        'comment_field' => '<p><textarea id="comment" name="comment" cols="45"
          rows="8" aria-required="true"></textarea></p>',
        'comment_notes_after' => '',
    ) );
?>
```

That's it, a closing `div` and you're all set.

Most of the time, this basic comments.php template will do the job. However, sometimes you want something more, such as Facebook Connect integration or similar features. Sometimes those special cases are managed by plugins, but not always, so it is a good idea to get acquainted with the comments.php file.

WRAPPING UP: FOOTER.PHP

Finally it's time to close the whole thing, with the footer.php template file. This one wraps up all the tags from header.php, and adds some copyright information and such. But it also features four widget areas, which we'll get to in just a second, and two hooks: `notesblog_above_footer()` and `notesblog_below_site()`, for inclusion of code.

```php
<?php
    // Use this hook to do things above the footer
    notesblog_above_footer();

    // The widgets are in sidebar-footer.php
    get_sidebar('footer');
?>

</div><!-- /#blog -->
```

```php
<div id="copy">
    <div class="widecolumn left">
        <p>
            Copyright &copy; <a href="<?php echo home_url(); ?>">
            <?php bloginfo('name'); ?></a><br /><em>
            <?php bloginfo('description'); ?></em>
        </p>
    </div>
    <div class="column right">
        <p class="right">
            <?php _e('Built on', 'notesblog');?>
            <a href="http://notesblog.com" title="Notes Blog">Notes
            Blog</a> <?php _e('by', 'notesblog'); ?>
            <a href="http://tdh.me" title="TDH">TDH</a><br />
            <?php _e('Powered by', 'notesblog');?>
            <a href="http://wordpress.org" title="WordPress">
            WordPress</a>
        </p>
    </div>
</div>

<div id="finalword">
    <span>&uarr;</span> <a href="#top" title="To page top">
    <?php _e('That\'s it - back to the top of page!',
        'notesblog');?></a>
    <span>&uarr;</span>
</div>

    </div>
</div>

<?php
    // Use this hook to do things below the site
    notesblog_below_site();

    // WordPress ends
    wp_footer();
?>
</body>
</html>
```

Remember to always put `wp_footer()` at the very end of your footer.php file, just before the closing of the body tag. This is the WordPress wrap-up, and just like `wp_head()` it is important.

The four widget areas aren't actually in the footer.php file (although they could be). To keep things nice and tidy I'm using `get_sidebar('footer')` to include sidebar-footer.php, where the widget areas are in fact located. Let's take a look at sidebar-footer.php as well:

```php
<?php
    // Only show widget areas if there's anything in them
    // Thanks Twenty Ten
    if (   ! is_active_sidebar('footer-column-a')
        && ! is_active_sidebar('footer-column-b')
        && ! is_active_sidebar('footer-column-c')
        && ! is_active_sidebar('footer-column-d')
    )
        return;
    // If we get this far, we have widgets. Then we move on!
?>

<div id="footer">
    <div class="footer-column-container">
        <ul class="footer-column widgets">
            <?php dynamic_sidebar('footer-column-a'); ?>
        </ul>
        <ul class="footer-column widgets">
            <?php dynamic_sidebar('footer-column-b'); ?>
        </ul>
        <ul class="footer-column widgets">
            <?php dynamic_sidebar('footer-column-c'); ?>
        </ul>
        <ul class="footer-column widgets">
            <?php dynamic_sidebar('footer-column-d'); ?>
        </ul>
    </div>
</div>
```

If you've played with the Twenty Ten theme you'll recognize the code. Basically it is four widget areas that just show up when there's something in them. Nothing too fancy.

THE EVER IMPORTANT FUNCTIONS.PHP FILE

The functions.php file has evolved a lot over the years. Not only do you declare your widget areas in it, but you also set a number of important settings, create your hooks, enable menus and custom backgrounds, and so on. Notes Blog does all this, except for adding the custom header feature which isn't a part of the current version (that's covered in Chapter 6).

Basic Settings in functions.php

The functions.php file can be a bit overwhelming, so let's start from the top.

```php
// Localization support, fetches languages files from /lang/
load_theme_textdomain( 'notesblog', TEMPLATEPATH . '/lang' );

// The default content width
if ( ! isset( $content_width ) ) $content_width = 640;
```

```
// The visual editor will use editor-style.css
add_editor_style();

// Add default posts and comments RSS feed links
add_theme_support( 'automatic-feed-links' );

// Add custom background support
add_custom_background();

// Add post thumbnails support (920x250px)
add_theme_support( 'post-thumbnails' );
set_post_thumbnail_size( 920, 250, true );

// Add some post formats
add_theme_support( 'post-formats', array( 'aside', 'gallery', 'quote' ) );
```

This code includes the basic settings for some standard WordPress features. First, you load the `textdomain` used for localization and tell WordPress that the language files are located in the lang folder in the theme:

```
load_theme_textdomain( 'notesblog', TEMPLATEPATH . '/lang' );.
```

Then you set the default width for content to 640 pixels. This is used for media and embeds.

Moving on, `add_editor_style()` will load editor-style.css to tweak the visual editor in admin to be more like the actual site, and `add_theme_support( 'automatic-feed-links' )` adds default RSS feeds. This code also enables custom background images/colors for easy editing in the admin interface with `add_custom_background()`.

To get the featured image feature for posts and Pages, you set `add_theme_support ( 'post-thumbnails' )`, and obviously you want these images to look alike so set the image size to 920x250 pixels, enforced, with `set_post_thumbnail_size( 920, 250, true )`. In Notes Blog, the featured image, should it be present, is located at the top of the post or Page and covers the full width; that's why it is so big.

Finally, this code adds support for some post formats, which we touched on previously. You can use post formats to further control how your posts should look and behave. Chapter 6 covers them in more detail. Anyway, `add_theme_support( 'post-formats', array( 'aside', 'gallery', 'quote' ) )` adds support for three of the post formats: Aside, Gallery, and Quote. That means that you can choose any of those (or Standard) when writing posts.

Adding Menu Areas in functions.php

The following code is for declaring a menu area. As you probably know, WordPress has a menu interface, and while you can put your created menus in widgets and drop them anywhere, you can also create menu areas. Notes Blog only has one menu area, called Top Navigation, and unsurprisingly it is the top navigation in the theme.

```
// Add the Top Navigation menu
register_nav_menus( array(
        'top-navigation' => __( 'Top Navigation', 'notesblog' ),
) );
```

Chapter 6 covers menus in depth.

Adding Widgets in functions.php

Next, take a look at widgets. Notes Blog has a whole bunch of widget areas, all declared in the following code and then called for when needed in the other template files.

```
// WIDGET AREAS ->
// Beside the logo
register_sidebar( array(
    'name' => __( 'Beside the logo', 'notesblog' ),
    'id' => 'beside-the-logo',
    'description' => __( 'Widget area in the header, right of the logo.', 'notes-
  blog' ),
    'before_widget' => '<li id="%1$s" class="widget-container %2$s">',
    'after_widget' => '</li>',
    'before_title' => '<h2 class="widget-title">',
    'after_title' => '</h2>',
) );
// Global right column
register_sidebar( array(
    'name' => __( 'Global right column', 'notesblog' ),
    'id' => 'global-right-column',
    'description' => __( 'The global right column sits on top of every right column,
  leave empty if unwanted.', 'notesblog' ),
    'before_widget' => '<li id="%1$s" class="widget-container %2$s">',
    'after_widget' => '</li>',
    'before_title' => '<h2 class="widget-title">',
    'after_title' => '</h2>',
) );
// Front page right column
register_sidebar( array(
    'name' => __( 'Front page right column', 'notesblog' ),
    'id' => 'front-page-right-column',
    'description' => __( 'Right column widget area used on the front page.', 'notes-
  blog' ),
    'before_widget' => '<li id="%1$s" class="widget-container %2$s">',
    'after_widget' => '</li>',
    'before_title' => '<h2 class="widget-title">',
    'after_title' => '</h2>',
) );
// Posts right column
register_sidebar( array(
    'name' => __( 'Posts right column', 'notesblog' ),
    'id' => 'posts-right-column',
```

```
        'description' => __( 'Right column widget area for single posts.', 'notesblog'
    ),
        'before_widget' => '<li id="%1$s" class="widget-container %2$s">',
        'after_widget' => '</li>',
        'before_title' => '<h2 class="widget-title">',
        'after_title' => '</h2>',
) );
// Pages right column
register_sidebar( array(
        'name' => __( 'Pages right column', 'notesblog' ),
        'id' => 'pages-right-column',
        'description' => __( 'Right column widget area for Pages.', 'notesblog' ),
        'before_widget' => '<li id="%1$s" class="widget-container %2$s">',
        'after_widget' => '</li>',
        'before_title' => '<h2 class="widget-title">',
        'after_title' => '</h2>',
) );
// Archives right column
register_sidebar( array(
        'name' => __( 'Archives right column', 'notesblog' ),
        'id' => 'archives-right-column',
        'description' => __( 'Right column widget area for archive listings.', 'notes-
  blog' ),
        'before_widget' => '<li id="%1$s" class="widget-container %2$s">',
        'after_widget' => '</li>',
        'before_title' => '<h2 class="widget-title">',
        'after_title' => '</h2>',
) );
// Right column fallback
register_sidebar( array(
        'name' => __( 'Right column fallback', 'notesblog' ),
        'id' => 'fallback-right-column',
        'description' => __( 'Right column fallback widget area for the rest.', 'notes-
  blog' ),
        'before_widget' => '<li id="%1$s" class="widget-container %2$s">',
        'after_widget' => '</li>',
        'before_title' => '<h2 class="widget-title">',
        'after_title' => '</h2>',
) );
// Home column A
register_sidebar( array(
        'name' => __( 'Home column A', 'notesblog' ),
        'id' => 'home-column-a',
        'description' => __( 'The left column just below the menu on the front page.',
  'notesblog' ),
        'before_widget' => '<li id="%1$s" class="home-widget-container %2$s">',
        'after_widget' => '</li>',
        'before_title' => '<h2 class="widget-title">',
        'after_title' => '</h2>',
) );
// Home column B
```

```
register_sidebar( array(
    'name' => __( 'Home column B', 'notesblog' ),
    'id' => 'home-column-b',
    'description' => __( 'The middle column just below the menu on the front page.',
 'notesblog' ),
    'before_widget' => '<li id="%1$s" class="home-widget-container %2$s">',
    'after_widget' => '</li>',
    'before_title' => '<h2 class="widget-title">',
    'after_title' => '</h2>',
) );
// Home column C
register_sidebar( array(
    'name' => __( 'Home column C', 'notesblog' ),
    'id' => 'home-column-c',
    'description' => __( 'The right column just below the menu on the front page.',
 'notesblog' ),
    'before_widget' => '<li id="%1$s" class="home-widget-container %2$s">',
    'after_widget' => '</li>',
    'before_title' => '<h2 class="widget-title">',
    'after_title' => '</h2>',
) );
// Footer column A
register_sidebar( array(
    'name' => __( 'Footer column A', 'notesblog' ),
    'id' => 'footer-column-a',
    'description' => __( 'The far left column in the footer.', 'notesblog' ),
    'before_widget' => '<li id="%1$s" class="widget-container %2$s">',
    'after_widget' => '</li>',
    'before_title' => '<h2 class="widget-title">',
    'after_title' => '</h2>',
) );
// Footer column B
register_sidebar( array(
    'name' => __( 'Footer column B', 'notesblog' ),
    'id' => 'footer-column-b',
    'description' => __( 'The left middle column in the footer.', 'notesblog' ),
    'before_widget' => '<li id="%1$s" class="widget-container %2$s">',
    'after_widget' => '</li>',
    'before_title' => '<h2 class="widget-title">',
    'after_title' => '</h2>',
) );
// Footer column C
register_sidebar( array(
    'name' => __( 'Footer column C', 'notesblog' ),
    'id' => 'footer-column-c',
    'description' => __( 'The right middle column in the footer.', 'notesblog' ),
    'before_widget' => '<li id="%1$s" class="widget-container %2$s">',
    'after_widget' => '</li>',
    'before_title' => '<h2 class="widget-title">',
    'after_title' => '</h2>',
) );
```

```
// Footer column D
register_sidebar( array(
    'name' => __( 'Footer column D', 'notesblog' ),
    'id' => 'footer-column-d',
    'description' => __( 'The far right column in the footer.', 'notesblog' ),
    'before_widget' => '<li id="%1$s" class="widget-container %2$s">',
    'after_widget' => '</li>',
    'before_title' => '<h2 class="widget-title">',
    'after_title' => '</h2>',
) );
```

Widget areas are registered with `register_sidebar()` and then defined with an array of settings. You can control obvious things like name and ID for your widget area, but also the description that will show up in the widget interface in WordPress admin and hence help your users understand what the particular area is meant for. Other things you can fiddle with include how the widget title, should there be one, should be wrapped, as well as the widget itself. See the Codex entry at `http://codex.wordpress.org/Function_Reference/register_sidebar` for more information, such as the default values for `register_sidebar()`.

Including Hooks in functions.php

Remember all those hooks that you can use to insert code into the theme? They are declared in functions.php as well, are created by `do_action()`, and they look like this:

```
// NOTES BLOG HOOKS
// Create the inside head wrap hook
function notesblog_inside_head() {
    do_action('notesblog_inside_head');
}
// Create the above wrap hook
function notesblog_above_site() {
    do_action('notesblog_above_site');
}
// Create the below menu hook
function notesblog_below_menu() {
    do_action('notesblog_below_menu');
}
// Create above single post hook
function notesblog_above_post() {
    do_action('notesblog_above_post');
}
// Create above post title in listings hook
function notesblog_above_post_title_listing() {
    do_action('notesblog_above_post_title_listing');
}
// Create below post title in listings hook
function notesblog_below_post_title_listing() {
    do_action('notesblog_below_post_title_listing');
}
// Create above post title in single post view
```

```
function notesblog_above_post_title_single() {
    do_action('notesblog_above_post_title_single');
}
// Create below post title in single post view
function notesblog_below_post_title_single() {
    do_action('notesblog_below_post_title_single');
}
// Create above page title in single page view
function notesblog_above_page_title_single() {
    do_action('notesblog_above_page_title_single');
}
// Create below page title in single page view
function notesblog_below_page_title_single() {
    do_action('notesblog_below_page_title_single');
}
// Create the between post and comments hook
function notesblog_below_post() {
    do_action('notesblog_below_post');
}
// Create the above footer hook
function notesblog_above_footer() {
    do_action('notesblog_above_footer');
}
// Create the below site hook
function notesblog_below_site() {
    do_action('notesblog_below_site');
}
// <- ENDS
```

Hooks are covered in Chapter 6, but if you look at the following code you'll get a sense of how they work:

```
// POSTMETA BELOW POST TITLE
function notesblog_add_postmeta_below_title() { ?>
    <div class="entry-meta">
        <?php _e( 'Written by', 'notesblog' ); ?> <?php the_author_posts_link();
          ?> &bull;
        <?php the_time( __( 'F j, Y @ g:i a', 'notesblog' ) ); ?> &bull;
        <?php _e( 'Filed under', 'notesblog' ); ?> <span
          class="meta-category"><?php the_category(', '); ?></span>
        <?php
            // Check for tags, output if there are any
            if ( has_tag() ) {
                _e('and tagged ', 'notesblog');
                the_tags('<span class="meta-tags">', ', ', '</span>');
            } ?>
        <?php
            // If the comments are open we'll need the comments template
            if (comments_open()) { ?>
                <span class="comments-link">
```

```
              <br /><?php comments_popup_link( __( 'Leave a comment',
                'notesblog' ), __( '1 comment', 'notesblog' ),
                __( '% comments', 'notesblog' ) ); ?>
          </span>
    <?php } ?>
    <?php edit_post_link( __( 'Edit', 'notesblog' ), '<span
      class="meta-sep">&bull;</span> <span class="edit-link">', '</span>'
      ); ?>
  </div>
<?php }
// Add to listings and single post view
add_action('notesblog_below_post_title_listing',
'notesblog_add_postmeta_below_title');
add_action('notesblog_below_post_title_single',
'notesblog_add_postmeta_below_title');
```

The function `notesblog_add_postmeta_below_title()` contains the postmeta data
(post author, date published, and so on), and then you apply that to two hooks using
`add_action()`. You could say that you're sneaking in all the postmeta stuff that lives in
`notesblog_add_postmeta_below_title()` where you want it by adding it to the
corresponding hook. Again, you'll learn more about this in Chapter 6 so don't worry if it still
sounds strange.

Controlling Comments in functions.php

The last bit of code in the functions.php file is the one that controls how comments look.
Remember that `wp_list_comments()` had a callback to `notesblog_comment()`?
That's actually a function, and it contains everything needed to output comments.

```
// COMMENTS
function notesblog_comment($comment, $args, $depth) {
   $GLOBALS['comment'] = $comment; ?>
  <li <?php comment_class(); ?> id="li-comment-<?php comment_ID() ?>">
    <div id="comment-<?php comment_ID(); ?>" class="comment-body">
     <div class="comment-author vcard">
        <?php echo get_avatar($comment,$size='32',$default='<path_to_url>' );
          ?>
        <?php printf(__('<cite class="fn">%s</cite>'),
        <span class="says">says:</span>'), get_comment_author_link()) ?>
     </div>
     <?php if ($comment->comment_approved == '0') : ?>
       <em><?php _e('Your comment is awaiting moderation.') ?></em>
       <br />
     <?php endif; ?>

     <div class="comment-meta commentmetadata">
        <a href="<?php echo htmlspecialchars( get_comment_link(
          $comment->comment_ID ) ) ?>">
        <?php printf(__('%1$s at %2$s'), get_comment_date(),
          get_comment_time()) ?></a><?php edit_comment_link(__('(Edit)'),'
```

```
                 ','') ?>
        </div>

        <?php comment_text() ?>

        <div class="reply">
            <?php comment_reply_link(array_merge( $args, array('depth' => $depth,
            'max_depth' => $args['max_depth']))) ?>
        </div>
    </div>
<?php }
```

This is a bit messy, but it's basically a post-like output that will be used in the comment loop, so to speak. The comment_text() template tag outputs the actual comment (much like the_content() does on posts), and comment_reply_link() will only be used if threaded comments are activated. Not much sense in commenting on individual comments otherwise, is there? Thanks to the enqueing of the comment-reply JavaScript in header.php, that will look snappy, though.

You may be feeling a bit overwhelmed by functions.php file in Notes Blog right now. You should return to it every now and then, as you learn more, and things will fall into place.

UNDERSTANDING TEMPLATE FILES

A theme consists of template files. There is some confusion about this at times because people refer to the theme as a "template." That's wrong; a theme is a theme, which in effect is a folder (that needs to be situated in the wp-content/themes/ directory to be used) containing several files. The style.css stylesheet is a template file, and so are the header.php, footer.php, index. php, functions.php files, and so on that resides in the theme folder.

Template files can be used in a wide variety of ways. Their exact use depends on what you put in them, of course. You can make them behave in almost any way you want by changing the loop or leaving it out altogether, and you can use template tags to generate a specific behavior. Likewise, you can make pages a lot more dynamic by using conditional tags, and if you really want to shake things up you can always use plugins to extend WordPress beyond any of the built-in functionality.

There are a few things you need to know up front about template files. First, you need to know which ones are necessary for the basic functionality. Second, you have to work out which template file is used when. Third, you should figure out which template files are necessary for what you want to achieve.

Suppose you want the home page to be the same as the index.php pages, except with an added image or welcome text. Should you use a home.php template in addition to index.php? It would be a lot more convenient to add an is_home() conditional tag in index.php to output the additions on the front page only. The same goes for single posts: if there is not much difference between single post view and the front page, you can use is_single() to alter the parts that need to be different (like not linking the post title, for example).

93

WHICH TEMPLATE FILE IS USED WHEN?

Table 4-1 lists the various template files and describes the uses of each.

Table 4-1 **Template File Uses**

Template	Function
archive.php	Template for archives based on author, category, and date, overridden by respective individual template. Also archive-[post type].php for specific post type (i.e., archive-persons.php for the Persons post type)
attachment.php	Template for any post attachment, usually images but any mime type will do. Custom styling is done with [mime-type].php; for example image.php or video.php
author.php	The author template
category.php	Template for category view listings; category-[id].php and category-[slug].php can be used to target specific categories
comments.php	Comment display and posting template; if not available the default comment template will be loaded
comments-popup.php	Comments in a popup; rarely used anymore
date.php	Template for any date-based listing (per year, per month, and so on)
404.php	Page not found 404 error message template
home.php front-page.php	Used for the home page and the front page, respectively, should a static Page be set as home
index.php	The main template. Must be included as a fallback to every page should it not have a template file;, should most likely include the loop
page.php	The template for page view; individual page templates can also be created, and page-[slug].php as well as page-[id].php can be used to target specific pages
search.php	Search result/error message template
single.php	Single post view template; single-[post type].php (i.e., single-persons.php for a post type called persons) used for specific post types
style.css	Stylesheet file, must be included with a theme info header at top. Put everything CSS here
tag.php	List display for a tag; tag-X.php will be used for the tag with the slug X
taxonomy.php	For custom taxonomies; taxonomi-[taxonomy]-[term].php for specific term in specific taxonomy (i.e., taxonomy-monsters-godzilla.php for Godzilla in Monsters), taxonomy-[taxonomy].php for specific taxonomy (i.e., taxonomy-monsters.php), and taxonomy.php for general view

Remember, a theme doesn't need to include all the possible template files. In fact, you shouldn't use more of these than you really need to, since that only means that you'll have more files to maintain should WordPress change or if you want to alter something in your design.

Some of these templates may be confusing. Take a look at the category.php template, for example. By default this template displays the post listing from any given category. However, should there be a category-X.php template, where X is the ID of the category in question, that template file will be used rather than the category.php template. The same goes for tags: tag-X. php is displayed before tag.php. The same goes for category and tag slugs, so the category Monkeys with the slug `monkeys` and an ID of 42 can be reached at category-monkeys.php as well as category-42.php.

In short, WordPress will look for a specific template file, and if that one isn't present it will fall back to the next best template file, and lacking that, fall back again, and so on.

Keep in mind that page.php and Page templates are actually two different things. You may have noticed that you can set a template when creating WordPress Pages. These are Page templates, not controlled by page.php but rather sporting their own header information much like style.css. They can be very useful, so we'll play with them in a little while.

TEMPLATE HIERARCHY

Now that you know what the template files are, you need to know which one is loaded when, and what happens if there is no template at all. As you know, index.php is the fallback template for everything, and you can settle for using only that. Figure 4-3 illustrates the hierarchy of the template files.

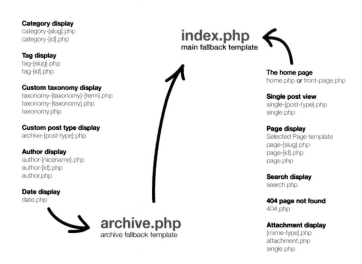

Figure 4-3: The hierarchy of template files

PAGE TEMPLATES

WordPress Pages are meant for static content that is less time-dependent than your average blog post (which probably is static, after all). The Pages can have subpages, which are typically used for information about the site, contact forms, and so on. However, you can take it way beyond that if you want. First, you can give the page.php template a nice styling that fits the kind of content you want to display on your Pages (rather than just have them mimic your blog posts). Second, you can create Page templates that you can apply to individual Pages from the Write page section in WordPress admin.

These Page templates are basically normal template files, except that they need a little code snippet at the top of the file before the actual code begins so that WordPress can find them (much like your theme's style.css, in other words).

Just put the following lines on top of the Page template file, which you can name whatever you like as long as it is suffixed with .php:

```php
<?php
/*
Template Name: My Page Template
*/
?>
```

This one, for example, could be named mypagetemplate.php. It may be a good idea to name Page templates pagetemplate-[something].php for semantic reasons, but that's entirely up to you. Just keep in mind that you shouldn't name them page-[something].php since page-[slug].php is a template file that WordPress might look for, and you could get a clash there.

With that code snippet on top, and then any kind of template file content you like, the Page template will show up in the Page template box in the Write page section in WordPress admin. Just pick it, save, and there you go.

A common usage for Page templates is an archive page. Maybe you want to have a link to your archives that displays all authors, categories, tags, and the 50 latest posts using template tags. This just won't work with a normal Page, because you can't put template tags within the post itself through WordPress admin (at least not without using plugins that open up the editor), so you need a Page template. Here's a sample, pagetemplate-archives.php from Notes Blog, designed for use with simple blog archives:

```php
<?php
/*
Template Name: Archives
*/
?>

<?php get_header(); ?>
```

```php
<?php
    // Check for post thumbnail
    if (has_post_thumbnail( $post->ID ) ) { ?>
    <div id="post-thumbnail">
        <?php echo get_the_post_thumbnail( $post->ID, 'post-thumbnail' );
            ?>
    </div>
<?php } ?>

<div id="content" class="widecolumn">
<?php
    // The basic loop
    while ( have_posts() ) : the_post(); ?>

    <div id="post-<?php the_ID(); ?>" <?php post_class(); ?>>
        <?php
            // Use this hook to do things above below the page title
            notesblog_above_page_title_single();
        ?>
        <h1 class="entry-title">
            <?php the_title(); ?>
        </h1>
        <?php
            // Use this hook to do things above below the page title
            notesblog_below_page_title_single();
        ?>
        <?php edit_post_link( __( 'Edit', 'notesblog' ), '<div
          class="entry-meta">', '</div>' ); ?>
        <div class="entry-content">
            <?php the_content(); ?>
            <h2><?php _e('Browse by Month:', 'notesblog');?></h2>
            <ul>
                <?php wp_get_archives('type=monthly'); ?>
            </ul>
            <h2><?php _e('Browse by Category:', 'notesblog');?></h2>
            <ul>
                <?php wp_list_categories('title_li='); ?>
            </ul>
            <h2><?php _e('Browse by Tag:', 'notesblog');?></h2>
            <?php wp_tag_cloud('smallest=8&largest=28&number=0&orderby=
                name&order=ASC'); ?>
        </div>
    </div>

    <?php if (comments_open()) { ?>
        <?php comments_template( '', true ); ?>
    <?php } ?>
```

```php
<?php
    // End the loop
    endwhile; ?>
</div>

<?php get_sidebar(); ?>
<?php get_footer(); ?>
```

Other common uses are Pages created just to display a specific loop. You can just take your index.php template file, for example, and make a Page template out of it (put the code snippet on top), and then change the loop to output whatever you want using `query_posts()`. You can also have a Page containing multiple loops, or perhaps PHP code that isn't related to WordPress at all.

Putting Page templates to good use is a huge step toward creating the site you want using WordPress.

THE 404 TEMPLATE

The 404.php template differs a bit from the other template files. It is only displayed when someone either clicks a faulty link to your WordPress powered site, or when someone misspells something. In other words, 404.php is used when stuff isn't working, and nothing can be returned.

That means that the 404.php template won't use the loop unless you want it to. A good 404 page, no matter what system you're running, should be informative and offer the lost visitor a way to get back on track. That can be a quick link to the site's front page, a search form, or a list of the 20 latest updates. Or all that, as it were.

What follows is a somewhat generic 404 error message that you can adapt for your own 404. php if you like. It does all the things you may need to help the visitor on their way.

```php
<?php get_header(); ?>
<div id="content" class="widecolumn">
    <h1 class="listhead">This is a <strong>404 Page Not Found</strong></h1>
    <div class="post single">
        <h2>There's nothing here!</h2>
        <p>
            We're sorry, but there is nothing here! You might even call this a
            <strong>404 Page Not Found</strong> error message, which is
            exactly what it is. The page you're looking for either doesn't
            exist, or the URL you followed or typed to get to it is incorrect
            in some way.
        </p>
        <p>
            <strong>Why don't you try and search for it?</strong> Use the
            search box and try to think of a suitable keyword query, and
            you'll probably be fine.
        </p>
```

```
    <p>
        You're sure that it should be here, that page you were looking
        for?
        <a href="/contact">Then tell us about it!</a>
    </p>
    <h3>Something to read?</h3>
    <p>Want to read something else? These are the 20 latest updates:</p>
    <ul>
        <?php wp_get_archives('type=postbypost&limit=20&format=html'); ?>
    </ul>
    </div>
</div>
<?php get_footer(); ?>
```

If there's no 404.php template to call, the index.php template will be used. In fact, you'll see the error message from the loop that was so painstakingly included in several loop examples in Chapter 3. You can style those individually using conditional tags as shown in the following snippet; is_404() will output something only if someone got something wrong.

```
<?php if (is_404()) { ?>
    <h1 class="listhead">This is a <strong>404 Page Not Found</strong></h1>
    <div class="post single">
        <h2>There's nothing here!</h2>
        <p>
            We're sorry, but there is nothing here! You might even call this a
            <strong>404 Page Not Found</strong> error message, which is
            exactly what it is. The page you're looking for either doesn't
            exist, or the URL you followed or typed to get to it is incorrect
            in some way.
        </p>
        <p>
            <strong>Why don't you try and search for it?</strong> Use the
            search box and try to think of a suitable keyword query, and
            you'll probably be fine.
        </p>
        <p>
            You're sure that it should be here, that page you were looking
            for?
            <a href="/contact">Then tell us about it!</a>
        </p>
        <h3>Something to read?</h3>
        <p>Want to read something else? These are the 20 latest updates:</p>
        <ul>
            <?php wp_get_archives('type=postbypost&limit=20&format=html'); ?>
        </ul>
    </div>
<?php } ?>
```

You can also handle 404 messages with a check on have_posts(), as I'm doing in Notes Blog:

```php
<?php
    // 404 Page Not Found or empty archives etc.
    if ( !have_posts() ) : ?>
    <div id="post-0" class="post error404 not-found">
        <h1 class="entry-title">
            <?php _e( 'Not Found', 'notesblog' ); ?>
        </h1>
        <div class="entry-content">
            <p>
                <?php _e( 'Sorry, there is nothing here. You might want to try
                    and search for whatever it was you were looking for?',
                    'notesblog' ); ?>
            </p>
            <?php get_search_form(); ?>
        </div>
    </div>
<?php endif; ?>
```

Whether you prefer to manage 404 errors through a 404.php template, or rely on code in index.php is entirely up to you. Just make sure you make it a good error message; just displaying 404 Page Not Found will certainly let the lost visitor know that something went wrong, but it won't be much help to them in finding the correct destination.

USING FUNCTIONS.PHP

One theme template file you haven't touched very much yet is functions.php. It is a bit mysterious, and most people take a brief look at it and then shy away. Not all themes have functions.php files, but the ones that do usually support widgets and may even have their own options page inside WordPress admin, as you saw in the functions.php files from Notes Blog earlier in this chapter. This is all possible thanks to the functions.php file.

What, then, does functions.php do? Basically, it does whatever you want it to, since it more or less acts like a plugin that is called within the WordPress initialization, both when viewing the public site and when loading the admin interface. Because of that, you can add admin functionality to functions.php.

You'll look at widgets and how to set up widget areas in a little while, but first, add a simple function to functions.php:

```php
<?php
    function hellomate() {
        echo 'Hello mate, how are you doing?';
    }
?>
```

If you put that simple little code snippet in functions.php, and then call the function somewhere within your theme, it will output the "Hello mate, how are you doing?" text. You call the function like you would call any PHP function:

```
<?php hellomate(); ?>
```

So that would echo the text. Not very useful, perhaps, but it does show you something that functions.php can do. If you have code snippets you use all the time, and want them easily accessible, this is your solution.

Many themes use admin options pages to let the user set their own color schemes, font styles, or perhaps change the header. This is all managed with functions.php. You'll get to create your own theme options pages later on.

SETTING THE DEFAULT WIDTH

A commonly forgotten feature is the content width setting. Content width, which is a simple little snippet added to functions.php, will tell WordPress the maximum width that the theme can manage, which in turns means that the theme will resize the image accordingly. Sure, you have Media Settings in the WordPress admin interface, where you can control the size of images (Figure 4-4), but the user may forget to change these things when changing themes.

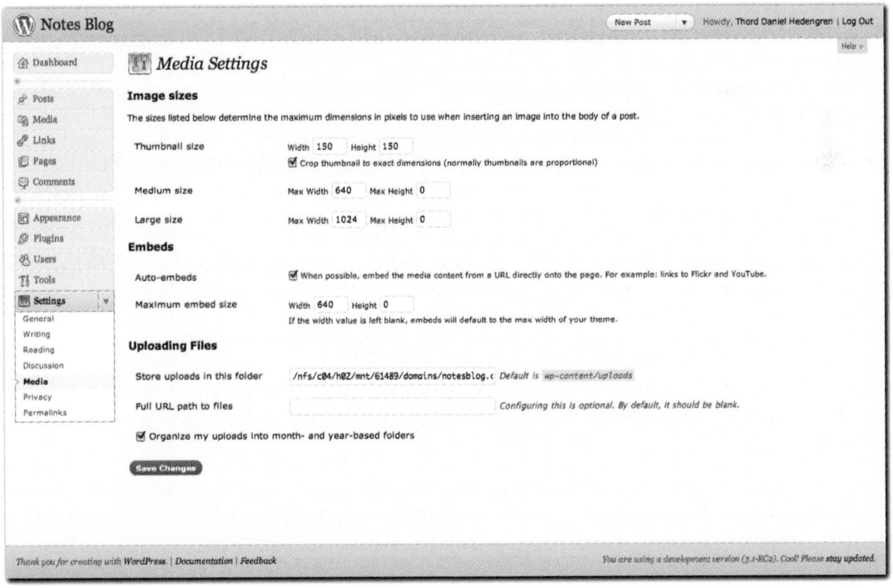

Figure 4-4: The Media Settings in WordPress admin isn't the only way to control image width

This is where $content_width comes in. It sets the width for large-sized images. Remember, when uploading an image to WordPress you get a total of four images; the ones listed on the admin page, and the original one. And with $content_width, the large image will fit perfectly with your theme.

It is easy to add. Just put this snippet in functions.php (within the PHP tags of course):

```
$content_width = 580;
```

580 is the width in pixels, so you need to change that to whatever is the maximum width for content in your theme.

INSERTING PROMOTIONS WITH FUNCTIONS.PHP

A lot of blogs and sites show promotional elements after the post, usually to get people to subscribe to the RSS feed. This is easily done in the theme's template files, but it can also be handled by your functions.php file and some action hookery.

Say you want to encourage your readers to subscribe to your RSS feed. You want to output a div with the class promotion, and within it an h4 header and a line of text. Thanks to the magic of CSS you can style it graphically any way you want just by applying styles to the div. Maybe something like this:

```
div.promotion { background: #eee; border: 1px solid #bbb; padding: 10px; }
div.promotion h4 { color: #f00; font-size: 14px; margin: 0 0 5px 0; padding:
0; }
div.promotion p { font-size: 12px; color: #444; margin-bottom: 0; }
```

That would probably look decent. To really bling it up you should add a background image featuring a nice RSS graphic or something to the div, but forget about that for now. This is the full HTML you want to output after your marvelous posts:

```
<div class="promotion">
    <h4>Never miss a beat!</h4>
    <p>
        Our smashing <a href="http://notesblog.com/feed/">RSS feed</a> keeps
        you up-to-date!
    </p>
</div>
```

How, then, do you get this thing to output itself without hacking the template files? Easy enough: you can use functions.php and attach it to the the_content() template tag. (You know, the one that outputs the actual content, after which you want to add it.) Here's the functions.php code:

```
function Promotion($content) {
        if(!is_feed() && !is_home()) {
            $content.= '<div class="promotion">';
            $content.= '<h4>Never miss a beat!</h4>';
            $content.= '<p>Our smashing <a href="http://notesblog.com/feed/">
                RSS feed"</a> keeps you up-to-date!</p>';
            $content.= '</div>';
        }
        return $content;
}
add_filter ('the_content', 'Promotion');
```

The function creates a variable called `Promotion`, which you're storing with the HTML code. Naturally, you can just as easily write the whole HTML in one long string, rather than having four lines of `$content`, but this way makes it a bit simpler to write. Then you return `$content`, which means that `Promotion` is now stored with the HTML you want to output. Finally, you use `add_filter` to add it after `the_content`.

And there you have it; whenever it is not a home page or a feed listing (see the `if` clause — you may want to add more conditions there by the way), you'll output the promotional box that asks the reader to subscribe to the RSS feed.

Why would you do this rather than just hack the template files? The only real reason for this is that this method is pretty theme-independent, so you can just copy and paste it between your themes and just add the necessary CSS to the stylesheet. Having a set of functions for the most common content you want to output, and even hooking them onto template tags when possible, is a way to streamline your WordPress themes even more.

As you can see, functions.php can be very handy, and it is certainly a lot more than just the widget declarations that just about every theme has these days. That said, the widgets are the most commonly used feature originating from functions.php, so we'll look at those next.

UNDERSTANDING WIDGETS AND WHEN TO USE THEM

Widgets add drag-and-drop functionality that allows the administrator to add features to a WordPress site from within the admin interface. This can be anything from a simple text block in the sidebar, to category listings, recent comments, or the latest updates from RSS feeds. That is just core widget functionality built into WordPress; add widget-ready plugins and you get a lot more.

When used correctly, widgets can be a great asset for a site administrator, since the hands-on way you use and alter them makes them really easy to work with. In the coming chapters you'll see how you can use widget areas for tasks other than just displaying a lot of clutter in the sidebar of typical blog 1A. In fact, you may remember that Notes Blog has a widget area called Submenu in the header, in which users easily can add a simple menu should they want to. That's just a small taste of what widget areas can do for you.

DECLARING WIDGETS

It is easy to make your theme widget-ready. Do so using functions.php within your theme, where you declare the widget areas, and then add the necessary code in your various theme files (usually sidebar.php) where you want the widget area to show up.

This is the simplest way of doing it, just creating the default sidebar widget in functions.php:

```php
<?php register_sidebar(); ?>
```

Then, add this to the part of sidebar.php where you want the widgets to show up. It should go within the `ul` tags:

```
<ul id="sidebar">
<?php dynamic_sidebar(); ?>
</ul>
```

For a more detailed example of how the sidebar.php can look with default content within, see the "Side Order: sidebar.php" section of "A Closer Look at Notes Blog" earlier in this chapter.

MULTIPLE WIDGET AREAS

Some themes have more than one widget area. You can accomplish this by declaring the widget areas in functions.php a little differently. If you want two sidebar areas, a header area, and a footer area that are widget-ready, just add the following code to functions.php:

```
<?php
    register_sidebar(array('name'=>'Sidebar 1'));
    register_sidebar(array('name'=>'Sidebar 2'));
    register_sidebar(array('name'=>'Header'));
    register_sidebar(array('name'=>'Footer'));
?>
```

Speaks for itself, right? This is basically the same declaration as for one (default) widget area, but with the names of every area defined. This will have to carry on to the code that defines the actual areas in the template files. That doesn't require any fancy footwork; just add the widget area name to the first PHP tag for defining an area, like this:

```
<?php dynamic_sidebar('The-Widget-Area-Name'); ?>
```

So the footer area would look like this:

```
<?php dynamic_sidebar('Footer'); ?>
```

Simple and straightforward. Naturally, anything that goes for single widget areas can be used when you have multiple widget areas, so if you need them to behave differently by all means go for it. Again, take a look at the Notes Blog example previously in this chapter and you'll see some more elaborate use of widget areas.

CUSTOMIZING WIDGETS

Sometimes you may not want the widgets to output the way they do by default. Maybe you want to enclose them in `div` tags, for example. To do so, register them in functions.php using an array:

```
<?php
    register_sidebar(array(
        'before_widget' => '',
        'after_widget' => '',
        'before_title' => '',
```

```
        'after_title' => '',
    ));
?>
```

The wrapping code goes inside the single quotation marks at the end of each line.

Now, wrap the widget in a `div` with the class `customwidget`, and enclose the title in a `div` with the class `customtitle`:

```php
<?php
    register_sidebar(array(
        'before_widget' => '<div class="customwidget">',
        'after_widget' => '</div>',
        'before_title' => '<div class="customtitle"',
        'after_title' => '</div>',
    ));
?>
```

You should use this custom stuff with caution. After all, most themes and widgetized plugins are created with the unlimited list in mind.

Now that you've gotten deep into the theme's template files, and have looked into how to widgetize areas, you can do something about those comments. Yes, you did indeed look at the comments.php template file earlier in this chapter, but there is more to comments than just getting the functionality working. They need to look good.

MAKING COMMENTS LOOK GOOD

Not all sites need comment functionality, but chances are that a lot of the sites you'll be building with WordPress will. Most blogs allow readers to comment on the posts, and the same goes for the vast majority of editorial sites out there, from newspapers to magazines. It is just a good way to connect with the readership, and while the sites in question may have different motives for doing this, and may have different comment policies, the basic functionality remains the same.

From a WordPress theme designer's point of view, comments can be a bore, mostly because making them look good can be a problem. The actual code isn't all that hard though, and if you like the default comment view (as featured in the default WordPress theme) you won't even have to create the comments.php template file. You had a close look at such a file in the "A Closer Look at the Notes Blog" section earlier in this chapter, so I'll gloss over that part for now and look at the comments from a less technical point of view for a little while.

The following list notes the most important considerations for designing the comments section of a site:

- Clearly delineate the comment section from other content. You don't want the readers to mix up comments with the editorial content.
- The comments need to be easy to read, just like the rest of the site.
- Proper spacing between comments, along with alternating colors or dividing lines, helps provide visual separation. Any method that accomplishes this separation is fine.
- The comment author must be evident.
- The post comment form should be obvious to use, properly tabbed, and use a readable font in a decent size. Think about it: if you want the readers to write long and insightful comments, you should make it as easy on them as possible to do so.

A few less essential points come to mind as well:

- What's the comment policy? Link to it or put it in small print along with the Post Comment button.
- Do you allow HTML code? If so, which tags are acceptable?
- Do the comments go into moderation before publication? If they do, you should let the readers know, or at least output a big note when a posted comment goes into moderation.
- Do you require signup and/or login to comment? Then make that process as simple and obvious as possible.

Think the comment functionality through and you'll be fine. You'll also have a much easier time designing it, and possibly altering the functionality when required as well.

THREADED COMMENTS

Threaded comments were introduced in WordPress 2.7 and require activation from within the WordPress admin interface, under Settings → Discussion. Any theme that uses the proper template tag for listing the comments, which is `wp_list_comments()`, supports threaded comments should you want them. See the "Soapboxing" section of "A Closer Look at Notes Blog" earlier in this chapter for more on comments.

If you activate threaded comments you'll get a reply link at the end of each comment. Clicking it will alter the post comment section somewhat and add a Cancel Reply link as well. This is all built-in stuff, so you needn't worry about it.

What you do need to consider, however, is the following:

- How deep will the threaded comments go? This is an admin setting, and you need to make sure you support it within your design.
- You need to ensure the Reply link is properly styled.
- You need to ensure the Cancel Reply link is properly styled.

Replies to comments end up within that particular comment's `li`, inside a `ul` with the class `children`. The comment hierarchy is basically like this (with some code cut out to illustrate the point):

```
<li>
    [The top level comment content]
    <ul class="children">
        <li>
            [First level reply]
            <ul class="children">
                <li>
                    [Second level reply]
                </li>
            </ul>
        </li>
    </ul>
</li>
<li>
    [Next comment on the top level]
</li>
```

How many `ul`'s with the `children` class are allowed is determined by the threaded comment depth setting in admin. Five is the default, so your themes should support that many at least. The whole concept of threaded comments is built on hierarchy, so you should probably set the margin or padding for the `children` class to 10 pixels or so. It all depends on your theme, but you should make every reply indent a bit.

Styling the Reply link is easier. The link resides in a `div` with the class `reply`, so just style that any way you want. You can make it float to the right and in a font size of 12 pixels easily enough by adding this to the stylesheet:

```
div.reply { float:right; font-size: 12px; }
```

The same applies to the Cancel link that is outputted just below the Post a Comment header in the Respond section of the comment area. Again, this all depends on how your comments. php template looks, of course, but usually you'll find it here. It is in a `div` with the `cancel-comment-reply` class by default. You can make that bold just as easily as you managed the Reply link:

```
div.cancel-comment-reply { font-weight:bold; }
```

If you want to place this link somewhere particular, you can control it by placing the `cancel_comment_reply_link()` template tag wherever is suitable for your theme. Naturally, it should be close to the respond form, since that is where the link will be

107

outputted. The default `div` listed above needs to be in the template too, so this is what you'll be moving around:

```
<div class="cancel-comment-reply">
    <?php cancel_comment_reply_link(); ?>
</div>
```

Threaded comments are a great way to make longer conversations more manageable, so do consider using them if the topics on the site in question spark debates.

AUTHOR HIGHLIGHTING

Highlighting the post author's comments is a good idea, especially if the site is of the teaching kind. Say, for instance, you're doing tutorials. The readers may have questions, in which case it is a good idea to be very clear about which comments are the author's.

Comments are listed in a list, (`ol`) with every comment being a list item (`li`). This is where you can make a difference, since `wp_list_comments()` applies some CSS classes to each `li`. Among those classes are `bypostauthor`, if it is in fact the post author who wrote a comment. That means that the post author need to be logged in when commenting, otherwise WordPress won't recognize him or her.

Give the post author comments a yellow background by adding this to style.css:

```
li.bypostauthor { background: yellow; }
```

Now, all comments by the author of the original post will have a yellow background. You may want do something fancier as well, but changing the background of the comment is a good idea, as is upping the font size and/or color a bit. And if you want, you can take it really far since everything related to the particular comment is found within the `li.bypostauthor` tag. That means that you can change the way the avatar is displayed (`img.avatar` is the CSS class you're looking for), or alter the comment metadata (`div.comment-author` and `div.comment-meta`) as well as the actual comment text. Set the comment text font size to 18 pixels, just for the fun of it, and keep the comment background yellow:

```
li.bypostauthor { background: yellow; }
li.bypostauthor div.comment-body p { font-size: 18px; }
```

Use post author highlighting with caution. After all, it is not always all that important that the post author's comments are highlighted this way. A smaller note, however, will never hurt.

ADDING CUSTOM FIELDS

Custom fields open up even more advanced options to the theme and plugin designer. They provide a way to store custom data in the database, and that in turn means that they can open up new functionality. See the Custom Fields section in Chapter 3 for hands-on examples on how custom fields work; in this section I explain what you can do with them as a designer.

COMMON USAGE

Custom fields were initially thought of as a way to store metadata for a post, and that's still the way it is presented in the Codex, as well as how the default output (which we'll get to) behaves. However, that is not the most common usage for custom fields these days. Most often, custom fields are used to apply an image to a post, and use it in listings, or to achieve what is often referred to as magazine-style headlines. However, custom fields needn't be limited to managing magazine-style headlines or showing off post thumbnails in listings. You can use custom fields for a number of things, such as applying custom CSS styles depending on the post, as a way to add further unique styling to the posts. Or you can use custom fields to create and identify a series of posts (key would be Series and the value would be the various series' names), and then create a Page template with a custom loop that limits the output to posts with a specific Series value.

Another image-based custom field implementation would be to not only apply headline and listing images for the post, but also alter the complete body background!

Custom fields can be taken pretty far, and whenever you need to step outside the boundaries of traditional WordPress template tags and functions, custom fields are definitely worth a look.

THE USABILITY FACTOR

My main gripe with custom fields is that they look so messy. Just look at that custom fields box in WordPress admin; it isn't at all as user-friendly as the rest of the interface. Just the "key" and "value" nomenclature, and then the whole design of the box. . . . No, it just isn't something I'd trust a client with.

This is the most serious issue with custom fields, in my view. After all, when you've used it once it is easy enough to pick the key you need and copy and paste the image you want in the value field, for instance. But while that may not seem daunting to you, a client may feel differently.

This is something you need to keep in mind when doing work for clients. Is it feasible to assume that the person(s) updating the site can handle custom fields? The most common usage of custom fields is, after all, headline images and things like that, and they almost always involve finding a URL to the image and copying and pasting it to the value field of the appropriate key. Can the client handle that?

Custom fields are great, but until they are presented in a more user-friendly way, they are limited to the more Web-savvy crowd that isn't afraid to do some manual inputting. You probably fall into that category, but whether or not your clients (or partners, collaborators, or whatever) do is up to you to decide. If not, you are probably better off finding another solution. Luckily there are a few plugins that solve this (which we'll get to later in the book), so you have alternatives while you wait for WordPress core to make custom fields more user-friendly.

DEVELOPING A CORE THEME

If you're a theme designer, or just an aspiring one, and you want to develop WordPress-based sites, you really need a basic core theme. Here's why:

1. **It is a time saver.** Every time you need to start a new WordPress project, you have a basic and easy to edit/alter/break theme to begin with.
2. **It is familiar.** When you've spent hours and hours hacking a theme, possibly for several different projects, then you'll feel right at home when going at it again and again.
3. **It is easy to keep up-to-date.** If you keep your core theme up-to-date, you won't have to struggle with new functionality all the time: just update once, and there you have it.
4. **It may make client updates easier.** Assuming you're building your sites as child themes standing on your core theme's shoulders, updating client sites with new functionality shouldn't be a problem.

As you will discover in Chapter 5, child themes are your friends. If you set up a solid core theme that you build your WordPress sites on, you'll make everything easier on yourself.

The examples in this book rely on the Notes Blog theme (by yours truly). You can use it as your own basic core theme to build upon, whether you do this by hacking the theme directly to fit your needs, or by applying the child theme concept to it. The theme is free to use in just about any way you like, for personal sites or a basis for commercial projects.

Should you not want to use Notes Blog, you can either create your very own basic core theme from scratch (or copy and paste your way, with sensibility of course), or find a theme framework that fits you. There are several to choose from online, and a quick search will give dozens of promising hits. You must pay attention to the license for any theme you choose, since you want to be able to use your basic core theme any way you like without paying for every setup. If your core theme of choice is a premium theme, there is most likely a developer's license that gives you these rights, but if you're reading this book chances are you're better off spending some time creating your very own core theme.

So what should your core theme do? Well, everything you think you need on a regular basis, and absolutely nothing more. The last thing you want is a bloated core theme that may look good in itself, or perhaps suit one kind of WordPress site, but be entirely overkill for others. It is a better idea to keep an extras library with stuff you won't need all the time, from custom code to small code snippets and template files, and deploy these things only when needed. After all, you want the final theme to be as tight as possible, without being hard to maintain.

To sum up:

- Analyze your needs, and set up a basic core WordPress theme based on those needs.
- Use an existing theme framework, if possible, to save time.
- Pay attention to theme licenses!

Say you're the generous kind and want to share your brilliant core theme, or a variant of it at least, with the general public. Good for you, that's very much in line with the open source spirit. But if you're gonna do it, then let's make sure you do it right!

RELEASING A THEME

The WordPress community always appreciates the release of a new theme. The official theme directory offers theme installation from within the WordPress admin interface, which makes it all the more interesting to host your theme there. That way, the WordPress site will also make sure that sites use the latest version of the theme, or offer users the option to upgrade automatically through the admin interface. That is assuming you keep your theme up-to-date in the directory, of course.

When you release a theme, it should, of course, be fully functional, preferably validated, and not a complete copy of someone else's work. See the following theme checklist for more details on what you should consider before releasing your theme.

It may be tempting to sell your theme. Commercial (or premium, as they are sometimes called) themes are a reality, and there are licenses for sale with support programs, as well as other solutions that work around the GPL license that WordPress carries. Why should that matter to you and the theme you want to sell? Well, since WordPress is licensed under GPL, that means everything relying on WordPress is also covered. This is rocky ground to say the least, and you should carefully consider how you license your theme. It may also be good to know that the directory on `wordpress.org` only accepts themes compatible with the GPL license, which has (happily) sparked a mass conversion of premium themes to GPL.

THEME CHECKLISTS

When releasing a WordPress theme, and to some extent also when delivering one to a client or rolling out one of your own projects on a theme, there are some mandatory elements. Naturally, the theme needs to work, that's the first thing, and that means you need at the very least the style.css file with the theme information at the top, as well as the index.php file, and whatever other template files you may want to use.

But that's not all. Before releasing your theme, you should ensure that it meets all the standards in the following checklist. This checklist can help you avoid the mistake of releasing a theme and then having to patch it right away.

Development Issues

- Does the theme validate?

- Is there a proper doctype in the header?

- Do you call `wp_head()` and `wp_footer()`? (Because you really should!)

- Is there an RSS feed link in the header declaration? Web browsers need that to see the feed and add that pretty little icon to the right of the URL.

- Have you gotten rid of everything from your local development environment? This can be anything from local image references, to code relating to your svn.

- Are you using JavaScript properly? Remember, a lot of themes are shipped with Word-Press and there is even a `wp_enqueue_script()` function for this purpose, see Chapter 12 for more.

- Are the widget areas working as they should, and do they display default content? If they are, make sure the content is relevant and appropriate, otherwise they shouldn't output anything at all.

- What about menu areas? Are there any and how are you handling them? The menu feature in WordPress helps end users a lot, so you should use it if you can!

- Have you added Edit links to posts, Pages, and possibly even comments that display only when administrators are logged in? This is very handy.

- Do the Gravatars work properly?

- Did you remember to add CSS for threaded comments, even if you don't think you'll use it? It should support at least three, and preferably five, comments in-depth.

- Is your theme ready for localization? Should it be?

- Are all the dates and times displaying properly? Try not to code this into the template files by passing parameters to `the_date()` and `the_time()`: it is a lot better to having the user control these elements in the WordPress admin settings.

- Have you set the content width variable in functions.php?

- Are you supporting custom backgrounds and custom headers? Should you?

- Have you enabled support for post format? Do you need it?

- What about all the other nice things you can add support for: feeds, and a custom stylesheet for the visual editor in WordPress admin?

- If you have built-in support for plugins, have you made sure the theme works even when the plugins aren't installed?

- Are your readme.txt and the theme information in style.css up-to-date? Do you fulfill whatever demands your license of choice puts on the theme?

- Have you done the basic tests to make sure that the correct posts are displayed in listings, posting comments works, and things like that? Don't forget the most basic stuff: you can break a lot of WordPress functionality with your theme, so test it from the ground up!

Things the User Will Notice

- Is there proper 404 error handling?
- Is there a search form, and is the search results page actually usable?
- Are all the archives templates in your theme, or have you considered them in any other way? Make sure that archives for categories, tags, author, dates, and so on work in the way you want.
- Do nested categories and Pages display correctly when used? If there are widget areas where they should not be used at all, have you made sure the user is aware of this?
- Have you styled the single post view properly?
- Have you styled the Page view properly?
- Did you make sure you're not using `the_excerpt()` anywhere you should be using `the_content()`?
- Is pagination working: previous/later posts on post listing pages, and possibly previous/next post links on single posts?
- Does the author name display the way you want?
- Have you checked that all attachments (images, videos, and so on) are displayed properly? You may need to make a template file for this if your design is limited in any way.
- Do image galleries look good?
- Have you enabled featured images?
- When comments are turned off, what happens? Make sure that it looks good and displays a message the way you'd like it to.

Formatting

- Have you styled every element from the visual editor in WordPress admin to display properly? This includes block quotes, tables, and both ordered and unordered lists.
- Do block quotes, lists, and so on work within the comments?
- Are you styling comments and trackbacks differently? And do you highlight author comments?
- Have you put in special styling for sticky posts? Is special styling needed?
- Have you checked that headings 1 to 6 look good (even if you don't expect to use them all)?
- Do images inserted from within WordPress display properly? This includes images floating to the left and right as well as centered images.
- Do image captions work?
- What happens if an image that is too wide gets published? Does it break the design?

Naturally, there are a ton of things that are directly related to your theme that you need to test out as well. You need to check whether menu links work and that all text is readable. The preceding checklists will help you avoid common WordPress-related mistakes with your theme. You should add anything that is related to your design and code to those checklists for even more assurance that your sites will look good and work as expected.

COMMERCIAL THEMES AND THE GPL LICENSE

Commercial (or premium) GPL themes cannot be submitted to `wordpress.org` at this time. However, if you're a theme reseller you can get featured on the commercial themes page, which currently is just a links page containing screenshots of some popular themes, but no hosting. In other words, that means that the commercial GPL'd theme you're selling won't work with automatic updates from within the WordPress admin interface, since `wordpress.org` won't let you host it there unless you make it free for all to download. Naturally, if you do that hosting may be approved, and you can make money on providing support or customizations to the design, or whatever your theme business is all about.

The commercial themes page is a fairly new addition to wordpress.org, and the debate on how commercial GPL themes should be managed continues. If you intend to profit from commercial GPL themes in any way, you should keep up-to-date on developments in this area. Read more at `http://wordpress.org/extend/themes/commercial/`.

SUBMITTING TO WORDPRESS.ORG

If the theme checklist didn't raise any obstacles, and your theme is licensed under a GPL compatible license, you can submit it to the `wordpress.org` theme directory. Hosting your theme there is good for several reasons, the most prominent being the ability to reach WordPress users through the official channel, which incidentally now also resides within the admin interface. It also brings version control and hosting, as well as nice linkage with the `wordpress.org` support forums.

Your theme needs to be complete and saved in a single zip file. This should contain all the theme's template files, where style.css is extremely important. This is where the version is listed, along with the tags that are used to sort your theme. You also need to include a screenshot.png file, which has to be a screenshot of your theme in action, not a logo or similar. Other rules include `Gravatar.com` and widget support, exposed RSS feeds, showing the blog title and tagline, as well as listing both categories and tags by default.

Remember the Tags label in the top of style.css? That's where you define how your theme will be sorted on `wordpress.org`, should it be approved. Tags are separated by commas, like this (from the Notes Blog theme's style.css):

```
Tags: light, two-columns, right-sidebar, fixed-width, threaded-comments, sticky-
    post, translation-ready, custom-background, custom-menus
```

That would go at the top of the style.css file, along with the other things that define the theme. If you need a refresher, see the Notes Blog stylesheet earlier in this chapter.

Here are the tags currently used for sorting your theme on `wordpress.org` (a definitely up-to-date version is available at `http://wordpress.org/extend/themes/about/`):

Colors

- Black
- Blue
- Brown
- Green
- Orange
- Pink
- Purple
- Red
- Silver
- Tan
- White
- Yellow
- Dark
- Light

Columns

- One-column
- Two-columns
- Three-columns
- Four-columns
- Left-sidebar
- Right-sidebar

Width

- Fixed-width
- Flexible-width

Features

- Custom-colors
- Custom-header
- Custom-background
- Custom-menu
- Editor-style
- Theme-options
- Threaded-comments

- Sticky-post
- Microformats
- Rtl-language-support
- Translation-ready
- Front-page-post-form
- Buddypress

Subject

- Holiday
- Photoblogging
- Seasonal

Take good care to make the tags as accurate as possible, because it is via these tags that people will find your theme in the wordpress.org theme directory, whether they're browsing it from the wordpress.org Web site or from within their WordPress install (under Appearance and then Add New Themes).

Submit your theme at `http://wordpress.org/extend/themes/upload/`.

MOVING ONWARD WITH THEMES

Now you know how the WordPress syntax is constructed (Chapter 2), how the loop works (Chapter 3), and also how a theme is built from the ground up. The Notes Blog theme is meant as a framework for you to build on, so you should definitely get acquainted with it. You'll find it used in examples throughout this book, proving that it is good to build upon.

At this point you may have started to consider creating your own core theme, tuned to your needs. By all means go for it, and be sure to pick the best from the themes you like as well as altering the code to fit your needs. There is no reason for you not to start fiddling with themes now, although the following two chapters may open up some more doors for you.

Next up are child themes, a way for you to build upon a theme without actually altering it. Think about that, and the possibilities, for a while, or just turn the page and get on with it.

5

THE CHILD THEME CONCEPT

AS A WORDPRESS designer, one of the things you need to keep in mind is the addition of new features with new versions of WordPress, and in turn the deprecation of old ones. A theme created a few years ago will probably still work, but it will definitely be lacking some of the newer functionality of more modern themes. And the further question is, will it still work in another few years? The backward compatibility in WordPress is pretty extensive, but there is a limit.

Compatibility is one of the many reasons why you create core themes to build on, and why using child themes to extend them is such a great idea. In a way, the child theme concept is all about moving the individual styling for the sites you create another step from the code, since the child theme will consist mostly of visual enhancements and changes to the core theme. That means that the user can update the core theme without breaking anything.

This chapter is dedicated to the brilliance of child themes and how you can use them effectively for your own projects.

THE BRILLIANCE OF CHILD THEMES

Child themes let you create themes that rely on other themes, called *parent themes*, as templates, by changing parts of the parent theme to suit your own needs. For example, say you love a particular theme, but dislike the fonts and colors. You may also think that it needs a few Page templates to meet your needs. There are two ways to tackle this problem. The most obvious method is the direct route: just open the theme's files and edit them to your heart's content. In this case, that would mean making some changes in style.css (for the fonts and colors), and adding a couple of Page templates. No big deal, right?

Wrong. What happens when the theme author updates the theme with brand-new functionality, and you, giddy with joy, upload the new version and see all your edits go away? Obviously, your edits, with the colors you changed and your Page templates, aren't included in the original author's theme, so now you'll have to re-create all your adaptations so that the theme fits your needs again. You can of course keep notes of what you change, and back up your altered files, but the new version of the theme may have several changes and (re)applying your edits will be at best a nuisance, at worst tricky and time consuming.

Hacking a theme may be a simple solution, but if you want to be able to upgrade it with new versions with your edits intact, there is a better way. You can create a child theme, using the original theme as the parent theme (or template, as it is called when defining it). The child theme sits in its own folder, and so do all its associated files, so when you upload the new version of the original theme that you've built your site upon, you'll only overwrite that theme's files, and not your child theme, which contains all your changes. In other words, none of your edits will go away on updating the main theme. The whole idea is to separate the main theme functionality, code, and content from your own edits and adaptations. And since those will reside in your child theme's area they are safe from the parent theme's updates. Figure 5-1 illustrates the child theme concept.

HOW CHILD THEMES WORK

Any theme can be the parent of a child theme. the parent theme must be located in your wp-content/themes/ folder (because otherwise you can't use its files), and the child theme in its own folder, just like a regular theme. For example, to use the Notes Blog theme as a parent theme, make sure it is in the wp-content/themes/ folder, and then add your very own Small Notes child theme (or whatever you want to call it) in its own folder, also within wp-content/themes/.

After that, you need a style.css file to tell WordPress that it is a theme, and in fact a child theme, and point to the parent theme. Whenever a template file is called for, WordPress will look for it within the child theme, and if it isn't there, it'll load up the one in the original parent theme.

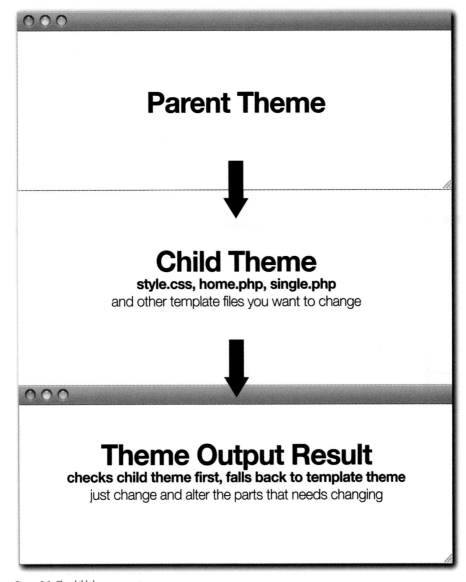

Figure 5-1: The child theme concept

Here's the basic style.css for just about any theme:

```
/*
Theme Name: Your Theme Name
Theme URI: http://your-theme-homepage.com
Description: Oh what a lovely description of your theme you'll put here!
Author: Your Name
Author URI: http://your-website.com
Template: If this is a child theme, you'll set the parent theme's folder name here,
```

119

```
  otherwise remove
Version: A version number
.
Any general information, license statements, plugin requirements, or any other
  information you may want to share.
.
*/
```

You need the Template line if you want the stylesheet to declare that it is a child theme; otherwise you'll just leave that out. However, don't write the parent theme's *name* in your child theme's style.css header; write the name of the *folder* in which it resides. Here's the style. css file again, filled out with dummy content to fit the hypothetical Small Notes child theme for Notes Blog:

```
/*
Theme Name: Small Notes
Theme URI: http://notesblog.com/blog/small-notes/
Description: This is Small Notes, a child theme for Notes Blog.
Author: Thord Daniel Hedengren
Author URI: http://tdh.me
Template: notes-blog
Version: 1.0
.
You need to have both Small Notes and Notes Blog in your wp-content/themes/ folder
  for this theme to work.
.
*/
```

> *The default WordPress theme is located in wp-content/themes/default/ so to use that as your template for your child theme, write* `default` *in the Template line.*

Remember, this is the child theme's style.css file. You can activate it just like a normal theme from the Appearance page in WordPress admin.

Now that you have your stylesheet for the Small Notes child theme, you can change those fonts and colors. First, you must decide whether to completely replace the parent theme's style.css file (Notes Blog in this case), or build upon it. for this example you will build on the Notes Blog style. css, so you need to import the stylesheet from Notes Blog. You do that with the `@import` tag:

```
@import url("../notes-blog /style.css");
```

Add that line below the style.css theme header information, and add anything you want to alter below it. Change some colors and some fonts, just for the fun:

```
@import url("../notes-blog /style.css");

div#content { font-family: Georgia, Times New Roman, serif; }
ul.sidebar ( color: #444; }
```

Nothing fancy there, but you will have the font-family starting with Georgia on everything in the `div` with `id="content"`, and the color of type in the `ul.sidebar` tag will be dark grey. This will be read *after* everything in the stylesheet from Notes Blog is read; that's why you put the `@import` as high as possible in the style.css file.

So the full style.css file for the Small Notes child theme, with the changes mentioned so far, would look like this:

```
/*
Theme Name: Small Notes
Theme URI: http://notesblog.com/blog/small-notes/
Description: This is Small Notes, a child theme for Notes Blog.
Author: Thord Daniel Hedengren
Author URI: http://tdh.me
Template: notes-blog
Version: 1.0
.
You need to have both Small Notes and Notes Blog in your wp-content/themes/ folder
for this theme to work.
.
*/


@import url("../notes-blog /style.css");

div#content { font-family: Georgia, Times New Roman, serif; }
ul.sidebar ( color: #333; }
```

Remember the Page templates you wanted? Creating them is easy. Just create them like you would if you hacked the Notes Blog theme, and put them in the Small Notes child theme folder. Now they are available for use whenever the Small Notes child theme is activated, just like with a regular theme.

Every file in the child theme is ranked higher than its equivalent in the parent theme. That means that even though there is a sidebar.php in Notes Blog parent theme, your sidebar.php from Small Notes will be loaded instead. If you don't want to make any changes to the sidebar. php file from parent theme, then just don't add that file to the child theme.

There is one exception to this rule, and that is functions.php. The parent theme's functions. php file will be loaded even if there is a functions.php in the child theme folder, but should they clash then the child theme's functions.php comes out on top. This is a good thing because it means that you can use the child theme's functions.php, which takes precedence over the parent theme's functions.php, to alter whatever features and functions you'd like from the parent theme. In other words, if you want to do something slightly different in your child theme you can override parts of the parent theme's functions.php by just altering the particular code that's bothering you in your child theme's functions.php, leaving the rest of the parent theme's functions.php fully functional. The great advantage to this process is that only changes go in your child theme, so that whenever the original parent theme is updated, you can update your parent theme too, knowing that your changes are intact in the child theme. Better

121

yet, your child theme will reap the benefits of the parent theme update, while otherwise remaining untouched.

THE WONDERFUL LOOP.PHP TEMPLATE

WordPress 3.0 introduced the loop.php template. Essentially, the loop.php template allows you to separate the loop from the other template files, as covered previously. This really helps when it comes to child themes, since it lets you pinpoint a specific loop in your child themes, instead of overwriting a complete template file.

Suppose you want to alter the loop on category archives. Your parent theme of choice has a fully functional category.php file, which in turn includes a loop template called loop-category. php, with this now familiar code snippet:

```php
<?php get_template_part('loop', 'category'); ?>
```

As you know, this will first look for loop-category.php, and failing that, loop.php.

Previously, you would have to create a brand new category.php template file to get to the loop used there, but no more. If you want to alter the actual loop in your child theme, just put a loop-category.php template file in there. Because the child theme's file will take precedence, the loop-category.php file that your parent theme's category.php wants to include will be pulled from your child theme instead (assuming you've put it there, of course). In other words, you can get to the loop included in the parent theme's category.php without having to put a complete category.php template in your child theme, just the loop. Sweet, huh?

EVENT CHILD THEMES

One of the cooler, albeit not as groundbreaking, usages of child themes is the possibility of short-term event themes. Think about it: if you have a theme that you're happy with, but suddenly want it full of snow and reindeer and such to celebrate that cold time of the year, then why not just create a child theme that swaps out the colors, background images, and even the graphics?

Or, to be blunt, say you want to make money by selling parts of your design to a company for promotion. Background images, slightly altered header files, and the like are all a breeze using child themes. Site-wide ads and roadblock-like functionality is easily implemented in this way.

Using child themes for minor events, promotions, and other custom hacks is a great way to keep the main theme clean. Any good theme designer will be doing this in the future, and some are probably employing it already.

A Few Words on Theme Semantics

Child themes can certainly spin things around. Say that you love a particular theme, and it has a class called `column-right`, which is used to place the ever-present sidebar to the right side of the main content, in a suitable column. Fair enough. Problem is, you want it on the left side, which you can easily fix by just applying `float:left` in the style.css file of your child theme. It works, but it is ugly to have an element named `column-right` positioned to the left.

This may seem a bit nerdy, even trivial, but writing code that makes sense is important when several people are collaborating on a project, and also good form in general. The whole point of naming elements in design after what they actually are supposed to be is that you, and the people you work with, will have an easier time finding your bearings in the design.

So `column-right` should really be on the right side. That's where you'll look for it, thanks to the name.

Another popular example of this is the sidebar. A lot of people think that the sidebar.php template, or at least the actual term "sidebar," should be retired. It is something of a relic from the past, from the time when WordPress was about blogging only. Today WordPress is a CMS, and you use it for a lot more than just publishing blog posts. Why call it sidebar, why not sidecolumn? You can take the reasoning another step; what says that it will be on the side of things at all? Single column designs often position the sidebar.php content at full width below the main content, above the footer. There's nothing wrong with that, other than that the sidebar obviously isn't to the side.

Now, perhaps that's taking it a bit too far. WordPress and its community will most likely keep using the sidebar lingo for quite some time, but that doesn't mean that you need to name things `column-right`. It is something to think about when designing themes, because while a certain name may make a lot of sense in the present context, there's nothing to say that you won't be moving that `column-right` to the left side. And if someone were to use your theme as a parent template theme for a child theme, that is even more likely to happen.

So think about the semantics. It'll make things easier on everyone.

123

THE FLIPSIDE OF INHERITANCE

You already know that every file in a child theme takes precedence over its parent theme's counterpart. A child theme's style.css trumps the style.css of the parent theme, and so does the child theme's index.php compared to the parent theme's index.php, and so on.

The child theme inherits the contents of the parent theme, but only if it needs it.

This brings up some issues, the most obvious probably being "what if they don't match, design-wise?" Well, the whole idea with child themes is to make customizations to themes you like. In other words, if you create a child theme based on a parent theme that you end up changing altogether, with new template files for just about everything, you may have defeated the purpose. After all, that is just like taking the original theme and making a new version of it, which means that you're missing out on the smooth upgrading perks that child themes can claim.

A child theme is most warranted when most of your changes go in style.css and possibly in functions.php. The former can alter the look and feel of the theme, while the latter can change the necessary functionality.

So what's the verdict, are child themes a good idea? In most cases, yes. If you discover you're creating a brand-new theme rather than making stand-alone changes to an existing one, you're better off creating what you need from scratch, or rather, from that core theme you may have ended up creating by now.

COMMON ISSUES TO KEEP IN MIND

There really are just two things with child themes that can cause confusion. The first is purely user-based, and that is the fact that the child theme just won't work unless the parent theme is in the wp-content/themes/ folder. This is pretty obvious when you think about it, but most users are used to just uploading a theme and then activating it, and that won't work with a child theme unless the parent theme is there. Or, rather, it may work but it will definitely look awful and behave badly too.

The second issue with child themes is technical, and it involves the template path. Most of the time when you want to point to the theme directory, for example to display an image, you'll use `bloginfo()` and pass the `'template_directory'` parameter. That won't work in a child theme, as the template directory is in fact the parent theme's directory! Hence this code, to display an image, would point to the parent theme's theme folder rather than the child theme's folder:

```
<img src="<?php bloginfo('template_directory'); ?>/images/the-image.gif" alt=
"My image" />
```

Luckily, there is a solution to this. By passing the parameter `'stylesheet_directory'` rather than `'template_directory'` in your child theme, WordPress will look in the folder with the theme's stylesheet instead. And guess what, that's your child theme! So the code above would have to be altered to this to work in a child theme:

```
<img src="<?php bloginfo('stylesheet_directory'); ?>/images/the-image.gif"
alt="My image" />
```

This is a common issue, with images suddenly not working or perhaps the wrong one being displayed because of it existing in the parent theme as well.

MANAGING SEVERAL SITES USING CHILD THEMES

If you're one of those people running your own blog network, or just a series of sites built on the same basic design, then child themes are just right for you. Think about it: you can put more resources into creating features and deploying new functionality in the parent theme, and store all the custom stuff for the various sites in child themes. That way, you'll speed up development and make upgrades easier.

MANAGING DESIGN FOR MULTIPLE SITES

First, find the common elements in your design. Granted, since most people don't launch a series of sites built on the same basic look, but rather pilfer themes and designs left and right, it may even be a better idea to start from scratch and create a basic design to build upon and customize. There are several big-name blog networks that employ this method today, so look around.

Second, after finding all the common elements your sites will need, you should wireframe the main parent theme design. Make room for everything, think about what may go where, and plan ahead.

Third, create the parent theme. This should be as simple and stripped down as possible, containing only the things that *all* your sites will use. If an element isn't common to all your sites, ignore it and define it in the child themes instead. A common mistake is to overstyle the parent theme, since it just looks bland and boring otherwise. Don't do that; you'll just end up overriding your own code in the child theme's template files, and that is code that has already been read once. Why make your themes slower to load, after all?

After these three steps, things get a bit more fluid. Start creating child themes that fit the various sites in your network and roll them out. When your network is built completely on child themes, and you want to add a common feature, you only have to do that in the main parent theme. Upgrade it across the network, and suddenly all the sites will have this new feature. Compare that to having to actually implement it in every theme, which is at best a tedious copy-and-paste exercise, and you'll understand that there is time and potentially money to be saved by using child themes.

DON'T FORGET ABOUT FUNCTIONS.PHP

It is not just on the design front where you can benefit from using one main parent theme and any number of child themes across your network: pure functionality can gain from this too. Remember, you can have your very own functions.php file for every theme, both the main one and the child themes, which means that if you're PHP-savvy, you can create plugin-like functionality on the theme side of things.

Another of the things people running multiple sites need to tackle is the maintenance of plugins. Granted, this is a lot easier these days, with upgrade functionality from within the WordPress admin interface, but some of the tasks you use plugins for can in fact be done just as well from within your themes. And while you can have those cool things in your theme's template files, whether it is a parent or child theme, it just isn't all that convenient. Besides, the whole idea with themes in the first place is to separate design from code, so filling the template files with more PHP snippets than usual kind of works against that purpose.

This is where functions.php may be an acceptable middle ground. After all, it is a template file outside of the design part of the theme, existing purely to add extra functionality through PHP coding. So it may be a better idea to write general functions in the functions.php file of the main parent theme rather than maintaining plugins that do the same thing across all sites. This strategy can also help reduce the maintenance burden for a network with several sites.

125

WHAT ABOUT THEME FRAMEWORKS?

There's been a lot of recent buzz regarding theme frameworks within the WordPress community. You may wonder how child themes fit with that notion, and the answer is, of course, perfectly well. Most so-called theme frameworks are semi-blank themes that are designed for you to modify, using either child themes or similar concepts. Some want you to put custom code in folders within the theme, for example, so it pretty much depends on how the theme designer envisions the usage of the creation.

However, that doesn't mean that you're limited to doing only what the designer intended. Any theme is really a theme framework, and any theme can be used as the parent theme for a child theme. You can always just use the theme as the parent theme, and then create your own child theme.

Some of the functionality in these themes designed to be used as frameworks for your own creations rely on *action hooks*. This is basically a way for the theme to pass implementation and data to the theme using functions.php. Then, your child theme (or pseudo-functions file within the theme framework if that's the solution of choice) can do things with these action hooks, including removing them should they not be wanted. We'll get to action hooks in the next chapter.

So any theme is a theme framework, and the themes that try to pass themselves off as theme frameworks are basically just creations more suited for being used as the basis for new designs. That is worth keeping in mind, I think.

TAKING THEMES TO THE NEXT LEVEL

Understanding child themes is the first step in taking WordPress theme development to the next level, or at least expanding it to a wider scale. You can put all your core functionality in one theme, everything you usually put into themes anyway, and then lean on that one theme by using a child theme that builds on it.

I'm a firm believer in saving time and making updating easier, so I think child themes are a great idea in most cases, although there are exceptions. For example, with a very traffic-heavy blog you would want to cut down on anything that adds bandwidth, and in such a case you should consider as tight a theme as possible.

6 ADVANCED THEME USAGE

TO MOVE BEYOND traditional WordPress sites, which build upon the platform's blog basics, you need to be aware of some of the more advanced features that are available to the theme developer. Most of these features build upon the template tags and conditional tags that you have been using thus far, but the usage may differ. Some techniques, however, will change or add to the functionality of WordPress from within your theme, which may not be such a good idea if you're looking to release it for general use, but may be a good fit for the project you're working on right now.

That's what it all boils down to, really: taking WordPress and putting it to good use for the task at hand. Building a WordPress theme and releasing or even selling it is one thing, but building a fully fledged WordPress-powered site is something completely different. This chapter is all about taking that extra step and putting WordPress to good use. This includes having a sound theme concept, styling the content the way you want, adding custom features such as custom headers and backgrounds, and working with custom taxonomies when the default categories and tags won't cut it. It also covers adding even more hooks to your theme for easy inclusion of more features. Yes, there really is a lot you can do with your WordPress theme, so let's get to it.

OUTLINING THE THEME

The first things you should do when you're starting a new WordPress project is consider what functionality you need from the theme. Simple blog designs usually aren't very complicated — you just start from the top and go from there — but if you want to build a newspaper-like site using WordPress you will have to consider other factors. One of the most obvious concerns is how you make the site look customized, because although we all love WordPress one of the reasons for developing your own themes is to make your site look the way you want, rather than just relying on the default theme.

Before starting to design and code a site, you need to figure out a few basics, outlined in the following list.

- **The main Web site layout.** What sections, pages, and major elements do you need to make room for, and how will you populate these with content from WordPress? This usually involves planning multiple loops and determining what template files are needed where.
- **Sorting the content.** This is usually all about what categories to choose, and which parts of the site are static enough to be Pages. Also, will there be a need for public tagging? If not, you can use tagging for customizing post designs and similar tasks without having to think of public tag archives.
- **The small stuff.** Will you need dynamic elements in this site, where you can drop poll widgets and special promotions? These areas should probably be widgetized.
- **Commenting.** Most, but not all, modern Web sites with editorial content have commenting functionality, so you need to decide whether to incorporate commenting functionality for your project.
- **Special functionality.** Is there anything you need that WordPress can't do out of the box? If so, you need to figure out if there is a plugin that can help (or develop your own), or perhaps even find an external service to integrate into the site.

Knowing what you want to pull off is essential to outlining the perfect theme for a more advanced project. When you have worked through these items, you can start mocking up, doing paper sketches, playing around with code snippets, and whatever else is in your workflow when creating fabulous Web sites.

I've been developing WordPress sites on a professional basis since version 1.5, and I've been a user since before that. My sites range from simple blogs to magazines to things entirely different. Later in this book you'll learn how to create completely different things using WordPress, showing that it can be a framework as well as a CMS, but for now all you need to know is that I'm constantly trying to push it to do new things.

When I start up a new project, I always consider what it needs to do and how I can meet those needs: what types of content will be presented, and how will it be displayed to give the user the best possible experience? The following three sections outline my top three tips for doing this. This approach likely won't fit everyone or every project, but it will help you think through your own approach.

RULE #1: STYLE BY CATEGORY, SORT BY TAG, TUNE WITH POST FORMATS

Categories are great for rough sorting, like a category for Music and another for Books, but they should never be too niche. Tags, on the other hand, can be as precise as needed, which means that a book review may belong to the category Books, and have tags that identify the book's author, genre, title, publishing house, and so on. The purpose of this isn't just nomenclature; there are technical reasons behind the decision. First, it's easy to create custom looks for category listings using the category.php and even category-X.php (X is the ID) template files. These can let you list one kind of content in one way, and a second kind in another.

Tags, on the other hand, are niched in themselves and should be viewed partly as search keywords that get grouped together, and partly as descriptions of the content. They can be useful as both, especially when you want to collect all those J. K. Rowling book reviews without having to force a traditional (and not so exact) search. By carefully considering how you set up categories and tags, and how they relate to each other, you can achieve a great deal.

Need more control? Sometimes the default category and tag taxonomies won't cut it. That's when you create your own taxonomies to provide even more specificity. Custom taxonomies are great because while you can use them for additional organization, much like tags and categories, you can also keep them completely hidden from the visitor. Using a custom taxonomy to add more control over post styling is great, for example.

Need even more? Post formats give you additional control over posts and how they can be styled and managed. In typical blog fashion, this is often a more suitable solution than using categories for styling, so weigh these against each other.

129

RULE #2: CAREFULLY CONSIDER CUSTOM FIELDS

Custom fields are very useful. They can store data as well as images, and they can fill in the blanks when you need more than just a title, a slug, the content, and an excerpt, or when you want to sidestep the categories and tags. That's great. They are not, however, very user-friendly, as I've already argued, and that means you need to be wary. A lot of funky WordPress-powered sites need to rely heavily on custom fields, but in such cases you need to educate the people running them. A plugin, which can do the same thing but just not show it, may be a better idea.

> *Keep in mind that using custom fields to do simple stuff like asides is completely unnecessary, thanks to post formats. Use custom fields primarily for data.*

RULE #3: BUILD WITH PAGES, EXTEND WITH CUSTOM POST TYPES

Pages have a great strength in that you can have just about as many as you want, and each one can have its own Page template if you like. That means that anything you can do with WordPress can be accessible at the address of your choosing. Hence, most of my Page templates don't include the actual Page's content nor the traditional WordPress loop at all. Rather, they do other things, and while they may be a bit rough to manage by themselves — you have to hack the template file since there's nothing more than a title and a slug in WordPress admin — they can step outside the box.

Think about it. Say you need to show off your work stored at another service. You can include it by using the service's own JavaScript widget code, and you can even have it exist in itself that way; all functionality is included. Unfortunately, WordPress wouldn't let that code through. The solution is to just create a Page template and put the code there. The same goes for Google Custom Search Engine result listings, for showing off RSS feed content, or your lifestream.

The Page template is a powerful tool. Use it wisely.

Need even more control here? You can always add custom post types tailored to your needs. Want a completely separate hierarchy of Pages-like, err, pages? No problem; just create your own custom post type mimicking Pages. Custom post types are an excellent solution when you need more control over your content and how it is organized in the install as well as on the site.

IS THAT ALL?

No, of course not, but those are the main points I tackle when I start to build a site using WordPress. Other things to consider include whether the user should be able to subscribe to RSS feeds, what screen resolutions I should design for, and if I need additional support for mobile devices. There's more as well, depending on the site you're building, such as the search needs of the user, and not to mention how heavy the site can be — not everyone has a broadband connection. Keep an open mind and try to look at the site from your target audience's point of view.

INDIVIDUAL STYLING TECHNIQUES

Adding some individual styling can make both posts and Pages more interesting. At first glance this may seem hard to accomplish, especially when it comes to posts since they are all governed by one single template file: single.php. Luckily, there are great methods to add a little extra flair to the posts, thanks to the excellent addition of the `post_class()` template tag, and some nifty little CSS.

But first, you need to understand the more obvious individual styling technique. I'm talking about Pages, which can be easily styled to act in any way you like, since all you really need to do is create a Page template that behaves in the way you want. You can take it even further than is possible with blog posts by loading different sidebars, headers, footers, or whatever you want, really. The strength of the Page template is that it can be set up any way you want, and all you need to do is create it and choose it for your Page.

The same applies to category and tag listings. If you want to add a header graphic to a specific category, for example, all you need to do is alter that particular category's template file. You may remember that category-X.php takes precedence over category.php (which in turn beats first archive.php and then index.php), and that X is the category ID or category slug. So category-37.php would be the template file whenever a listing of posts in the category with ID 37 is called for, just like category-cows.php is the template file of choice when viewing the Cows category. And hence you can just edit the category-37.php (or category-cows.php) template file to reflect how you want that listing to look.

In short, it is easy enough to add a little extra styling to the parts of your site where there are template files to control that style. Consult Chapter 4 for more information on which template file is loaded when, and take that information into account when shaping up your site.

STYLING THE POSTS

Styling the individual posts may be a bit trickier. They are all governed by single.php, which means that you need other means of making them stand out when needed.

Enter the `post_ID` and `post_class()` template tags, which go in your `div.post` container, like this:

```
<div id="post-<?php the_ID(); ?>" <?php post_class(); ?>>
<!-- The post output stuff goes here -->
    </div>
```

You'll find this (or something similar, at least) in most WordPress themes. The `the_ID()` template tag returns the post ID, giving the `div` container the ID of post-X, where X is the returned ID. That means that this is a way to catch a specific post and make it behave the way you want. ID 674 would hence give you a `div` with `id="post-674"` to play with. Style it any way you like.

Most of the time, however, you don't want to style individual posts per se, but rather posts belonging to a certain category. You can check for this using a conditional tag and a short PHP snippet, of course, but `post_class()` already has you covered. The template tag returns a line of classes for you to style any way you want, depending on where the post belongs and so on.

First, you'll get the post ID as a class as well, so your post with `id="post-674"` will also have the class `post-674`. You'll also get every category that the post belongs to, with `category-` in front of the category slug. So a category called *Website news*, which usually gets the slug website-news, would return the class `category-website-news` from `post_class()`. The same goes for tags; if you tag something with "funny" you'll get that returned as the class `tag-funny`.

You'll also get the classes `post` and `hentry`, the former making sure that `post_class()` is compatible with older WordPress themes, which usually describe the `div` containers for posts with the post class, and the latter tells us the div belongs to an entry. In fact, that usage is still there too.

So what good does this do? First, you can change the category styling, which is probably the most common usage for these classes. Say you've got a news category called News, with the slug news; hence you'd get `class="category-news"` from `post_class()` whenever it was used. And say you want the links in this category to be green, and why not put a green border line to the left side as well, to really make it obvious? This can be easily achieved:

```
div.category-news {
    padding-left: 20px; border: 5px solid green; border-width: 0 0 0 5px;
}
div.category-news a { color: green; }
```

Now every post belonging to the News category would get green links and a green border line to the left. This is great, since categories can be used to control design elements, and tags in turn should be used to further sort the posts. For example, I might have a tag for My Fave, a feature I'm running. Every post that is one of my faves will get a My Fave graphic in the top right; not clickable or anything, just a marker so that people know it is one of my favorites:

```
div.tag-my-fave { background: url(myfave.gif) top right no-repeat; }
```

This would output a background image, myfave.gif, in the top right corner (and not repeat it) every time `post_class()` returns the tag with the slug `my-fave`. Naturally, it is no lucky coincidence that that is the actual slug for my My Fave tag, now is it?

Finally, you can pass a specific class to `post_class()`, which may be useful at times. Maybe you want to add the class `stars` to single posts? If so, just edit your `post_class()` code in the single.php template to this:

```
<div id="post-<?php the_ID(); ?>" <?php post_class('stars'); ?>>
```

As you can see, adding a class to `post_class()` is as easy as adding a parameter. A similar solution is used when you need to retain post-specific styling through `post_class()`, but it acts outside the loop. Then, you need to tell `post_class()` to return the ID, which is done by altering the code to this:

```
<?php post_class('',$post_id); ?>
```

As you can see, `post_ID()` can let you add pinpointed style to one particular post, but `post_class()` is more useful since it lets you style sets of posts, and also that one post should you need to. In fact, one can question if the `post_ID()` part is still needed, but as long as it is in the default theme it obviously is, and it may be useful in the future.

BODY CLASS STYLING

Another way to apply some styling to various parts of a WordPress site is the `body_class()` template tag, introduced in version 2.8. Basically, it is for the body tag what `post_class()` is for the blog post div container. This is how you use it:

```
<body <?php body_class(); ?>>
```

Depending on where you are on the site, the body tag will get different classes. Say you're reading a post with the ID 245, and you're logged in. That would return this body tag:

```
<body class="single postid-245 logged-in">
```

A category listing would return other classes, and a tag listing another set again. Pages, the front page, search — every imaginable part of your site will return more or less different classes for your body tag.

Why is this good for you? Say you want a different size for your h2 headings depending on whether they are loaded in a listing, or in a single post. You can define this by adding classes to the various template files, or you can do it in CSS with the classes outputted by `body_class()`.

First, you need to find out what classes are returned and when. See the class listing later in this section to get a bearing of what you have to play with, but for now it is enough to know that the class `single` is passed to the body tag when viewing a single post, and `archive` is passed universally for all listings pages (much like the template tag archive.php, which is called for both category and tag listings should category.php and tag.php not be present in the theme). That means you'll work with these classes. Here is the code you may want to put in your stylesheet:

```
body.single h2 { font-size: 48px; }
body.archive h2 { font-size: 36px; }
```

This indicates that whenever `body_class()` returns the `single` class, which is in single post view, you get 48-pixel h2 headings, whereas whenever `body_class()` returns `class="archive"` you get 36-pixel h2 headings.

Body class styling can be taken a long way, since the addition of body classes depending on whereabouts on a site you are is placed so high up in the hierarchy. Most themes designed prior to the addition of the `body_class()` template tag won't be able to truly put this to good use, but if you reconsider your CSS code you'll see that you can control more of your design from the classes passed to body, rather than by adding classes to every element in the template files.

The following classes are available (and are listed in order of importance), depending on where you are on the site. Most likely you don't have to style them all.

- `rtl`
- `home`
- `blog`
- `archive`
- `date`
- `search`
- `paged`

133

- `attachment`
- `error404`
- `single-postid-X` (where X is the post ID)
- `page-id-X` (where X is the Page ID)
- `attachmentid-X` (where X is the attachment ID)
- `attachment-MIME` (where MIME is the MIME type)
- `author`
- `author-USER` (where USER is the author's nicename)
- `category`
- `category-X` (where X is the category slug)
- `tag`
- `tag-X` (where X is the tag slug)
- `page-parent`
- `page-child parent-pageid-X` (where X is the Page ID)
- `page-template page-template-FILE` (where FILE is the template file name)
- `search-results`
- `search-no-results`
- `logged-in`
- `paged-X` (where X is the page number, refers to listings)
- `single-paged-X` (where X is the page number, refers to listings)
- `page-paged-X` (where X is the page number, refers to listings)
- `category-paged-X` (where X is the page number, refers to listings)
- `tag-paged-X` (where X is the page number, refers to listings)
- `date-paged-X` (where X is the page number, refers to listings)
- `author-paged-X` (where X is the page number, refers to listings)
- `search-paged-X` (where X is the page number, refers to listings)
- `tax-X` (where X is the taxonomy name)
- `term-X` (where X is the term name)
- `admin-bar`

Utilizing the classes outputted by `body_class()` is a great way to add more precise visual control to the various sections of a site. A lot of template files in older themes have become redundant because of minor visual tuning now being easily managed by the classes outputted by `body_class()`. That's a lot better than resorting to template file specific classes.

STICKY POSTS

When sticky post functionality was introduced way back in WordPress 2.7, you needed to add the `sticky_class()` template tag to your post `div` containers. That added the class 'sticky', which could then be styled accordingly. You don't need that anymore, thanks to post_class(). In addition to the various tasks already mentioned, post_class() also applies the 'sticky' class to posts that are marked as sticky from within WordPress admin.

Making the sticky posts stand out a bit is easy enough; just add something to div.sticky in your stylesheet:

```
div.sticky { padding: 20px 20px 8px 20px; background: #f8f8f8; }
```

Nothing fancy there, as you can see (see Chapter 3 for more on sticky posts). The only thing to keep in mind when it comes to sticky posts is that you don't know how many of them will be used. If there are two sticky posts, the most recent one will end up on top, and then the next newest one below. That means that several sticky posts need to look good when placed together.

What are sticky posts good for? The most obvious use would be in a traditional bloggish site, nailing the larger, important posts at the top using the sticky feature, and un-stickying them whenever there's something new to lift to the top. Something of a limited headline area, so to speak.

Another obvious usage is for announcements. If you're selling e-books, for example, you can stick the "Please buy my e-book for $9 so that I can pay the rent" post up on top, as shown in Figure 6-1. More traditional announcements like new site launches or a call to action for an important cause would also work well.

Figure 6-1: When this book comes out you may see this on notesblog.com

Finally, you can go a step further by using the `is_sticky()` conditional tag. You can query WordPress (using a loop, and `query_posts()` to get the desired effect) for your sticky posts and manage them separately. One idea is to have a headline area outside the normal loop, and just include a set number of sticky posts in it, excluding everything else. In fact, you can use sticky posts to manage a full headline, but the same effect can be achieved with either custom fields or a specific tag, for example, and since the sticky post checkbox is more or less hidden away, the former may be a better call.

FANCY CUSTOM FEATURES

It may be misleading to call these "custom" features, since support for custom menus, custom headers, and custom backgrounds, is built into WordPress, albeit not in every theme. It's easy to add support for these elements in your theme, and having them can be very useful for the user. The following sections take a look at these pieces.

CUSTOM MENUS

Adding support for menus is really simple. Start by adding a menu area for your theme, called Smashing Menu in this example. Do this in functions.php:

```
register_nav_menus( array(
    'smashing-menu => Smashing Menu,
) );
```

That's all there is to it. Now the user can add a menu to the Smashing Menu area in the theme as well, using the `wp_nav_menu()` template tag, like so:

```
<?php wp_nav_menu('smashing-menu'); ?>
```

This will let you populate this particular menu from the menu interface found under Appearance → Menu in the admin interface. That's it. Simple, huh?

CUSTOM HEADERS

Adding support for a custom header isn't particularly complicated but it does require a few lines of code in functions.php. First, you declare the header's text color as well as the default header image, and then tell WordPress the width and height of the images, like so:

```
define('HEADER_TEXTCOLOR', 'ffffff');
define('HEADER_IMAGE', get_bloginfo('stylesheet_directory') . '/img/header-
  default.jpg');
define('HEADER_IMAGE_WIDTH', 940);
define('HEADER_IMAGE_HEIGHT', 130);
```

We also need to define how the header should be outputted.

```
// The site header function
function site_header_style() { ?>
```

```
<style type="text/css">
        div#header {
        background: url(<?php header_image(); ?>);
    }
</style><?php
}
```

This is simple CSS, using `header_image()` as the background. That's a template tag that does only one thing: outputs the URL to the header image. You could put the tag to other use as well, such as putting `header_image()` in your theme. The preceding code would apply the chosen custom header image as the background for `div#header`. You can change that to whatever suits your theme.

Because the headers are managed in the admin interface, you need to make it look decent there:

```
// The admin header function
function admin_header_style() { ?>
    <style type="text/css">
        #headimg {
            width: <?php echo HEADER_IMAGE_WIDTH; ?>px;
            height: <?php echo HEADER_IMAGE_HEIGHT; ?>px;
        }
    </style><?php
}
```

The `#headimg ID` is used in the admin interface, but it needs the proper width and height, hence the added styles.

Finally, you enable the whole thing. Without that, you have no custom header functionality, so don't forget this little bit of code:

```
// Enable!
add_custom_image_header('site_header_style', 'admin_header_style');
```

CUSTOM BACKGROUND IMAGE

So what about the custom background image? It's simple: the following code in functions.php is all you need:

```
// Enable custom backgrounds
add_theme_support('custom-background');

// Activate the admin panels
add_custom_background();
```

That's it. Any settings, be it a background image or just a background color, will be added to `wp_head()` in a stylesheet. Enabling custom background must be the easiest thing so far, right?

MASTERING ACTION HOOKS

Action hooks are all the rage these days, just like theme frameworks. Actually, they are probably so hot *because* of the theme frameworks, because the frameworks are littered with these babies. But I get ahead of myself. First you need to understand what an action hook is.

Your theme is most definitely already using action hooks. The familiar `wp_head` and `wp_footer` calls in the header.php and footer.php template files are action hooks. They are there so developers can hook in and add stuff to the beginning of WordPress, or after it has finished loading. Plugin developers use these all the time, and I imagine that any of the Web statistics plugins utilizing Google Analytics, Woopra, or whatever hook on to either the `wp_head` or `wp_footer` action hook and add their tracking code.

You can add your own hooks as well, something you no doubt saw when we went through Notes Blog in Chapter 4. This is the primary way theme framework designers use hooks, basically adding a number of hooks to various parts of the theme, and then letting the user or child theme developer alter the look and add features by hooking onto them. Hooks can be used for a multitude of tasks, from populating a menu or advert spot with proper coding, to actually removing elements from the design. In a sense, it is a good way to make a very complete design, and then let the users decide which parts of it should be used. Add an admin options page that does this for you, and you don't have to worry about hacking functions.php as a user, as naturally that's where all the action is.

I tend to lean the other way, though. While it may be tempting to just add everything imaginable and then have the users check or uncheck boxes to decide what should be displayed, this practice can quickly bloat the theme. In my opinion, a good framework is something to build on, not to cut away from.

Either way, with action hooks you can add functionality, either by adding your own (we'll get to that in a little bit), or by freeloading the hooks from WordPress. There are a lot of piggy-back possibilities within WordPress, with helpful hooks such as `wp_head` (which you'll find referenced in most themes' header.php file) and `wp_footer`. There are way too many to list here, so I'll just point you to the (hopefully up-to-date) Action Reference page in the WordPress Codex: `http://codex.wordpress.org/Plugin_API/Action_Reference`.

HOOKING ON

If you want to hook on to one of WordPress's action hooks, say by adding some Web statistics code to the `wp_footer` hook, you do it in functions.php. You write a PHP function containing the stuff you want to add, and then you add it to the hook.

Let's start with the function. The actual analytics script code is just nonsense, so if you want to use this particular hook you should, of course, swap the code for your own.

```php
<?php
function my_webstats()
```

```
{ ?>
    <script for your web statistics tracker />
<?php } ?>
```

This gives you the `my_webstats()` function to use, loaded with the (obviously faulty) script tag. This is what you want to hook on to `wp_footer`. Notice how I cut the PHP tag to make it easier to manage the HTML. You do that by using the `add_action` function, and placing it before the actual function:

```
add_action('wp_footer', 'my_webstats');
```

You're telling `add_action` that you want to add to `wp_footer` (first parameter), and then you tell it to add the function `my_webstats`, which you define below. The full code would look like this, in your functions.php file:

```
<?php
    add_action('wp_footer', 'my_webstats');
    function my_webstats()
{ ?>
    <script code for your web statistics tracker />
<?php } ?>
```

That would add the script at the end of your theme when loaded. Some excellent WordPress hookery right there.

CREATING YOUR OWN ACTION HOOKS

Creating your own action hooks is easy. First, you create your PHP function like you did before. It can be anything, really: a simple echo, or something way more advanced. The only difference between creating and using your own action hooks, compared to the built-in ones, is that you need to add them to your theme. Remember, `wp_head` and `wp_footer` already sit there, so no need to add them, but your brand-new action hook won't be so lucky.

The code for adding action hooks is simple:

```
<?php do_action('the-name-of-the-function'); ?>
```

Just put in your function's name (which would be `my_webstats` if you wanted to use the one from the previous example), and put the code wherever you want it in your theme. If your function is named `'welcome_text'`, that means you'll put this wherever you want to output the contents of the `welcome_text` function:

```
<?php do_action('welcome_text'); ?>
```

No need to use the `add_action()` function since you have the `do_action()` snippet in the theme telling WordPress to run the function for you. It's as simple as that: a custom action hook is created. You now need to hook on to it so it actually displays something. In the previous example, an options page within the WordPress admin interface where you can save your welcome text would be prudent. Then you just hook on to the `'welcome_text'` hook like you normally would.

To recap: `add_action()` is used to add actions to hooks, most likely in functions.php, whereas `do_action()` creates your own hooks and resides in your theme files.

REVISITING NOTES BLOG

You probably remember from Chapter 4 that Notes Blog features a bunch of hooks unique to the theme, declared in functions.php. If you look at the theme files, you'll find hooks in header. php, footer.php, and in the loops. The whole idea with adding hooks like this is to make it easy for child themeand plugin developers to add functionality without having to alter the files. However, the hooks are not only for people building upon Notes Blog; the theme actually employs the hooks as well. The postmeta under the title (as seen in Figure 6-2) on single posts and Pages are actually code residing in a function, and then added to the corresponding hook.

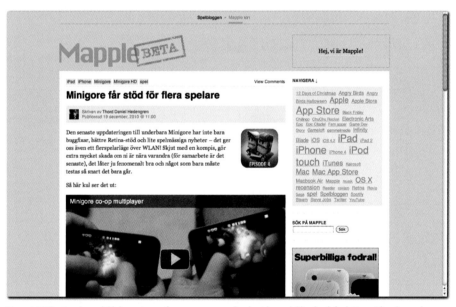

Figure 6-2: The Mapple.se child theme inserts fancy postmeta under the title much like the default Notes Blog theme does

Take a look at the code, starting with loop-single.php which is the loop used in single.php, the template file for single post view:

```php
<?php
    // The basic loop
    while ( have_posts() ) : the_post();

    // Use this hook to do things between above the post
    notesblog_above_post();
?>
```

```php
<div id="post-<?php the_ID(); ?>" <?php post_class(); ?>>
    <?php
        // Use this hook to do things above below the post title
        notesblog_above_post_title_single();
    ?>
    <h1 class="entry-title">
        <?php the_title(); ?>
    </h1>
    <?php
        // Use this hook to do things above below the post title
        notesblog_below_post_title_single();
    ?>
    <div class="entry-content">
        <?php the_content(); ?>
        <?php wp_link_pages( array( 'before' => '<div class="page-link">'
            . __( 'Pages:', 'notesblog' ), 'after' => '</div>' ) ); ?>
    </div>
</div>

<?php
    // Use this hook to do things between the post and the comments
    notesblog_below_post();

    if (comments_open()) { ?>
    <?php comments_template( '', true ); ?>
<?php } ?>

<?php
    // End the loop
    endwhile; ?>
```

You'll find four hooks in loop-single.php: `notesblog_above_post()`, `notesblog_above_post_title_single()`, `notesblog_below_post_title_single()`, and `notesblog_below_post()`. The one we're interested is `notesblog_below_post_title_single()`, which is located just below the title.

Now take a look at functions.php, and this function:

```php
// POSTMETA BELOW POST TITLE
function notesblog_add_postmeta_below_title() { ?>
    <div class="entry-meta">
        <?php _e( 'Written by', 'notesblog' ); the_author_posts_link(); ?> &bull;
        <?php the_time( __( 'F j, Y @ g:i a', 'notesblog' ) ); ?> &bull;
        <?php _e( 'Filed under', 'notesblog' ); ?> <span
          class="meta-category"><?php the_category(', '); ?></span>
        <?php
            // Check for tags, output if there are any
            if ( has_tag() ) {
                _e('and tagged ', 'notesblog');
                the_tags('<span class="meta-tags">', ', ', '</span>');
```

```
        } ?>
    <?php
        // If the comments are open we'll need the comments template
        if (comments_open()) { ?>
            <span class="comments-link">
                <br /><?php comments_popup_link( __( 'Leave a comment',
                    'notesblog' ), __( '1 comment', 'notesblog' ),
                    __( '% comments', 'notesblog' ) ); ?>
            </span>
    <?php } ?>
    <?php edit_post_link( __( 'Edit', 'notesblog' ), '<span
      class="meta-sep">&bull;</span> <span class="edit-link">', '</span>' );
      ?>
    </div>
<?php }
// Add to listings and single post view
add_action('notesblog_below_post_title_listing',
'notesblog_add_postmeta_below_title');
add_action('notesblog_below_post_title_single',
'notesblog_add_postmeta_below_title');
```

The function, `notesblog_add_postmeta_below_title()`, contains the code to output the postmeta. Your tags, dates, author, categories, and so on are all there, stored in the function. Now you want to hook the function to the `notesblog_below_post_title_single()` hook. That's done with this little line:

```
add_action('notesblog_below_post_title_single',
'notesblog_add_postmeta_below_title');
```

The `add_action` hook attaches `notesblog_add_postmeta_below_title()` to `notesblog_below_post_title_single()`, and that is all there is to it. If you want it above the title instead, you can use `notesblog_above_post_title_single()` instead, which would look like this:

```
add_action('notesblog_above_post_title_single',
'notesblog_add_postmeta_below_title');
```

(In that case, it would probably be prudent to rename the function, since it says "below the title".)

This is as easy as it gets, and very useful. I suggest you take a look at the various template files in Notes Blog, especially the loop and the header.php and footer.php file to see where I've placed hooks for easy addition of features and content. Hooks are great, aren't they?

USING TAXONOMIES

Taxonomies are both cool and useful. Basically, they enable you to create your very own versions of categories or tags. That means you can have several different sets of tags, for example (see Figure 6-3).

By adding taxonomies, you add more ways to categorize and tag your posts. You could say that the default categories and tags are both taxonomies that are there by default, so you have one taxonomy called Categories and one called Tags to start with. Suppose you want more, say a separate way of tagging posts, called Topics; you can add that, which gives you two tagging taxonomies that can each take their own set of tags, separate of each other. And finally, you may want a third one called Frequently Asked Questions, which would leave you with three tagging boxes: the default one and the two new ones.

Figure 6-3: Multiple tag taxonomies

Naturally, there is a template file for taxonomies, called taxonomy.php. Create it and treat it like any other archive, which means that it needs the loop, of course, and it will be used for post listings generated by a click on a taxonomy link. You cannot, however, create a taxonomy-X.php template file for a specific taxonomy tag, as you can with tag.php or categories.php. So if you want some special treatment for a particular custom taxonomy tag, you need to write a PHP snippet to check for it, and then output according to the result.

An example is the best way to describe how this works. Say you want to create a site about videogames, focusing on Xbox 360, PlayStation 3, and Wii. You'll have news, reviews, and previews, which will be your categories. This lets people view the latest news without worrying about the platform. There are a lot of things you can take into account here, but the following example focuses on what most gamers are most interested in: the games themselves.

Games may be available across platforms, but sometimes they are not. In fact, some games are only available on a specific platform, like the Super Mario games from Nintendo only being released on the Nintendo platform (which is the Wii in this example). This means that you may want to make something of a games database in tag form, but since the same game can be available for several platforms and you want to be able to tell them apart, you can't use regular tagging.

1. Start by creating a tagging feature for each of the video game platforms: one for Xbox 360, one for PlayStation 3, and one for Wii, using taxonomies. That way, you can tag on a per-platform basis, which also means that you can output individual tag clouds. And, since tags are the way tags are, it means that The Super Game can be a tag for both PlayStation 3 and Wii, without them being mixed up. Figure 6-4 shows the Write Post page with the added taxonomies.

Figure 6-4: The taxonomies in action on the Write Post page in WordPress admin

You create your own taxonomies using functions.php, within the necessary PHP starting and closing tags as usual:

```php
add_action( 'init', 'videogames', 0 );
function videogames() {
    register_taxonomy( 'xbox360', 'post',
        array(
            'hierarchical' => false,
            'label' => 'Xbox 360',
            'query_var' => true, 'rewrite' => true
        )
    );
    register_taxonomy( 'playstation3', 'post',
        array(
            'hierarchical' => false,
            'label' => 'PlayStation 3',
            'query_var' => true,
            'rewrite' => true
        )
    );
    register_taxonomy( 'wii', 'post',
```

```
        array(
            'hierarchical' => false,
            'label' => 'Wii',
            'query_var' => true,
            'rewrite' => true
        )
    );
}
```

The first thing that happens is a simple action, added to the initialization and done so at first (the zero). It's called `'videogames'` here, but it could just as well have been `'new_taxonomies'` or something else.

Next you need to create the `'videogames'` function and register your new taxonomies. Take a closer look at the first one, for Xbox 360:

```
register_taxonomy( 'xbox360', 'post',
    array(
        'hierarchical' => false,
        'label' => 'Xbox 360',
        'query_var' => true, 'rewrite' => true
    )
);
```

I'm sure you can figure out what `register_taxonomy()` does, so move on to the actual parameters. First is `'xbox360'`, which is the name of the taxonomy (for internal purposes). Second is `'post'`, which tells `register_taxonomy()` what kind of content this particular taxonomy is for. For now, only posts work (hence `'post'`), but later on WordPress will most likely support Pages and possibly links as well.

After that comes an array, which first needs to be passed a value for `hierarchical`. In this case, it is set to `'false'`, which means that the taxonomy will behave like tags. If you set it to `'true'` it would in fact be hierarchical, and thus would work like categories instead.

Moving on within the array, you set the `label`, which is the way the taxonomy will be presented within WordPress admin, to `'Xbox 360'`, which just looks better than the taxonomy name `'xbox360'`. After that follows `'query_var'`, which is set to `'true'` here and hence will return the taxonomy name (`'xbox360'`, remember?) as the query variable for use with tags like `wp_tag_cloud()`, but you can set any text string here. Maybe you want it to be just `'360'`, in which case it would be presented exactly like that, as a parameter within single quotes, and not as `'true'` passed right now.

Finally is `'rewrite'`, which tells WordPress whether to try and make a pretty perma-link out of the taxonomy URLs or not. In other words, if you've got a The Super Game tag in the Xbox 360 taxonomy, it can either be the default `domain.com/?xbox360=the-super-game`, or it can be a pretty `domain.com/xbox360/the-super-game`. In other words, you probably want to have `'rewrite'` set to `'true'` since using perma-links is a good idea.

2. That's basically it. Now, assuming you've tagged your posts with these new taxonomies, which will show up as boxes along with the default tag box, you can start using these new

taxonomies. For single posts, use `get_the_term_list()`, which will return a list of tags, linked and all, just like the `the_tags()` template tag would do. It is, however, a bit trickier to use:

```
<?php echo get_the_term_list( $post->ID, 'xbox360', 'Xbox 360 games: ', ',
', '' ); ?>
```

As you can see, you need to `echo` it. The first part in the `get_the_term_list()` function is passing the ID of the actual post you're on, so that you have something to start from.Next you pass the taxonomy to be used (the `'xbox360'` one). Then you have the actual printed text before the list, `'Xbox 360 games: '`, which is what you were going to use these custom taxonomies for in the first place, remember? You'll recognize the setup: first you've got what goes before the list (again, the `'Xbox 360 games: '` text), then the separator, which is a comma and a spacing, and then what goes after, which is nothing at all passed.

You may say that `the_tags()` and echoing `get_the_term_list()` in the way shown above are the same thing. If the default tagging feature were named `'tags'`, you could put it in instead of `'xbox360'` and get the same result.

You can also use `the_terms()` to do this, but then the tags belonging to the taxonomy won't be linked.

3. Now spice up your site by outputting a tag cloud (Figure 6-5) for the `'xbox360'` taxonomy, displaying 25 tags (meaning 25 games in this example). To do this you use `wp_tag_cloud()`:

Figure 6-5: A simple tag cloud outputted from the Xbox 360 taxonomy using `wp_tag_cloud()`

```
<?php wp_tag_cloud( array( 'taxonomy'
 => 'xbox360', 'number' => 25 ) ); ?>
```

You need to put things in an array to properly pass all the data to the `'taxonomy'` parameter. Here, you're passing `'xbox360'` which is the name of the taxonomy in question, and then the number of tags to be shown.

4. Finally, you may want to put the taxonomy to good use in a loop. This is somewhat similar to `wp_tag_cloud()`, but you use `query_posts()` instead:

```
<?php query_posts( array( 'xbox360' => 'the-super-game', 'showposts' => 25
) ); ?>
```

Here you're querying for posts tagged with `'the-super-game'` in the `'xbox360'` taxonomy, and you'll display 25 of them.

That's it; now you've got an additional tag taxonomy that you'll use to input the game titles. This way you can get nice game archives without cluttering the regular tags with this content. In the case of a videogame site, additional taxonomies like these makes sense since the regular tags would be dominated by the format tags — just think about the number of posts that would carry tags like "Wii" and "Xbox 360"! It also means that you can build more specific solutions for the tag taxonomy, which in the preceding example means that you can show information about each game (for example, the taxonomy tag) in a way that differs from how your regular tags behave when someone clicks on them.

It goes without saying that being able to add new taxonomies, essentially new separate sets of tags, can come in handy. Sites looking to work with data in almost database-style can definitely put it to good use, as shown in the previous example, but it can also be a different way to tackle the sorting of content. In particular, the addition of more taxonomies can make it possible to further push the categories to a design-driven feature within the site. After all, tagging offers so much more focused control where it matters, and you get that when you add your own taxonomies as well. You can have a taxonomy for design tagging only, for example. The tags in this taxonomy would only be used by the theme, by adding classes to the post `div` or perhaps the body tag. There's no default support for this, but it can be used nonetheless by adding it to the theme using a few snippets of code.

You can also imagine some taxonomies overlapping with custom fields, since some usage of this feature is all about sorting posts. Taxonomies are better suited for this by nature. Taxonomies reach their full potential, however, when larger amounts of content need to be controlled. Taxonomies are, after all, a sorting feature and that means they work best when there is actually something to sort.

At first it can be a bit daunting to wrap your mind around the possibilities that custom taxonomies offer. This feature can be put to good use; no doubt several WordPress-powered sites are already putting taxonomies to useful work. You, as an end user, may not see it, but the developer may not have to write a bunch of plugins or strain the not so user-friendly custom fields to achieve the content sorting and presentation needed. So don't forget about taxonomies just because the documentation on them is limited and it isn't a function that is widely used yet; it is still a feature to be considered.

THEME OPTION PAGES

Sometimes you just need one place to provide the necessary data to make the site behave like you want it to. This data can obviously be coded into the theme's template files, but a popular alternative to having to hack the templates is to have an options page.

A theme option page is a page in the WordPress admin interface containing information or options for your theme. You create it by adding code to your theme's functions.php file, and actually build the whole thing from there. Theme option pages have been around for quite some time, and the default WordPress theme uses the technique to offer color customizations to the rounded header, among other things.

The specific options that will be available in your theme options page depend on the kind of theme you've built. Some themes let the user alter the design by changing default font sizes and similar elements, while others let you save custom code that will be outputted somewhere in the theme through action hooks. Either way, you should make sure you know why you may want an options page, and what you need it to do. This means you have to sit down and figure out what option settings makes sense for your theme, and build the option page from that. This will of course vary a lot from theme to theme. Some themes might benefit from font options, where others might need a feature to show or hide the sidebar via a setting on the option page.

CREATING A SIMPLE ADMIN PAGE

The admin options pages can more or less be used to do just about anything. You kick it off in functions.php, but then you can call other files or just put the whole thing there. Keep it somewhat limited, though, since functions.php is part of your theme and it may slow things down if you cram it too full of cool functionality that needs to run a ton of things at once.

We'll build a real simple page in WordPress admin using functions.php that you can tune and tweak to your own needs. First, you need to add the menu item to the WordPress admin. That means you need to add an action, and define the theme's option page:

```
add_action('admin_menu', 'smashingoptions_menu');

function smashingoptions_menu() {
    add_theme_page('Our Smashing Options', 'Our Smashing Options', 8,
        'smashing-options', ' smashingoptions _options');
}
```

Remember, all this is in between PHP tags within functions.php.

The first line adds an action, `admin_menu`, and then you add the `smashingoptions_menu` function to it. Next, you define the `smashingoptions_menu()` function and load it with `add_theme_page`. This in turn consists of the name of the page, the title of the page (obviously identical in this case), the user level needed to see the page, and then a nonexistent unique identifier (which can be a file as well as some identifying string), and finally the function for the actual page HTML content (which we'll get to next):

```
function smashingoptions _options() {
  echo '<div class="wrap">';
  echo '
          <h2>Smashing Options</h2>
          <p>This is a placeholder for upcoming admin options!</p>
      ';
  echo '</div>';
}
?>
```

Here, you basically just store the `smashingoptions_options()` function with the page you want to output in the admin interface. By putting a containing `div` with the `'wrap'` class around it all, you get the WordPress admin interface look. The three `echo` statements are simple enough; it is all normal HTML code, with backslashes in front of single quotation marks to avoid it breaking the echo string. Nothing fancy; it's just a placeholder theme options page, after all.

Here is the full code:

```php
<?php
add_action('admin_menu', 'smashingoptions_menu');

function smashingoptions_menu() {
    add_theme_page('Our Smashing Options', 'Our Smashing Options', 8,
        'smashing-options', 'smashingoptions_options');
}

function smashingoptions_options() {
    echo '<div class="wrap">';
    echo '
        <h2>Notes Blog Core</h2>
        <p>This is a placeholder for upcoming admin options!';
    echo '</div>';
}
?>
```

Want to save stuff and add cool functionality? We'll dig deeper into that in the following chapters, dealing with WordPress plugin development. That's basically where you are at this point: you're doing a WordPress plugin, but in your theme's functions.php file.

ISSUES WITH THEME OPTIONS

Besides the obvious issues faulty code can cause, there's really just one big consideration when it comes to theme option pages and using functions.php this way: speed.

Remember, functions.php always gets loaded, and if it is big and does a lot of things, then loading it will take time, and an otherwise snappy site may be sluggish for a short while. That's not good, of course, and is why I personally recommend keeping things as clean as possible in functions.php.

That being said, using functions.php is a great way for small options settings. More advanced things should be handled outside, by calling other files, or in a plugin. It is all a matter of what you want to do, so the only really good advice here would be that you have to consider if you're executing your actions the right way, and if you can, move the code (or at least parts of it) somewhere else if your functions.php is growing too much.

One thing you shouldn't cut down on, though, is localization, at least not if you plan on releasing your theme. We'll tackle that next.

MULTIPLE LANGUAGE SUPPORT

Just as you can get WordPress in your language of choice thanks to language files, you can do the same for your theme, and plugins as well for that matter. And just as with WordPress, you need to provide a .mo file that is tailored for your theme, which in turn is created from a POT file via the .po file. It is all a pretty messy business, since a lot of the tools used to generate these files are pretty clunky to use, but using the software is worth it.

First you need to understand why a certain language file gets loaded if it is available to WordPress. There is (usually) no menu setting for what language you want a specific theme or plugin to be in; rather, WordPress looks for the setting defined in the installation, which is to say the one you added to WPLANG in wp-config.php (see Chapter 1 for more detail). That means that if your WordPress install is in German, then a localized theme containing German language files will use those if possible.

The translation process consists of three steps. First you need to create a POT (Portable Object Template) file. The software of your choice (see the following "Working with Language Files" section for related links) will parse your theme and build a POT file containing all the words and phrases you have marked for translation.

Step two is to create a .po (Portable Object) file from your POT file. This process saves the original language (usually English), and the translated language in one file. This is where the translation actually occurs.

The third step in the translation process would be to create the .mo (Machine Object) file, using appropriate software. This file is created from the .po file, so that it becomes machine-readable, and that makes the translation a lot faster to read and hence output. The .mo file is the file used by WordPress and your theme.

But how does the software that generates the POT file know what should be made available for translation? This is where you come in, as the theme (or plugin) author. You have to mark the parts of your theme that should be up for translation by wrapping the word or phrase in a PHP snippet, and then applying it to a domain. The domain is really just a translation set, and that in turn will be defined in functions.php.

Say you want to make the text "Hello you!" available for translation. That would look like this:

```
<?php _e('Hello you!', 'mydomain'); ?>
```

That would output "Hello you!" as if written in plain text, but if there is a translation available and mydomain is defined in functions.php, you'll get that instead. If not, you'll just get "Hello you!" in plain old English.

You can also write it like this, using two underscores before the opening parenthesis rather than one and the e:

```
<?php __('Hello you!', 'mydomain'); ?>
```

Call up the trusty Notes Blog theme for an example. In the loop.php file you'll find the following result outputted (within PHP code tags, so skip them) whenever a search result is called for:

```
_e('Your search result:', 'notesblog');
```

That would output "Your search result:" if there was a defined domain called notesblog.

Sometimes you want these translations within tags. This is how you've done it with the `the_content()` template tag, to make the read more link outputted by the `<!-more->` code snippet in posts available for translation:

```php
<?php the_content(__('Read more', 'notesblog')); ?>
```

A double underscore, and then the translation. So why the double underscore method? Well, the `_e()` is an `echo` statement, while the double underscore, or `__()`, is a `return` statement. Doing `echo` within PHP functions can create some weird results since it prints out the content, whereas `return` saves it for future use

So how, then, do you tell the theme to use the translation file in the first place? Just dropping the translation file in the theme won't do it; you need to declare that a specific text domain should be used (`"notesblog"` in the earlier examples). Just add this line in the functions. php file (within the PHP tags of course, just like almost everything else in the functions.php file):

```php
load_theme_textdomain('notesblog');
```

This tells you:

1. That the theme is localized, otherwise there's not much point in using the `load_theme_textdomain` functionality.
2. That every translation string with the domain `'notesblog'` is considered.
3. That you still need a translation.

The actual translation should be in a .mo file, and that in turn comes from a .po file, which you created from a POT file. And the POT file is generated by your chosen software (again, see the following section for links and suggestions), which in turn has parsed your theme looking for your translation strings, the `__()` and `_()`.

WORKING WITH LANGUAGE FILES

There are several ways to work with the portable language files. One of the most popular programs available is PoEdit (`www.poedit.net/`), which is available across platforms. You can easily open and edit available .po files in PoEdit, and then save them as .mo files to be used with your theme or plugin.

Other software and services for working with .po files include GNU's very own gettext (`www. gnu.org/software/gettext/`) and LaunchPad (`https://translations. launchpad.net/`). However, neither of these are as easy to use as PoEdit and most often PoEdit is recommended.

When you release a theme or a plugin with a language file, be sure to also make the original .po file available so that the users can translate it into their own language as well. It is a good idea to encourage that, since others may benefit as well.

THE NAMING ISSUE

While it may not be entirely within your theme or plugin translation scope, a weird error arises when a widget area gets called, and it can't be found because the name has been changed by the translation. That is (or hopefully was, by the time you read this) the case with WordPress and the Swedish translation of "Sidebar," being a widget area located in sidebar. php no less. The translators translated "Sidebar" (to "Sidomeny," which somewhat misses the mark, but still) and by doing so the themes that made direct calls to the "Sidebar" widget area failed, since it was translated incorrectly.

Messy? Yes, it is. The point is, be wary so that you don't end up translating things that are used for calling up various features, functions, or whatever. At least not without making sure that the actual call for whatever it is, is also altered accordingly. You might want to take a closer look at the functions.php file in either Twenty Ten's or Notes Blog's and examine how the widget areas are localized there. By localizing both the area name (and description), and the actual call for the area, you're avoiding these issues.

Next up is conditional design, which is basically all about names, be they category or Page names. While those won't be translated without quite a bit of fiddling, it is a good idea to consider their names regardless.

CONDITIONAL DESIGN

Conditional tags are great because they let you create a more dynamic design that aligns itself with whatever situation the visitor is in. This means that you can serve up different things depending on the condition, hence the title.

The most obvious usage of conditional tags is to check where the visitor is on your site, and output something accordingly. This is used in the index.php template file in the Notes Blog Core theme, to keep it from having to have all the various archive template files (better you create them in your child themes, after all). This code checks where the visitor is and outputs something suitable:

```php
<?php
if (is_category()) {
    echo '<h1 class="listhead">';
    _e("Category", "notesblog");
    echo ' <strong>';
    single_cat_title();
    echo '</strong></h1>';
} if (is_tag()) {
    echo '<h1 class="listhead">';
    _e(„Tag", „notesblog");
```

```
    echo ' <strong>';
    single_tag_title();
    echo '</strong></h1>';
} if (is_search()) {
    echo '<h1 class="listhead">';
    _e("Your <strong>search result</strong>", "notesblog");
    echo '</h1>';
}
?>
```

The code goes above the loop, and outputs various h1 heading messages depending on where you are, using the conditional tags `is_category()`, `is_tag()`, and `is_search()`. These perform exactly as you may imagine: returning `true` if it is a category page, a tag page, or a search result. So when that is the case, the code will print the correct header.

And yes, `_e()` is used for localization, as you know by now.

Conditional design can be pretty useful, as you can see. You can make more distinctive alterations to the design as well, such as including different headers depending on where on the site you are, and so on. Or you can build a menu that highlights the Page or category you are on, as in the following example.

This example shows you how to build a simple conditional tag, and apply a specific class to the one menu item that is relevant, meaning the one that represents the page you're actually viewing.

1. Start with some basic markup for the menu:

   ```
   <ul>
       <li>a menu item</li>
   </ul>
   ```

   This is obviously an unordered list, and the idea is to have a menu item per list item. So adding more menu items would only mean more list items.

2. Next, add some links:

   ```
   <ul>
       <li><a href="/">Home</a></li>
       <li><a href="/category/music/">Music</a></li>
       <li><a href="/category/books/">Books</a></li>
       <li><a href="/category/games/">Games</a></li>
       <li><a href="/about/">About</a></li>
   </ul>
   ```

   Nothing fancy so far, just some plain links. The first link, Home, is obviously to the site's root. The Music, Books, and Games links are all to category archives, and About is to the About page. You probably read that from the links already.

3. Next, you add the `class="activemenu"` to the list item when the user is in that particular place. That way, you can style the class in your stylesheet and make it stand out. Maybe like this:

```
li.activemenu { background: yellow; }
```

That would give the active list item a yellow background. It could just as well be a background image showing an arrow, or a bottom border, or whatever really.

4. Next, add the conditional tags. The concept is easy enough, just check if you're in the place in question: if you are, output the class, otherwise don't. First, start by checking if you're on the home page, using the conditional `is_front_page()`. You might have used `is_home()` too, but there are some cases when that would return differently, so go with the front page here:

```
<li <?php if (is_front_page()) echo 'class="activemenu"'; ?>><a
href="/">Home</a></li>
```

If it is the homepage, PHP will echo the class. Otherwise, it won't — it's as simple as that.

5. Finally, complete the menu:

```
<ul>
    <li <?php if (is_front_page()) echo 'class="activemenu"'; ?>>
        <a href="/">Home</a>
    </li>
    <li <?php if (is_category('music')) echo 'class="activemenu"'; ?>>
        <a href="/category/music/">Music</a>
    </li>
    <li <?php if (is_category('books')) echo 'class="activemenu"'; ?>>
        <a href="/category/books/">Books</a>
    </li>
    <li <?php if (is_category('games')) echo 'class="activemenu"'; ?>>
        <a href="/category/games/">Games</a>
    </li>
    <li <?php if (is_page('about')) echo 'class="activemenu"'; ?>>
        <a href="/about/">About</a>
    </li>
</ul>
```

Most of these conditional tags take several types of parameters, from ID to the slug (used in this example) to actual Page and category naming. And whenever the glove fits, so to speak, the PHP code will apply the `class="activemenu"` on the list item. Simple!

Checking whether the visitor is on a specific Page or in a particular category can be very handy, since you can return what fits for your site. In the preceding example, you're just echoing a CSS class to mark a specific menu item differently using the `activemenu` class, but you can output anything you like. Maybe you want to have a category with beginner content, which would then output information on how to subscribe to the RSS feed, whereas the non-beginner would just get a traditional RSS feed icon and a brief text link.

WORKING WITH RSS FEEDS

RSS feeds are a great way both to deliver and to subscribe to content. WordPress supports the old 0.91 version, the 1.0 version, and, more up-to-date, the 2.0 version. There is also Atom support, but keep in mind that you need to activate Atom from the settings page should you want to use it.

Most themes have feed links built-in, and while the Web browser will tell your visitors discretely that there is a feed available, you really want to push it a bit harder than that. Take a look at just about any successful professional blogger and you'll see nice RSS graphics, often incorporating the feed icon, and pushing of the subscription services in premiere positions.

You should do the same if you want to gain subscribers. That's lesson one on RSS: position it well on your site, otherwise people will neither see it nor use it.

Lesson two is to seriously consider full feeds. You can choose whether you want to send out a full feed or one just featuring excerpts. Feeds containing just excerpts *will* have fewer subscribers, since people using RSS prefer to get the whole story. You'll find that a large number of these readers will click the links and visit your site anyway, but they may just opt out if you're not publishing full feeds. Then again, if you really, truly, definitely have to get people to your site, and having them read the content in a feed reader is a disaster, then fine. Just make sure you know what you're doing, and why, if you're strapping your feed.

The third and final lesson is to offer alternative subscription methods. The most popular alternative is e-mail subscriptions, usually delivered by Feedburner (`http://feedburner.com`), which is owned by Google. It puts together a daily digest from your RSS feed, delivering it to subscribers via e-mail. This is good because RSS feeds are still something mainly used by the technical crowd, so offering other subscription options is a good idea.

THE WORDPRESS FEEDS

WordPress outputs a number of feeds by default. You can get them easily enough, using the `bloginfo()` template tag:

```
<?php bloginfo('rdf_url'); ?>
<?php bloginfo('rss_url'); ?>
<?php bloginfo('rss2_url'); ?>
<?php bloginfo('atom_url'); ?>
```

These are for the 0.91, 1.0, and 2.0 RSS feed versions and the Atom feed, respectively.

You can also get the feed for your comments, as well as an individual post's comments. Naturally, you'd want to use these tags in your theme:

```
<?php bloginfo('comments_rss2_url'); ?>
<?php comments_rss_link('RSS 2.0'); ?>
```

The second one is for a specific post's feed.

However, I personally prefer to keep the PHP calls at a minimum. All these feeds can be found by directly inputting the URL. Since you understand the necessities of permalinks (or will, when you've finished reading this chapter), you've got your blog set up to use these. That means that these URLs will work for you:

- `http://mydomain.com/feed/`
- `http://mydomain.com/feed/rss/`
- `http://mydomain.com/feed/rss2/`
- `http://mydomain.com/feed/rdf/`
- `http://mydomain.com/feed/atom/`

The first one is the default; you'll even find it in some themes, although that is a bad idea since it requires permalinks to be set up and not all hosts support that. The following, however, will always work, but don't look as pretty:

- `http://mydomain.com/?feed=rss`
- `http://mydomain.com/?feed=rss2`
- `http://mydomain.com/?feed=rdf`
- `http://mydomain.com/?feed=atom`

But there's more! These are just for the main feeds, but there are actually feeds for just about everything in WordPress. Author feeds, category feeds, and tag feeds all come very in handy sometimes. There's even one for comments to a particular post. Assuming you've got your permalinks setup, this is how they are built up:

- `http://mydomain.com/author/USERNAME/feed/`
- `http://mydomain.com/category/SLUG/feed/`
- `http://mydomain.com/tag/SLUG/feed/`
- `http://mydomain.com/POST-PERMALINK/comments/feed/`

So if my username is "tdh" on notesblog.com, and I want to pull out all my posts via RSS, this would work: `http://notesblog.com/author/tdh/feed/`.

BUILD A CUSTOM FEED URL

Sometimes you may want your feed to exclude a category, or consist of a couple of tags only, perhaps. You can accomplish this by hacking the feed URL, which actually takes some parameters. Then, if you want to, you can run that feed through a service such as Feedburner, since the URLs tend to be pretty long and ugly.

For example, say you want to exclude the category with ID 47 from your custom feed. Then the URL would look like this:

```
http://mydomain.com/feed/?cat=-47
```

That would output the full RSS feed, but nothing in the category with ID 47. Notice the minus sign in front of the ID; it works here just as it does in most other cases.

How about a feed for a search query? Just as simple:

```
http://mydomain.com/feed/?s=keyword1+keyword2
```

Or maybe you want to just run category 39, and show the tag with the slug `ninja`? Do it like this:

```
http://mydomain.com/feed/?cat=39&tag=ninja
```

Basically, you add parameters to the URL, and work from there. The accepted parameters are shown in Table 6-1.

Table 6-1 Accepted Parameters

Parameter	Description
author	Author ID
cat	Numeric ID
tag	Tag slug
keyword	Search keywords
year	The year (for example, 2009)
day	The date (for example, 15)
monthnum	The month by number (for example, 3 for March)
hour	The hour (for example, 19)
minute	The minute (for example, 45)
second	The second (for example, 13)
p	The post ID
paged	A specific page relating to the front page post listing

BASIC SEO IMPLEMENTATIONS

Getting the most out of the search engines is a topic for a book in itself. The cold, harsh truth is that the best SEO optimization is manually edited on per-post and per-page basis, rather than automatically generated. However, there are some things you can do in your theme from the start to get better SEO results.

Here are some tips to consider when setting up your theme:

- **Validate!** Valid code is better. You can check it here: `http://validator.w3.org`.
- **Permalinks, obviously.** Permalinks change those ID-based, ugly URLs to more user-friendly as well as search-engine-friendly ones. The earlier keywords in your permalinks get picked up first, so you should really get the post and page title slug in there (not the

157

ID), and possibly the category as well. Some claim that having date-based data in the permalinks helps the search engines as well, and that may very well be true if the site is updated often enough. The big bump, however, will be when you switch to permalinks, so make that a must in every setup.

- **Tags and keywords.** Tagging your posts not only helps describe the content for your readers, it is also an opportunity to tell the search engines more about them. You can use a plugin to populate the meta keywords field with your tags (not linked of course), or similar.

- **Generate a sitemap.** The most heralded solution for this is the Google XML Sitemap Generator plugin: `http://www.arnebrachhold.de/projects/wordpress-plugins/google-xml-sitemaps-generator/`.

- **The title tag.** Your title tag should include both the post name (first) and the site name (last). A divider between the two helps differentiate.

- **Headings.** On the front page, your blog's name should be in an `h1` block. When viewing single posts or Pages, the title of the post or Page should be in the `h1` block. On archive listings (search, categories, tags, and so on), I tend to set the listing title as `h1`, and have the post titles returned as `h2`.

- **Reconsider links.** Links are only good when they are relevant, so pushing that massive blogroll in the sidebar all the time may not be good. This is a bit fuzzy, however, so consider it wisely. Relevant links are always good.

- **Related posts are relevant links.** There are numerous related post plugins out there, and as long as they return relevant links to your posts, they are a good thing.

- **Breadcrumbs.** Breadcrumbs are links, usually on the top of the page, showing where the page is located, for example Home → Reviews → Smashing WordPress. They are not only helpful for the user, they also help the search engine read your page. You need to use a plugin for this functionality. This one is popular and easy enough to add: `http://yoast.com/wordpress/breadcrumbs/`.

- **Load time.** It is not only users that appreciate a fast-loading site, search engines do too, so clean up your code. You may even want to consider a caching plugin, although some of these may end up creating duplicate content so be sure you read up on it accordingly.

Also, be sure to check out the plugin lists later in the book for links and advice on good SEO plugins that make your WordPress site even more attractive to the search engines. Naturally you'll want your theme to be as search-engine-friendly as possible, since a lot of traffic comes that way.

TRIMMING WORDPRESS ON THE THEME SIDE

All sites should be as fast-loading as possible. You can do quite a lot on the theme side of things, but the question is how much you really want to do. If you take it to the extremes, you'll end up with one-line files that will be completely impossible to edit, which means you'll need a non-optimized workfile that you later optimize. This usually applies to stylesheets, which can be smashed together quite a lot, and hence you'll save a few bytes, but it also means that you won't be able to scan them easily when looking for something.

With that in mind, what can you do to speed up your theme? Try these tips:

- **Clean out unnecessary code.** Most themes can use another going-over or two after they appear to be finished.
- **Minimize PHP usage.** Direct links to images in your theme directory, usually called with `bloginfo('template_directory')`, will save you several PHP calls. There are a lot of those in most themes, as there is automatic output of the site's name and things like that. If you expect large amounts of traffic, hardcode that into the theme instead.
- **Beware of plugin overload.** Plugins are great, but sometimes they aren't all that well designed. At the very least, they represent one or more PHP queries and possibly database processing. You should consider each of them carefully.
- **Outside services.** This is not strictly in your theme, but outside services such as chat widgets or Twitter badges take time to load and will impact the performance of the site in the eyes of your visitors.
- **Accelerate and cache PHP.** Your hosting solution of choice may offer PHP accelerators and caching for often-called functionality. Talk to your hosting provider for options, and then make sure that they are compatible with WordPress; all may not be.
- **WordPress caching.** There are caching plugins for WordPress that store static files rather than serving data from the database all the time. This can actually speed up a site, so it may be worth considering.
- **Tighten the files.** You can Google your way to both HTML and CSS compressors, which tighten your files but make them a whole lot harder to read. Be sure to check the output to ensure that the compressors' scripts haven't added something malicious. You can never be too sure.

In the end, tightening a WordPress theme is more or less the same as tightening any site. Good and tight code, preferably valid, will load faster than clunky and bloated code, so get it right from the start.

And if you're doing everything right but your WordPress site keeps chugging slowly, then maybe you've outgrown your host. After all, when all the PHP calls are minimized, the code is tight and valid, and you've got your accelerators and caching, then there's just not much more that you can do other than crank up the voltage to power your beast.

THEMES VERSUS PLUGINS

The themes are not only the look and feel of a site these days, they are also simple plugins. You use themes to get everything to display where you want, and to break the normal flow of posts provided by the loop. You can achieve a lot using the template and conditional tags, and by adding extra functionality in functions.php, by using action hooks (and by being crafty overall), you can build just about anything.

As I've hinted at in this chapter, cramming functions.php full isn't always such a great idea. A lot of things you do in that file can just as well be done by a plugin, and while that is unnecessary or even redundant at times, sometimes it truly is the best decision. After all, the whole idea with various skinning concepts in publishing systems is to separate as much design from the code as possible. When it comes to WordPress themes, it means that you'll have to break that rule a bit if you want to do crafty things.

A lot of those things can be handled by plugins rather than code in the themes, which fits better with the whole dividing design and code concept. You'll learn a lot more about plugins in the next few chapters.

III

USING PLUGINS WITH WORDPRESS

7

ANATOMY OF A WORDPRESS PLUGIN

IT GOES WITHOUT saying that plugins are different from themes, but they have a lot in common. You could say that when you're adding functionality to your theme by adding code to the functions.php template file, you're actually writing a plugin.

But there is a huge difference. Themes are there to display the WordPress site, using the tools available. Plugins, on the other hand, are used when you need to extend the WordPress functionality with additional features. You should remember that, because bloating your theme's functions.php with features isn't always the best way to go.

In this chapter you'll look at plugins from a slightly different standpoint than you did with the themes chapters. The reason for this is simple: your plugin can do anything. It is basically a way for you to add whatever functionality you want; compare that to doing funky stuff with a select few template tags, and you see the difference.

With plugins, it is not a matter of what you *can* do, it is more a question of *why* you would want to do it. So that's where we'll start.

PLUGIN BASICS

A plugin's essentials are similar to a theme's essentials:

- The main plugin file needs to be a PHP file with a unique file name, or a unique folder name if your plugin consists of several files inside a folder.
- The PHP file needs an identifying header, just like a theme's style.css does, so that WordPress can recognize it as a plugin.

Then you can expand by adding even more functionality outside of the main plugin PHP file if you want, just like you add template files to the child theme's style.css.

> *Before you move on with plugin basics, you should know that writing plugins are usually a lot more demanding than working with WordPress themes. You need a firm knowledge of PHP, so if you're lacking that I suggest you brush up on your skills before embarking on any larger plugin writing adventure*

Giving your plugin a unique file name or folder name is very important, since plugins reside in wp-content/plugins/ and you don't want any conflicts. Name it appropriately, and in such a way that there is no doubt which plugin it is should someone need to find it using FTP but only know it by the name it is displayed with from within the WordPress admin interface.

The identifying plugin header block will look familiar. The following is a dummy:

```php
<?php
/*
Plugin Name: My Smashing Plugin
Plugin URI: http://my-smashing-plugin-url.com
Description: This is what my Smashing Plugin actually does.
Version: 1.0
Author: Thord Daniel Hedengren
Author URI: http://tdh.me
*/
?>
```

Actually, only the plugin name line, the first one within the comment notations, is mandatory. The rest should be there, however, so that the user knows what the plugin is, where to get updates, version numbering, who made it, and so on.

You should include licensing information as well. This is the standard GPL licensing info dummy text that is recommended in the WordPress Codex:

```php
<?php
/*  Copyright YEAR  PLUGIN_AUTHOR_NAME  (e-mail : PLUGIN AUTHOR E-MAIL)

    This program is free software; you can redistribute it and/or modify
    it under the terms of the GNU General Public License as published by
```

```
        the Free Software Foundation; either version 2 of the License, or
        (at your option) any later version.

        This program is distributed in the hope that it will be useful,
        but WITHOUT ANY WARRANTY; without even the implied warranty of
        MERCHANTABILITY or FITNESS FOR A PARTICULAR PURPOSE.  See the
        GNU General Public License for more details.

        You should have received a copy of the GNU General Public License
        along with this program; if not, write to the Free Software
        Foundation, Inc., 51 Franklin St, Fifth Floor, Boston, MA  02110-1301  USA
*/
?>
```

Naturally, you'd want to change YEAR, PLUGIN_AUTHOR_NAME, and PLUGIN AUTHOR E-MAIL to the correct information. You can also include the full license as a text file, aptly named license.txt of course. Obtain the license from www.gnu.org/copyleft/gpl.html.

And that's about it. All you need for WordPress to find the plugin is this, one single file with an identifying header. Dropping it in wp-content/plugins/ will result in it being listed in the Plugins section within WordPress. Activate it from the Plugins admin page, and it will be available to you in your theme, and from WordPress's actions themselves.

This is where the fun part begins, because now you have to figure out what you need to do, and how you'll accomplish it.

Whether you're planning on writing the plugin you think will change the way you use WordPress, or just need some extra functionality for your latest project, you should go through the following plugin checklist before getting started. It may just save you some time and headaches.

- Is there a plugin for this already? If there is, consider using that instead, or forking/hacking it if it nearly does what you want.
- Make sure you've got a unique name for your plugin. Don't just check the wordpress.org plugin directory; Google it to make sure. One way to ensure a unique name is to add your company's initials to the front of the plugin name, such as acme_pluginname.
- Decide on a unique prefix to all your functions, and stick to it. That way you're doing your part in eliminating any unnecessary conflicts due to similar naming structure.
- Do you want to internationalize your plugin? You really should; it works the same way as with themes and is pretty easy after all.
- Should this plugin have widget support? If it should, what kind of settings should it have?
- Do you need a settings page within the admin interface?
- What license should the plugin have? Keep in mind that it has to be GPL-compatible to get hosted by the wordpress.org directory.

- Don't forget the final check. Is the header up to date? Is the version number correct? Do all the links work? Is every necessary file in the package? And last but not least, have you spell-checked your plugin?

METHODS FOR INCORPORATING YOUR PLUGINS

Writing plugins is more like traditional PHP coding than working with WordPress themes. While you may use both template and conditional tags, most likely you'll be writing a lot on your own as well, not relying so much on the built-in features that WordPress tags offer you. Of course, it all depends on what your plugin does, but overall plugin development is more you than WordPress.

The usual way you do WordPress plugins relies on creating functions, and then applying them to hooks and filters. By inserting your function where you need it to be, perhaps when wp_head is loaded, or when the comments are getting loaded, you can trigger your plugin code at the appropriate time.

The following sections describe three ways you can write and work with plugins, starting with the ever important hooks.

USING HOOKS

Remember the action hooks from the previous chapter? *Action hooks* are triggered by specific events when a WordPress site is running, such as publishing a post for example, which would be the `publish_post()` hook. A second type of hooks, *filter hooks*, on the other hand, are functions that WordPress passes data through, so you'd use them to do stuff with the data. Useful filter hooks include `the_excerpt()`, `the_title()`, and so on. You ought to recognize them from the template tags.

Hooks come in handy for plugins as well, not just for themes. Thanks to hooks, you can add your cool plugin functionality to the appropriate part of WordPress, such as `wp_head()` or `wp_footer()`. The Web statistics example in the previous chapter, where you added a function in the theme's functions.php template file and then added it to the `wp_footer()` hook using `add_action()`, is very much the way a plugin might work.

Often, you'll end up writing a function in your plugin, and then you'll add it to one of the hooks. This is how `add_action()` works:

```
add_action ('hook-name', 'function-name', X, Y );
```

The `'hook-name'` is of course the name of the hook you want to add the action to. What happens is that WordPress, when encountering that hook when running the code, will check to see if there are any added functions registered for that hook. If there are, the function will run, if not, it won't. And the function is, of course, the one you've defined in `'function-name'`.

As an example, this code snippet would cause the `'smashing-shortcode'` function to run when `wp_head()` is executed:

```
add_action ('wp_head', 'smashing-shortcode');
```

X and Y are optional integers. The first, X, is the priority argument (which defaults to 10), used to sort actions when there are several added to a specific action hook. The lower the number is, the earlier the function will be executed, so if you need to make sure that something happens before or after something else, this is where you control that. Y, on the other hand, is the number of arguments your function can accept (defaulting to 1). If you need the function to handle more than one argument, you can set it by entering another number here.

Most of the time you won't see the priority or number of arguments in plugins, but they come in handy when needed. As they are optional, you can just leave them out when you don't need them. At other times you really need the priority since you might clash with other plugins otherwise. If that seems to be the case, it's a good idea to adjust the priority to make sure your plugin loads first, or last for that matter.

Filters work more or less the same way, but you use `add_filter()` rather than `add_action()`. The parameters are the same, and you pass them the same way as well. The only difference is that you can't use the action hooks with `add_filter()`, you use the filter hooks instead. Other than that the two behave in the same way.

Adding functions to a hook, whether it is of the action or filter kind, is easy enough, but what about *removing* functionality? Sometimes you don't want an action or filter hook to run, and that means you need to make sure it gets removed. This is done with `remove_action()` and `remove_filter()` for action and filter hooks, respectively. The syntax is simple:

```
remove_action('action-hook', 'the-function')
```

And the same for `remove_filter()`:

```
remove_filter('filter-hook', 'the-function')
```

This is not just used to remove functionality you have added, you can also remove core functionality from within WordPress with these. Any action or filter function can be removed this way, from pinging to deleting attachments, so some plugins may actually be designed only to limit WordPress functionality, rather than extend it, all depending on what your goal is.

CREATING YOUR OWN TEMPLATE TAGS

Another way to access your plugin functionality is by creating your own template tags, much like `bloginfo()`, `the_title()`, and so on. This isn't hard at all; in fact just by creating a function in your plugin (or in functions.php for that matter), you can access that function by a simple little PHP snippet:

```
<?php function-name(); ?>
```

Not very complicated, right? It really isn't, but that doesn't mean that it is the best way to include plugin content, even though it is by far the easiest method. With this method you don't need to add any hooks, and the function will be executed when the plugin template tag is loaded, which means that you'll just put it where you want it within your theme files.

One thing you need to keep in mind before going down this route is usability. Not everybody is comfortable with editing the theme files, and if you intend to release your plugin, or deliver it to a client, then it may not be a good idea to force template file hacking for usage. If you'll be doing the deployment yourself it really doesn't matter. However, if the end user will have to fiddle with the plugin's position or perhaps will need to pass parameters to it, then it is probably a better idea to look at other solutions.

At other times, just adding functionality using template tags won't cut it, and you need to overwrite parts of the core WordPress functionality. That's when you turn to the pluggable functions.

THE PLUGGABLE FUNCTIONS

Sometimes you may need to overwrite parts of the WordPress core functionality, perhaps to replace it with your own or just because your particular use of WordPress differs from the intended one. Maybe you don't want localizations to work in WordPress admin, for example, in which case you'd need to get rid of `load_textdomain`, or perhaps you want to replace the admin footer with your own. Just removing a hook won't do it. That's when you turn to pluggable.php, located in wp-includes. Naturally, you won't hack it, because that would be a tedious thing to manage with updates; instead you'll write a plugin that does the override. Now this is dangerous stuff. First of all, you can only do an override once, so if two plugins do different overrides on the same pluggable function, the site will misbehave (at best) or break (at worst). This means that two plugins both relying on overriding the same pluggable function can't be installed at the same time, which is a serious drawback. Therefore, you should probably keep your pluggable function stuff to sites you are in complete control of.

Also, to avoid unnecessary errors, you may want to wrap any code pertaining to a plugin relying on these things in a check to see if the function exists:

```
<?php if (!function_exists('function-name')); ?>
```

There are, naturally, times when the pluggable functions can come in handy. See the most up-to-date list of what functions you can get in this way in the Codex: `http://codex.wordpress.org/Pluggable_Functions`.

And use with caution, obviously. Just writing the plugin in the correct way, which is covered next, isn't enough when you're nulling out parts of the WordPress core. Don't be surprised when things stop working or conflicts come out of nowhere when you dive into these things. After all, the WordPress functionality you're bypassing is there for a reason.

MUST-HAVE FUNCTIONALITY FOR PLUGINS

Strictly speaking, the only thing your plugin really must have is a main PHP file containing the identifying header, and whatever code is needed to get the job done. However, in reality, you should probably take it a few steps further than that. After all, someone other than you may have to work with your plugin, and so it should be as simple and accessible as possible. That means that you should go to great lengths to make the plugin blend in nicely with the WordPress admin interface.

The same goes for whatever parts of the plugin will show to end users. Some plugins add visual functionality, and that should work with as many themes as possible if you intend to release the plugin. Naturally, if you've developed a plugin for use with a particular project only, this won't be an issue. The same goes for localization support; there's no need for that if there won't be any language support other than the default one, is there?

Finally, I think every plugin should come with a license, and some sort of instructions as to how the plugin should be used. Readme files are nice and all, but it's better still to build the instructions into the actual plugin since a lot of users are reluctant (or just too impatient) to read the attached readme files.

PLUGIN SETTINGS

Sometimes you want to save things in the database. You've got the freedom of any PHP script here really, which means that you can add full tables and so on to the database should you want to. I won't cover that.

I will, however, tell you how to use the WordPress options database and store small snippets of data in it. This is the wp_options table in the database. Remember, don't store too much data in there. If your plugin includes a lot of content, you should definitely consider other solutions. Some things that would be great to store include plugin settings that you can query, smaller code snippets that your plugin will output, and so on. The same goes for theme options pages by the way; wp_options is the place for storing smaller data amounts.

To demonstrate usage, let's turn to a really simple plugin called Footer Notes. What it does is add an admin page where the user can save some HTML code that is added at the end of posts (using a plugin-specific template tag). It also supports adding the HTML code at the end of post items in the RSS feed should the user want to. This manifests as a simple options page in the admin interface with two text boxes where the HTML code is pasted, and a Save button. That's it.

```php
<?php
/*
Plugin Name: Footer Notes
Plugin URI: http://notesblog.com/footer-notes/
Description: Footer Notes adds a simple code block to your posts and feeds.
Version: 0.1
Author: Thord Daniel Hedengren
```

```
Author URI: http://tdh.me
*/

// add menu to admin --
if (is_admin()){
    add_action('admin_menu', 'nb_footernotes_menu');
    add_action('admin_init', 'nb_footernotes_register');
}

// whitelist options --
function nb_footernotes_register() {
    register_setting('nb_footernotes_optiongroup', 'nbfn_post');
    register_setting('nb_footernotes_optiongroup', 'nbfn_feed');
}

// admin menu page details --
function nb_footernotes_menu() {
    add_options_page('Footer Notes Settings', 'Footer Notes', 8,
        'nb_footernotes', 'nb_footernotes_options');
}

// add actual menu page --
function nb_footernotes_options() { ?>
    <div class="wrap">
        <div id="icon-options-general" class="icon32"><br /></div>
        <h2>Footer Notes</h2>
        <p>
            This is the settings page for the
            <a href="http://notesblog.com/footer-notes/">Footer Notes</a> plugin.
            This plugin adds HTML code at the bottom of your posts and your feed
            items. Just add the HTML code you want for the two possible
            spots.
        </p>
        <p>
            Leave either of these <strong>completely empty</strong> if you do not
            want to return anything!
        </p>

        <form method="post" action="options.php">
        <?php settings_fields('nb_footernotes_optiongroup'); ?>

        <table class="form-table" style="margin-top: 20px; padding-bottom: 10px;
          border: 1px dotted #bbb; border-width:1px 0;">
            <tr valign="top">
                <th scope="row">
                    <h3 style="margin-top: 10px;">
                        Code to be added after posts
                    </h3>
                    <p>
                        The code below will be added where you put the
                        <code>nb_footernotes()</code> template tag in your theme,
```

```
                        on a per-post basis. It needs to be within the loop.
                    </p>
                </th>
            </tr>
            <tr>
                <td>
                    <textarea name="nbfn_post" style="width: 90%; height: 150px;
                        padding: 10px;">
                            <?php echo get_option('nbfn_post'); ?>
                    </textarea>
                </td>
            </tr><tr valign="top">
                <th scope="row">
                    <h3 style="margin-top: 10px;">
                        Code to be added after feed items
                    </h3>
                    <p>
                        The code below will be added at the bottom of each item
                        in your feeds.
                    </p>
                </th>
            </tr><tr>
                <td>
                    <textarea name="nbfn_feed" style="width: 90%; height: 150px;
                        padding: 10px;">
                            <?php echo get_option('nbfn_feed'); ?>
                    </textarea>
                </td>
            </tr>
        </table>

        <p class="submit">
            <input type="submit" class="button-primary" value="Save Changes" />
        </p>

        </form>
    </div>
<?php }
// custom hook for the posts --
function nb_footernotes() {
    do_action('nb_footernotes');
}
// and now for the post output --
add_action('nb_footernotes', 'nb_footernotes_post_output');
function nb_footernotes_post_output() {
    echo get_option('nbfn_post');
}
// feed output time --
function nb_footernotes_rss() {
    echo get_option('nbfn_feed');
}
```

```
// feed filters --
add_filter('the_excerpt_rss', 'nb_footernotes_rss');
add_filter('the_content_rss', 'nb_footernotes_rss');
// that's it! -- FIN//
?>
```

The plugin also consists of a license.txt and a readme.txt, as well as an uninstall.php file for cleaning out the database. For now, though, focus on the actual plugin.

At the very top is the plugin file header, which is the actual plugin description. Next is a check to see if you are in the admin role, and adding the nb_footernotes_menu() function defined further down. You'll recall that this is the way to create an options page in the WordPress admin; if you don't remember how this was done, see Chapter 6 for a more in-depth description.

The first code snippet of real interest is this one:

```
// whitelist options --
function nb_footernotes_register() {
    register_setting('nb_footernotes_optiongroup', 'nbfn_post');
    register_setting('nb_footernotes_optiongroup', 'nbfn_feed');
}
```

This code registers 'nbfn_post' and 'nbfn_feed', which are two pieces of options data that you want to save information to (into the database obviously), with the nb_footer-notes_optiongroup. This one is within the form further down on the page:

```
<?php settings_fields('nb_footernotes_optiongroup'); ?>
```

This saves a lot of time, actually, and does away with a bunch of hidden input fields that you had to use in previous versions of WordPress. All you need to do is register everything using register_settings and add it to an option group, and then you use settings_fields() within the form to get it working.

The options page is pretty straightforward. Remember that the form tag should have action="options.php" and if you want the table to act in a typical WordPress manner you give it class="form-table". The submit button at the very end is a simple submit, and it will do the job well enough. You can, of course, style it otherwise if you want.

In this case you've got two textareas where the idea is to have the user put some HTML code. The one for 'nbfn_post' looks like this:

```
<textarea name="nbfn_post" style="width: 90%; height: 150px;
padding: 10px;">
    <?php echo get_option('nbfn_post'); ?>
</textarea>
```

The interesting part is `get_option('nbfn_post')`, which means that it both collects (and outputs thanks to `echo`) and saves to `'nbfn_post'` in the database. The code in a typical input field would have the `get_option()` part as the value rather than between the opening and closing tag. Like this:

```
<input type="text" name="nbfn_post" value="<?php echo get_option('nbfn_post'); ?>"
  />
```

Now to output the stuff you've saved. First, you need the HTML code meant to go with the post content. To give the user freedom I opted to create a plugin-specific template tag to add to the theme, rather than to just append it to `the_content()`. This is the custom template tag:

```
<?php nb_footernotes(); ?>
```

And this is what creates it (the first part) and loads it with the content from `'nbfn_post'` That is where the HTML for its post is stored, remember? Echoing `get_option('nbfn_post')` will return the saved content:

```
// custom hook for the posts --
function nb_footernotes() {
    do_action('nb_footernotes');
}
// and now for the post output --
add_action('nb_footernotes', 'nb_footernotes_post_output');
function nb_footernotes_post_output() {
    echo get_option('nbfn_post');
}
```

You want the feed HTML code added to the bottom of each post in the RSS feed, so use a filter to do that. But first you need to store the content from `'nbfn_feed'` in the nb_footernotes_rss() function so you can add it:

```
// feed output time --
function nb_footernotes_rss() {
    echo get_option('nbfn_feed');
}
// feed filters --
add_filter('the_excerpt_rss', 'nb_footernotes_rss');
add_filter('the_content_rss', 'nb_footernotes_rss');
```

DATABASE CONTENT AND UNINSTALLING

When creating a plugin that stores data to the database, you need to consider what happens when someone doesn't want to use it anymore. Do you need uninstall functionality to clean up after yourself? You usually do if you have saved a bunch of things in the database, which shouldn't be sitting around full of unused data anyway.

There are a number of ways to remove unwanted functionality. One method is to include an uninstall.php file with your plugin. This file contains the uninstall code to delete the database content you have added:

```
delete_option('my-data');
```

This would delete the `my-data` field in the `option` database table. Since a lot of plugins store some option data in that table, it can get cluttered, and that's never a good thing. Naturally, you'd add whatever you need to remove to the uninstall.php file. This also applies for uninstalls made through the WordPress admin interface.

Take a look at the uninstall.php file for the Footer Notes plugin mentioned in the previous section. It contains this:

```php
<?php
// for old versions --
if ( !defined('WP_UNINSTALL_PLUGIN') ) {
    exit();
}
// delete the option data --
delete_option('nbfn_post');
delete_option('nbfn_feed');
?>
```

The first part is a check to see if the uninstall feature is present. This feature was not used in earlier versions of WordPress, so if you are not using WordPress 3.0 or later (which you obviously should!), the script will exit, not doing anything. That way, this file is backward compatible. The remaining code deletes the option data stored in the database: `'nbfn_post'` and `'nbfn_feed'`, as you'll recall. This is done when deleting the plugin from within the WordPress admin interface, and hence the user gets a cleaned-up database.

Naturally, you can do the same thing without an uninstall.php file, but then you need to do a little more coding. The `register_uninstall_hook()` can be used to do the same thing; just check for it like you normally do. If you're contemplating using the hook approach, chances are you have your own uninstall thing happening on the plugin's page within the WordPress admin interface. Or maybe you just don't want your plugin to contain an uninstall.php file, and prefer to build the uninstall process into the plugin itself, keeping it clean and tight.

The important thing is that you remember to add uninstall functionality should you have stored anything in the database. You may want to make it optional, however, to remove the data, since it may be useful later on. Also, it is probably a good idea to remove the data on deactivation, since that is recommended for all plugins when doing manual WordPress upgrades.

AFTER UNINSTALLING

It is easy to forget that when a plugin is uninstalled, it may leave a few things lying around. Database data is one thing, and hopefully the uninstall at least gave the user a chance to clean up after the plugin, but there is one thing that is even more pressing: shortcodes.

What happens when a plugin relying on shortcodes gets uninstalled? *Shortcodes* are snippets of code that output something within the post content. The most common shortcode that WordPress uses is actually the `[gallery]` shortcode, which you'll see when you include a gallery in a post and switch to HTML view in the Add New Post screen.

So what happens to shortcodes used by plugins when the plugin is uninstalled? The shortcode won't be parsed, hence it is outputted as regular text. Your `[myshortcode]` shortcode will end up printed just like that, in the middle of your post.

It won't look good.

So while the plugin may not be active, or even present anymore, you still need to maintain some sort of backward compatibility to it. That means that you should offer some sort of solution for the user to make sure the posts aren't littered with un-parsed shortcode. One way would be to run a SQL query and simply remove all the shortcode automatically, but that may be a bit drastic, and what happens if something breaks during this process? It may destroy the database. Or, more likely, how do you know that there isn't a human error within the post that for some reason causes the remove shortcode query to cut too much?

How you choose to handle redundant shortcode depends on the kind of usage you have introduced in your plugin. One ugly fix would be to include a plugin that changes the short-code from outputting whatever you had it doing in the first place to outputting nothing at all.

Obviously, not all types of plugins will need this treatment. For example, plugins utilizing widgets will just stop displaying the widget when removed.

ADDING WIDGET SUPPORT TO PLUGINS

Widgets make it easy to customize the contents of a blog or site. You can put them in the widget area(s), dragging and dropping it from within the WordPress admin interface. WordPress ships with a few widgets, such as one for outputting RSS, one displaying the latest posts, listing the Pages, the categories, and so on. These widgets may not be enough, however, and when you create a plugin you may want to give the user the chance to run it from within a widget area. This is a lot more user-friendly than having to put the plugin PHP template tag in the theme's template files, so it may be a good idea to widgetize your plugin if it should be displayed in a widget area.

Thanks to the widget API, creating widgets for your plugins isn't all that complicated. You extend the built-in widget class, called `WP_Widget`, give it some instructions, and then register it so it will show up, as shown in the following code:

```
class SmashingWidget extends WP_Widget {
    function SmashingWidget() {
        // The actual widget code goes here
    }
    function widget($args, $instance) {
        // Output the widget content
```

```
    }
    function update($new_instance, $old_instance) {
        // Process and save the widget options
    }
    function form($instance) {
        // Output the options form in admin
    }
}
register_widget('SmashingWidget');
```

In this example, you extended the `WP_Widget` class with your `SmashingWidget` widget. The first function, which is just `function SmashingWidget()`, is the actual widget with the functionality you want, so that's where the action is. The `widget()`, `update()`, and `form()` functions are necessary to get the widget to behave the way you want. Obviously, you wrap it up by registering the widget with `register_widget()`. Both the cancel link and the submit button are built into the widget API, so you needn't worry about them when it is time to save whatever changes you'll let your users meddle with.

CREATING A WIDGET

This section walks you through creating a simple widget. This widget will output some text to say hello to the visitor, and you'll also be able to rename the heading from within the admin interface.

1. Remember, all this code is within a plugin file, which is PHP and has the plugin identifying header. Unless you have a plugin you want to add this functionality to, you should create a brand new one with an appropriate name.

   Start with the widget class:

   ```
   class SmashingHello extends WP_Widget {
   ```

   The widget is named `SmashingHello`, so you can probably tell what's coming.

2. Next you get the widget function:

   ```
   function SmashingHello() {
       parent::WP_Widget(false, $name = 'Smashing Hello');
   }
   ```

3. Remember, you need `widget()`, `update()`, and `form()` to make cool things happen. This is the next step, starting with `widget()`:

   ```
   function widget($args, $instance) {
       extract( $args );
       ?>
           <?php echo $before_widget; ?>
               <?php echo $before_title
                   . $instance['title']
                   . $after_title; ?>
               Well hello there! Ain't that just Smashing?
           <?php echo $after_widget; ?>
       <?php
   }
   ```

You take `widget()` and extract the arguments. Notice the `$before_widget`, `$after_widget`, `$before_title`, and `$after_title` settings. These shouldn't be changed unless necessary. They are controlled by the widget API and default theming, so they make things look good.

So what happens? You echo the `$before_widget` and then the `$before_title`, without telling them to do anything fancy, so they'll just pick up the default code. Then there's the `$instance` title, which is the title you'll use as an input field in the widget interface within admin, so that people can write whatever they want there. Then you're done with the title, getting to `$after_title`, and then there's your lovely text that the widget will display: "Well hello there! Ain't that just Smashing?" Not high prose, of course, and you can put just about anything here, a WordPress loop query or whatever. Finally, the widget is all over and you get the `$after_widget`.

Again, these `before` and `after` bits are to make the widget behave the way the theme wants them to. This is something the theme designer can control, so if you want to keep your widget cross-compatible, you can stick to the defaults and worry about how it looks in the design.

4. Moving on, you need to make sure the widget is saved properly when updated:

```
function update($new_instance, $old_instance) {
    return $new_instance;
}
```

This is easy, since `update()` only takes `$new_instance` and `$old_instance`. Naturally, you want to return the `$new_instance`, which is whatever you changed. You may want to do some tag stripping with `strip_tags()` here if the kind of widget you're creating may run into some nasty HTML stuff. That's easy; just do something like this for an input field named `'music'`:

```
$instance['music'] = strip_tags( $new_instance['music'] );
```

See `strip_tags()` at work there? It makes sure no stray HTML code gets through. Very handy.

5. Now add one more setting to change the widget title:

```
function form($instance) {
    $title = esc_attr($instance['title']);
    ?>
      <p>
            <label for="<?php echo $this->get_field_id('title'); ?>">
                Title: <input class="widefat" id="<?php echo $this->
                get_field_id('title'); ?>" name="<?php echo $this->
                get_field_name('title'); ?>" type="text" value="<?php
                echo $title; ?>" />
            </label>
        </p>
    <?php
    }
```

The keys here are `get_field_name()` and `get_field_id()`. They handle which field does what. And then, when you've built your pretty little widget settings form, just save it (with the widget API automatically-created save button) and it does the trick.

177

6. Finally, you need to close the class curly bracket, and register the widget:

```
}

add_action('widgets_init',
    create_function('', 'return register_widget("SmashingHello");'));
```

Figure 7-1 depicts the widget.

There you have it, a widget where you can change the title and output some text. This can just as easily be something else, thanks to the fact that widget output is just PHP spitting something out.

Another thing to remember is that not all widgets need to take options. If you just want to drop an element in a widget area, with the ease it brings, then by all means just create the widget and forget about the settings. It is really all about what you need in terms of functionality.

Figure 7-1: The widget you just created, dropped in the sidebar widget area

DASHBOARD WIDGETS

Not only can you create regular widgets, there's support for Dashboard widgets as well. That means you can add widgets to the admin area of WordPress, commonly referred to as the Dashboard. All those boxes you see on the front page of the Dashboard are in fact widgets, and you can add your own.

To create a Dashboard widget, you need to create a plugin, and hence a file in which the code goes. This one is a simple reminder to the users of a group blog to visit the internal pages, and hence it only outputs some text and some links. First you need to create the function that does this:

```
function dashboard_reminder() {
    echo '
        Hey you! Don\'t forget the internal pages for important stuff:<br />
        &larr; <a href="http://domain.com/internal/forum">Forum</a><br />
        &larr; <a href="http://domain.com/internal/docs">Documentation</a><br />
        &larr; <a href="http://domain.com/internal/staff">Staff</a><br />
        OK THX BYE!
    ';
}
```

It's a simple function called `dashboard_reminder()` that echoes some HTML. This is what you want the widget to display. The next step is to add the Dashboard widget itself.

```
function dashboard_reminder_setup() {
    wp_add_dashboard_widget('dashboard_reminder_widget', 'Staff Reminder',
      'dashboard_reminder');
}
```

The key here is wp_add_dashboard_widget(), to which you pass first an identifying ID of the widget (which is 'dashboard_reminder_widget' in this case), and then the text label to describe the widget, and finally the name of the function containing the Dashboard widget's content (obviously the dashboard_reminder() function). It's worth knowing that the Dashboard widget ID, which is the first parameter passed to wp_add_dashboard_widget(), is also the class the widget will get should you want some fancy CSS stylings.

Pause for a moment and look at the wp_add_dashboard_widget() function. The first parameter is the widget ID, the second the widget name that you want to display, and then there's the callback of the function containing the actual widget content. There's a fourth parameter as well, called $control_callback, and it passes a null value by default, and is optional. You can use that to give your widget settings by passing a function containing whatever settings you want to let the user fiddle with. None are included in this example, but it may be a good idea to keep in mind that you can pass a fourth parameter for more functionality in your Dashboard widget.

Returning to the example, you need to add the widget action to the wp_dashboard_setup hook, using add_action():

```
add_action('wp_dashboard_setup', 'dashboard_reminder_setup');
```

There you have it, a Dashboard widget! (See Figure 7-2.) As of now there is no Dashboard widget order API so you widget will end up at the bottom in the Dashboard. The user can reorder widgets manually, of course, but you may want to force things to the top. There are some hacks available online, such as the one described in the WordPress Codex (http://codex.wordpress.org/Dashboard_Widgets_API) should you need to achieve this.

Figure 7-2: The Dashboard widget in all its glory

Now that you've gotten your hands a little dirty with plugins and widgets, it's time to discuss database usage. It is easy enough to store data in the options tables, but sometimes it is just not the best practice.

PLUGIN CONSIDERATIONS WHEN USING THE DATABASE

Storing data in the database is sometimes necessary to make your plugins function the way you want. From storing some simple options, to adding full tables with more data for the users to utilize, the database is truly a tool that should be put to good use. Putting data in the database means you can query for it easily; it is just very convenient.

However, it comes at a price. A cluttered database isn't very nice to maintain, and you have to make sure the user can uninstall the data stored by the plugin. And if that's not enough, you need to decide where to save this data. Either you use the *options* table created by WordPress, a nice solution for smaller settings, or you create your own table within the database for the plugin only. The latter solution is probably better if you need to store a lot of data, but it extends the database in such a way that it may create issues with other plugins doing database things, should you want to integrate with them in any way. It also means that there is a part outside WordPress that needs to be backed up, and should you want to move the install the Export/Import method won't cover the data.

So what's best? Data in options, or in its own table? It is entirely up to you depending on what you need to store. My personal guideline is that settings should go in options, and if it is actual content or larger amounts of data, I consider the external table option.

Just make sure you inform the user, and make sure that it is possible to clean up after uninstallation should it be necessary, and you'll be fine.

BACKWARD COMPATIBILITY FOR PLUGINS

Another aspect to consider when developing plugins is whether or not you want or need backwards compatibility. There are new functions and hooks added to WordPress all the time, and if you rely on the new ones, previous versions not featuring them naturally can't run the plugin. That's why you should be careful when using new features as they may just not work in older versions of WordPress.

However, it is not just WordPress functionality that changes; the system requirements have seen some revamps too. As of writing, PHP 4 is still supported (but will soon be dropped), while most PHP developers agree that PHP 5 is a lot better. The basic premise should be to support the hardware that WordPress runs on, but sometimes that's just not enough. You may need PHP 5, or want it enough to accept that hosts running PHP 4 will cause your plugin to fail, despite WordPress running just fine. If you take that route, be sure to output an error should someone try and run your plugin under PHP 4, when it really requires PHP 5. Technically, the same issue can apply to MySQL.

How far back you want to let your users go with your plugin is up to you. Since the addition of automatic updates one can only hope that the updating frequency of the end users is higher than it was pre-auto updates, but a surprisingly large number of blogs still run on older versions of WordPress, which is bad news for developers and for site owners. After all, older versions can lead to security issues as well as compatibility problems.

PLUGINS AND WORDPRESS MULTISITES

As of WordPress 3.0, the multi-user version of WordPress, previously called WordPress MU, is a part of the regular version. Now called WordPress Multisites, this feature is used to power multiple blogs at once. Most plugins (and themes for that matter) will work with the Multisites feature. The only time you may run into issues is if you add tables to the database, or possibly if you play with the core tables. You can activate this feature by adding a few lines of code to your wp-config.php file. To get you started, add the following line above the "That is all, stop editing!" line in the wp-config.php file of your install:

```
define('WP_ALLOW_MULTISITE', true);
```

This will enable the Network Admin link in your WordPress admin interface (see Figure 7-3). WordPress will then guide you through the simple steps needed to get your Multisite feature up and running. You can read more about that in the Codex at http://codex.wordpress.org/Create_A_Network.

Figure 7-3: The Network Admin looks something like this

Multisites can most easily be described as something of an umbrella that allows admin super-users to manage other blogs created underneath. On wordpress.com anyone can create a blog, but that isn't necessarily the way a WordPress Multisite install works; you can just as well run it to power multiple blogs (like a blog network, for example) and not let users register and/or create their own blogs.

DEVELOPING PLUGINS FOR MULTISITES

The process of developing plugins for WordPress using Multisites doesn't differ much from that for traditional WordPress plugins. The only differences are in the database, and to a minor degree, in the directory structure.

As for the directory structure, almost everything is the same as in the standard version of WordPress. The only real difference is the blogs.dir directory in the wp-content folder, which contains all the created blogs' data, such as images and uploads and such. You won't be using that folder much, since themes and plugins belong in the main wp-content folder, just like you're used to.

Your plugins can reside either in wp-content/plugins/, which you'll recognize, or in wp-plugin/mu-plugins/. The latter, which is a folder you'll create yourself, is something of an autorun for plugins; if you drop them there they won't show up on the Plugins page in the WordPress admin interface, and they'll be considered activated all the time. The only way to deactivate a plugin in mu-plugins is to delete it from the folder. Such plugins are known as *site-wide plugins*, and are covered in the following section. You can also activate plugins site-wide (as an admin super-user), bypassing the autorun in the mu-plugins folder.

Actual plugin development is just as for stand-alone WordPress. You do, however, need to be extra careful when creating new tables in the database or relying on content from core tables. Most of the time you'll be fine, but there are some differences in the database when you're running several sites in on WordPress install, so be watchful.

Another thing to consider when creating plugins for Multisites is how they are intended to be used. Because you can run a Multisites install in so many ways, open or closed, with plugins enabled for bloggers, just for admin, and so on, you may have to rethink the way the plugin works.

SITE-WIDE WORDPRESS PLUGINS

Plugins placed in wp-content/mu-plugins/ are called site-wide plugins, and they are always activated per default. To uninstall or even make them inactive you need to remove them, which makes them a bit special. After all, not being able to turn off a feature may change the way things work.

You can also activate plugins site-wide from within admin. This means that you can activate plugins located in wp-content/plugins/ to be active site-wide, just like the mu-plugins. This is of course a lot more user-friendly, so you should definitely consider managing site-wide plugin-powered features this way, rather than with mu-plugins. After all, since WordPress supports automatic updates, the more that are available at a click from within the admin interface, the better.

So that's it, you're writing a plugin. Now you can share it with the world by releasing it in the official WordPress directory.

HOSTING YOUR PLUGINS ON WORDPRESS.ORG

Just as with themes, there is an official plugin directory on `wordpress.org` where you can host your plugins. You don't have to post your plugins on that site, of course, but doing so allows users to get automatic updates so they can keep up-to-date with the latest fixes.

However, there are some terms that your plugins needs to fulfill to be hosted on `wordpress.org`:

- The plugins must be licensed under a GPL-compatible license.
- The plugin can't do anything illegal, nor be "morally offensive."
- The plugin must be hosted in the `wordpress.org` subversion repository.
- The plugin must have a valid readme file.

To get access, you need to be a wordpress.org user. Then, submit your plugin (`http://wordpress.org/extend/plugins/add/`) and wait for approval. This process can take some time, depending on the workload of the people involved.

When your plugin is approved, you'll get access to the subversion directory, to which you submit a zip archive containing the plugin, along with a valid readme file. A readme validator (`http://wordpress.org/extend/plugins/about/validator/`) makes sure that all the data needed for the `wordpress.org` directory to list the plugin information is there.

You should read the Developer FAQ for the Plugin Directory before submitting a plugin to make sure you have the most up-to-date information on the matter. This will almost certainly speed up the approval process. You can find the FAQ at `http://wordpress.org/extend/plugins/about/faq/`.

The benefits of being hosted in the `wordpress.org` repository are not only the automatic update functionality from within the actual users' admin interfaces, but also the statistics it adds. You'll see how many people have downloaded the plugin, get ratings, and you can get comments on it. Not only that, `wordpress.org` is also the central point for WordPress, which means chances are good that people will find your plugin, compared to just hosting it on your own site and hoping people come across it. Add the plugin search interface within the WordPress admin interface, and your plugin can be found from within any up-to-date WordPress system out there, and installed with just a few clicks.

That is, if you're in the `wordpress.org` repository. So get in there!

A FINAL WORD OF WARNING ABOUT CREATING PLUGINS

Developing WordPress plugins differs quite a lot from creating WordPress themes. Sure, there are a lot of similarities but in the end what you're really doing is writing PHP scripts that tap into the WordPress functionality. That means that while just about anyone with a little scripting knowledge can bend WordPress themes to their will, the same just doesn't apply when it comes to plugins. You need a working knowledge of PHP, and you need to be wary when working with plugins since you can cause a lot of damage, especially if you're tinkering with the database.

With that caveat noted, if you know a little PHP then developing plugins can be the solution to building the site you want, so knock yourself out.

The next chapter discusses when to use a plugin, and when to just rely on your theme's functions.php file.

8

PLUGINS OR FUNCTIONS.PHP?

WORDPRESS THEMES AND plugins typically work separately from each other, coming together only when it comes to implementing features. This cooperation is usually managed by having the correct widget areas available in the theme's template files, so that the user can drop the plugin's widget where it should be, or by actually putting plugin PHP code snippets into the theme. And sometimes the plugins will output or activate the functionality by use of the WordPress hooks, which in essence means that the theme only has to comply with WordPress to trigger the plugins. It is all pretty straightforward.

However, there is one case where themes and plugins collide, and that's when the functions.php file comes into play. The theme file can do more or less anything a plugin can, which means that it can be an optional solution for a publisher that normally would require a plugin. It also means that functions.php can clash with plugins, if used without caution.

This chapter explains when you should use a plugin and when to use functions. php instead.

WHEN TO USE A PLUGIN

When opting for the plugin solution over the functions.php option, or comparing the use of a plugin with a custom hack in the theme, you need to consider the following questions:

- Is the plugin really needed?
- Does the plugin extend WordPress functionality in a way that is either too complicated or so stand-alone that it really isn't an option to try and do the same thing in the theme files?
- Does the plugin need to work outside of the chosen theme?

A positive answer to all these means that you should go ahead with your plugin.

EXTENDING FUNCTIONALITY WITH PLUGINS

In short, there is a good basic rule as to when to use a plugin: everything that extends WordPress functionality should be a plugin. This means that if you add something to Word-Press that you wouldn't be able to do otherwise, you should do the actual addition with a plugin. Examples of such functionality range from added data management to integration with third-party apps.

However, there's a big gray area here. A lot of plugins are actually mimicking WordPress and its loop, such as recent post listings and similar solutions that exist so that the user won't have to create a lot of custom loops within the theme. The plugins can handle that for you, and they do it in a more user-friendly fashion, with options pages that set up the custom loop for you and widgets that let you drop them wherever you like. Compare that to having to actually write the loop code and put it in your theme file to be outputted where you want to. That may not seem like a big deal if you are a PHP expert, but for most WordPress users, it is a real hassle. In such cases, plugins aren't really extending functionality, but enabling users who might not otherwise be able to access that functionality.

Custom fields are another example of built-in functionality that might be better handled with a plugin. Custom fields are great for a lot of things, but at the same time they aren't exactly easy to use, with a bulky interface and so on. A plugin can do the same thing, and in fact use custom fields, but with a sleeker interface. That can potentially make updating your site easier.

CAUTION: PLUGINS CAN SLOW DOWN YOUR SITE

Nobody likes a slow-loading site, no matter how flashy it is. How fast your site needs to be depends on the target audience and kind of content being served. After all, Flash intro pages are still fairly common, and they should really not exist unless there is an audience for them.

No site should be slower than it needs to be, and a sure way to bloat your WordPress site is to fill it to the brim with plugin-powered functionality. Think about it: most plugins need to be initialized to work when the visitor encounters their functionality on the site, and that in turn can mean anything from running a PHP function (at the very least), to a full-sized loop with database queries. Say you have ten plugins on a page, and each one initializes a loop and outputs relevant database content. That will not only take time, it will also put additional strain on the server, possibly making it move sluggishly.

As mentioned earlier, a lot of plugins are really the loop in disguise. If you're displaying posts, comments, tags, or anything that builds around that, you're really querying the database. It is just like putting all those custom loops in your theme and watching them spin.

Now, a decent server won't usually mind the extra burden, but a lot of visitors at the same time can bring it to its knees. Database queries are heavy stuff, so you should be wary of having too many of those on the same page without the hardware to back it up.

The same is true for other types of functionality, from simple PHP functions to inclusion of third-party content. True, the biggest issue with these things comes whenever you fetch something from outside the server, which means that you'll be relying not only on your own host's hardware, but also the speed that the content can be reached (in other words, the speed of the Internet), and how quickly the target server can serve you the content. That is why a bunch of widgets pulling data from various services online will slow down any site out there.

The lesson is to not use too many plugins that put a strain on the server. That way you'll keep site load times as low as possible.

WHEN TO USE FUNCTIONS.PHP

When is it really a good idea to use functions.php? I have a rule for that too: only use functions.php when the added functionality is unique to your theme.

The reasoning around this is simple: functions.php is tied to one particular theme, which means that if you switch themes, your added functionality won't be available, forcing you to either re-create it in the new theme or abandon it altogether. This effectively disqualifies functions.php from any kind of use that controls output of content, since that would mean when you switch themes, the content would not be outputted or, at worst, it would render the site broken and full of errors.

Many of the things you do to extend your sites will be minor, and to be honest, you would probably be smarter to make those changes within the actual template files, keeping the plugin count to a minimum. However, some features are such big parts of the actual site functionality that they need to be added, because you'll probably need them in the long run. And while you may think that you just created the perfect theme, sooner or later you'll end up switching to the next perfect theme, and that means that you'll have to tackle the loss of whatever you've added to functions.php. True, you can just move the code from the old theme's functions.php file to the new one, but why bother with that?

The rule of just putting functionality in functions.php that is unique for the particular theme is a good one, I think. Examples of such functionality include layout settings (obsolete in a different theme) and theme option pages that would change slightly depending on how something is added and/or shown in the theme. Since putting that functionality into a plugin would make the plugin obsolete when you switch themes, functions.php is a better choice.

So, plugins are for extending WordPress functionality, and functions.php is for things unique to the actual theme. That pretty much wraps it up.

SOLVE IT WITH CHILD THEMES

Another way to solve the features problem is to use child themes. Assuming you've created or found the perfect theme to build upon, you can create child themes for the various iterations of your site. As always when it comes to child themes, keep your core features — which would include any cool functions.php features you've become reliant on — in your parent theme, and the design stuff and minor changes in the child theme you're using.

This means that whenever you need to relaunch your site with new modern looks, you can just create a new child theme without losing any of the functionality. No copy/pasting of functions.php code, as that all sits in the parent's functions.php.

You can read more about child themes in Chapter 5.

PLANNING FOR EXTENDED FUNCTIONALITY IN YOUR WORDPRESS SITE

Whenever you feel the need to extend the WordPress functionality on a project, you will have to figure out whether you can tweak the theme to pull off your ideas, or if you need to develop a plugin. More often than not, when stepping outside of the typical flow of content it is a mixture of both, and that's okay. The important thing is that there are solid ideas behind the choices being made. The obvious questions are:

- Do I need a plugin for feature X?
- Is it possible to extend feature X without completely overwriting it with new functionality?
- Will feature X work if/when the project gets a new theme?
- Will feature X perhaps become an issue when WordPress is updated?
- How will feature X integrate with the theme and other plugins/features?

The point is to establish a plan on how to build your WordPress site. This is true whether you just want to pimp your blog, publish an online newspaper, or do something completely different altogether with the platform. Naturally, the more extreme things you do, and the further you take WordPress beyond the blog, the more thought you'll need to pour into the project. For examples of what you can do, just look at the solutions in the next part of the book.

9

ESSENTIAL WORDPRESS PLUGINS

THE NUMBER OF plugins available for the WordPress platform is staggering; there is just no way to try them all, or even to keep up with all the changes taking place. This chapter is dedicated to just a smattering of the marvelous plugins that are available for WordPress. Each of the plugins covered here has reached the users, been thoroughly tested, and clearly fills a need. Still, they represent only a drop in the ocean compared to what's available.

Do keep in mind that plugins are always changing, just as WordPress is. That means that what works great today may not be so useful in the future. Along with using the information in this chapter, you need to continue researching and keep up with updates to make sure you find the right plugin to fill your needs.

Be advised: sometimes you'll get warnings when trying out a plugin, telling you that the plugin has only been tested up to this or that version of WordPress, and maybe not on the version that you're running. That doesn't necessarily mean it won't work for you, just that the plugin hasn't been tested with your particular version and/or the plugin author hasn't updated the plugin files. So don't be put off just because a plugin isn't tested with your version yet; set up a test blog and give it a go for yourself. Most plugins will work across versions, after all.

CONTENT-FOCUSED PLUGINS

It's all about the content; you want people to find it, get hooked, and then spend an afternoon enjoying your site. Wikipedia does it with links, and so can you. It's just a matter of making them interesting enough, and making it easy to dig into the archives. These plugins will help visitors get caught up in your content.

- **WP Greet Box** (`wordpress.org/extend/plugins/wp-greet-box/`): Whenever you get a new visitor from a social bookmarking site, it's a good idea to introduce yourself, or rather your site, to this person. That's what WP Greet Box does: it checks the referring URL and then outputs a message to the visitor. It can be something like, "Hi, welcome, please subscribe!" or something more tailored, like, "Welcome Digg visitor. Did you know I wrote a book on Digg? Get it here!" Very useful.

- **Yet Another Related Posts Plugin** (`wordpress.org/extend/plugins/yet-another-related-posts-plugin/`): The "Yet Another" part of this plugin's name is not only a flirt with code lovers out there, the number of related posts plugins is staggering, and that makes it hard to find the gold nuggets hidden among the rubbish. In my opinion this is a strong contender to the throne of related posts plugins, because it offers so many options and serves relevant links as well. For example, you can set the relevance threshold limits, so that a site with a lot of content can be stricter about what is considered to be related content. Other features include related posts in RSS feeds, support for Pages, caching, and also a template system that could be easier to use, but still offers nice customization options if you want to take things a step further.

- **Popularity Contest** (`wordpress.org/extend/plugins/popularity-contest/`): Do you know what is popular on your site? If not, this plugin is the solution, and even if you do it is a great way to promote the stuff visitors obviously like to others by outputting popular post lists using the plugin's widgets. Settings on how to weigh different factors can make the plugin work even better for your purposes.

  Showing the most popular content on a site, especially if it is weighing in the time element (so that outdated stuff doesn't suddenly pop up), is a great way to lead visitors through the site.

- **WP-PostRatings** (`wordpress.org/extend/plugins/wp-postratings/`): WP-PostRatings is an excellent plugin for rating posts. There are several different grade images included, and you can choose where you want to output it by using the [ratings] shortcode, or by adding the plugin's template tags to your theme. It also lets you get the highest and lowest rated posts, sorting by time or overall, as well as category and so on.

- **GD Star Rating** (`wordpress.org/extend/plugins/gd-star-rating/`): Another ratings plugin is GD Star Rating, which stands out with its support for several kinds of ratings per post (stars and thumbs up/down for example), as well as ratings for comments. It also features one of the flashier settings pages I've seen and a bunch of advanced settings. Well worth a look if you need ratings functionality.

- **PollDaddy** (`wordpress.org/extend/plugins/polldaddy/`): It should come as no surprise that the PollDaddy plugin fully integrates the hosted poll and service manager into WordPress, with the option of creating polls without having to leave the admin interface. Automattic owns PollDaddy, which is why it's so integrated, and that's at least one reason to consider this service as well since it has the backing infrastructure needed. If you want to get rid of all the PollDaddy links in your polls, however, you'll have to buy a pro account, so if that's an issue you may want to consider one of the native poll plugins instead.

- **WP-Polls** (`wordpress.org/extend/plugins/wp-polls/`): WP-Polls is a flexible poll plugin with archive support. You can either add it to your theme templates or use the widget to get the poll where you want it. It may take a while to set it up to fit your design, but it is a good alternative to the hosted PollDaddy solution.

MEDIA PLUGINS

Media most often means images when it comes to WordPress sites, and that's the case on the plugin side of things as well. It's not so strange when you think about it. After all, if you want to spread a video you put it on YouTube, right? That way it gets exposure and you won't have to worry about bandwidth costs for your HD masterpiece.

- **NextGEN Gallery** (`wordpress.org/extend/plugins/nextgen-gallery/`): NextGEN Gallery is a really cool gallery plugin that supports, well, a ton of things. You can have sortable albums, watermark your uploads, tweak the look with CSS, show a slideshow in the sidebar, and localize it. It supports zip file uploads, not to mention it lets your visitors browse your galleries in a smooth and user-friendly way. The admin interface is sleek, and you can easily get the shortcode needed to display the gallery, much like you would with the normal [gallery] shortcode. This is, all said, one complete plugin.

  The only caveat is that this plugin doesn't extend the normal image upload functionality, but rather works on its own. Images are stored in gallery folders residing in wp-content/gallery/ and while that's okay, it means that WordPress can't find them in the Media Library. Also, when deactivating NextGEN Gallery, you'll end up with a lot of shortcodes not being parsed anymore, hence not outputting the images, and since you can't get to the images from WordPress that can be a problem should the plugin be discontinued. Still, a very cool and well-made plugin.

- **Lightbox Gallery** (`wordpress.org/extend/plugins/lightbox-gallery/`): Lightbox Gallery adds the popular overlay lightbox effect to your gallery images, as well as making it possible to open any image by adding the `rel="lightbox"` tag to the link. You can do the same by implementing any of the available scripts out there, but this does it for you. Be aware that there are some hardcoded links in this plugin at the moment, so if you have moved your WordPress install to a subfolder but run the actual site in the root folder you may run into broken navigational images. Hopefully this will be remedied in the future; otherwise you might prefer another option.

- **Shutter Reloaded** (`wordpress.org/extend/plugins/shutter-reloaded/`): If you want to keep your lightbox overlay effects light, check out Shutter Reloaded. It checks for any link leading to an image file, and then gives it the lightbox treatment. Granted, it's not as flashy as many of the other options out there, but still cool enough.

- **Podcasting** (`wordpress.org/extend/plugins/podcasting/`): There was a time when podcasting with WordPress was synonymous with the PodPress plugin. Unfortunately it isn't really maintained anymore, which makes it even sweeter that there's a migration tool for PodPress users so that they can move to the Podcasting plugin. This plugin offers iTunes support and you can have both audio and video podcasts.

A few short and sweet media plugins to take a look at:

- **ThickboxAnnouncement** (`wordpress.org/extend/plugins/fsthickbox announcement/`) uses the Thickbox lightbox variant to overlay an announcement.

- **jQuery Lightbox** (`wordpress.org/extend/plugins/jquery-lightbox-balupton-edition/`) lets you add a lightbox-like overlay effect using jQuery and the `rel="lightbox"` to links leading to images.

- **PhotoQ Photoblog Plugin** (`wordpress.org/extend/plugins/photoq-photoblog-plugin/`) is another image plugin that keeps the images in its own structure, much like NextGEN Gallery.

- **AutoThumb** (`maff.ailoo.net/2008/07/wordpress-plugin-autothumb-phpthumb/`) uses phpThumb to give you more control over the images, looking only at the sizes and filters you add to the image source.

- **Featured Content Gallery** (`wordpress.org/extend/plugins/featured-content-gallery/`) adds an image carousel meant to be used to promote featured content on a front page.

ADMINISTRATIVE PLUGINS

By far the biggest section in this plugin compilation is the one for administrative plugins. That's probably because they range from backup solutions to statistics tools and WordPress admin fixes, as well as CMS-like functionality.

- **No Self-Pings** (`wordpress.org/extend/plugins/no-self-ping/`): If you're tired of seeing your own pings ending up on your own posts just because you're linking internally, then this is a must-have plugin. In my opinion, it should be in every WordPress install out there. If you want to crosslink internally, other than by the actual link in your post or Page, use a related posts plugin.

- **WP No Category Base** (`wordpress.org/extend/plugins/wp-no-category-base/`): WP Category Base gets rid of the default "category" in permalinks. You can customize it to say other things in the permalinks settings, like 'topics' or 'products', but you can't do away with it altogether. This plugin fixes that, making `domain.com/category/my-category` become `domain.com/my-category` instead.

- **WP-DB-Backup** (`wordpress.org/extend/plugins/wp-db-backup/`): You can never have too many backup solutions. This one uses the built-in WordPress pseudo-cron to e-mail you backups of the database, or stores them on the server for you in case something goes wrong. No matter what other backup solutions you may be running already, I encourage you to add this one as well. Remember, it just backs up the database, and only the default tables and any others you tell it to. Your uploaded files, plugins, and themes will need a different backup solution. Hopefully this plugin will be shipped with WordPress in the future, as I'm sure it would help a lot of people.

- **Maintenance Mode** (`wordpress.org/extend/plugins/maintenance-mode/`): This is a simple plugin that locks down your blog, displaying a message saying that the site is undergoing maintenance to every visitor except logged-in administrators. Remember that WordPress will put your site in its own maintenance mode when you're upgrading it, so this is for other stuff.

- **Shockingly Big IE6 Warning** (`wordpress.org/extend/plugins/shockingly-big-ie6-warning/`): Microsoft's Internet Explorer 6 is a scourge, and the only reason to run it is if your operating system is forcing you to. That would be Windows 2000, among others, since that particular OS won't run newer versions of Internet Explorer. However, there's nothing that stops users on these systems from installing any of the other Web browsers out there, it is just the newer versions of Internet Explorer that don't work. With this plugin you can educate your visitors to that fact, and make the Web a better place. Also, it will surely mean a better experience of your site for the user as well.

- **Branded Admin** (`kerrywebster.com/design/branded-admin-for-wordpress-27-released`): Branded Admin lets you customize the header and footer of the WordPress admin interface to better fit your brand. You may want to use the Branded Login plugin (`kerrywebster.com/design/branded-login-screen-for-wordpress-27/`) as well for even more customization.

- **Sidebar Login** (`wordpress.org/extend/plugins/sidebar-login/`): If you want a login form in the sidebar (or any other widgetized area) but don't want to hack the theme, then Sidebar Login is for you. It's straightforward, with no particular settings or anything to mess with.

- **Theme My Login** (`wordpress.org/extend/plugins/theme-my-login/`): The Theme My Login plugin replaces the traditional login page (wp-login.php) with a page in your theme instead. In other words, you get the login page integrated and therefore styleable, which can be a good idea if you want to give your users a login. You can also control where they'll end up after login, and add a login form to any widgetized area. Pretty useful.

- **Fast Secure Contact Form** (`wordpress.org/extend/plugins/si-contact-form/`): There are numerous contact form plugins out there. Unfortunately, many of them are prone to be plagued by spambots, so you should go with a plugin that addresses that problem. Fast Secure Contact Form has a good track record and is easy enough to work with, but there are a ton of other options out there as well.

- **TDO Mini Forms** (wordpress.org/extend/plugins/tdo-mini-forms/): This is a cool little plugin that lets you build your own forms for submission of content, which then end up in the WordPress database. You can use it to get user reviews or anything, really, and you can choose to trust some users to post directly, while others may have to be approved (which means that the posts they submit will be in draft status by default). The forms are highly customizable, and you can even have the users submit custom field values, or submit files. There's also both simple questions and CAPTCHA as well as IP banning to help fight spammers flooding you with nonsense. This plugin is featured in Chapter 15, where we look at non-bloggish sites relying on user content.

   A premium and more advanced alternative to TDO Mini Forms is Gravity Forms (www.gravityforms.com/), which does the same thing and more. If you need advanced forms and find TDO Mini Forms a bit lacking, then Gravity Forms is a good alternative, albeit not free.

- **Google Analyticator** (wordpress.org/extend/plugins/google-analyticator/): Google Analyticator makes it easy to get Google Analytics (google.com/analytics/) running on your blog without having to hack the theme's template files. It even offers some stats in the admin interface, which is nice for those of you not addicted to checking the Analytics page ten times a day.

- **Google Analytics for WordPress** (wordpress.org/extend/plugins/google-analytics-for-wordpress/): Another plugin for adding Google Analytics to your WordPress site without editing the theme files. Simple enough, with exclusions to make your statistics tracking more accurate.

- **WordPress.com Stats** (wordpress.org/extend/plugins/stats/): If you're used to the statistics served within the WordPress admin interface on wordpress.com, you'll love WordPress.com Stats. It's the same, but for your stand-alone WordPress install. It's nice and simple, but doesn't offer as much information as Google Analytics or any of the other "real" Web statistics options out there. It needs a (free) wordpress.com API key to work.

- **Broken Link Checker** (wordpress.org/extend/plugins/broken-link-checker/): This nifty little tool keeps track of your links. When installed, it will browse through your blogroll, Pages, and posts, looking for links that are broken. Then it lets you do stuff with them. Very handy, but I'm not sure I'd trust it to be running all the time. It rechecks every 72 hours by default, but you can have it check manually as well.

- **WP e-Commerce** (wordpress.org/extend/plugins/wp-e-commerce/): If you want to turn your WordPress site into a Web shop, or perhaps just enhance it to sell some merchandise, then WP e-Commerce will most likely be your first stop. The learning curve is a bit steep, but with some tweaking, both design-wise and settings-wise, you can get it to work the way you like. There is a lot of advanced functionality here, such as cross promotions, categorized products, and more. And if you want more you can always pay for the extensions, although the plugin will stand well enough on its own.

- **WordPress Simple PayPal Shopping Cart** (tipsandtricks-hq.com/wordpress-simple-paypal-shopping-cart-plugin-768): A less advanced solution to sell stuff using a WordPress site is to implement the WordPress Simple PayPal Shopping Cart.

Naturally, it connects to PayPal (only), and features a user-friendly shopping cart. You can add Add to Cart (or whatever text or image you like) anywhere you want by describing the product details in a shortcode fashion. That means that everything around the product, such as descriptions and images, will need to be managed manually.

The actual shopping cart can be added in a text widget or anywhere you like, which makes this plugin really flexible and easy to get working with just about any WordPress-powered site. Too bad it is PayPal only, but if you're fine with that you really should check this one out. There's a pro version too, if you need more bells and whistles.

- **Redirection** (`wordpress.org/extend/plugins/redirection/`): Redirection lets you set up redirects from your blog, so that `domain.com/smashing-company/` does a "301 moved" redirect to `smashing-company.com` instead, or whatever it is you need to do.

- **Pretty Link** (`wordpress.org/extend/plugins/pretty-link/`): If you want to shorten your URLs for use on Twitter, or just hide your affiliate links (that's naughty!), then Pretty Link is something to look into. Especially if you intend to roll things on Twitter and have a short domain name, because it even has the option to attach a "Pretty Bar," in a manner similar to what Digg and others are doing. Pretty Link is your own URL shortener with options, basically. There's a paid pro version as well.

- **Pods** (`wordpress.org/extend/plugins/pods/`): Pods is a plugin aiming to make WordPress even more of a CMS. The developers call it a CMS framework, and that's not too far from the truth. You can create content types, data structures, set up relationships, and so on. Building a site relying on Pods is sure to give you a lot of freedom. The only problem is it may be a bit daunting to get started with, especially if you're used to the straightforwardness of WordPress itself. Worth a look if you need WordPress to be more CMS-like.

- **WordPress Download Monitor** (`wordpress.org/extend/plugins/download-monitor/`): If you're interested in how many times a certain file has been downloaded, say a WordPress theme you've released or an e-book you're giving away, you can monitor it with the WordPress Download Monitor plugin. It offers upload of files (but you don't need to use that, you can just input the file URL), localization, categories, and easy addition of the downloads to posts and Pages. And statistics of course.

- **More Fields** (`wordpress.org/extend/plugins/more-fields/`): More Fields is an excellent plugin that makes custom fields not only easy to work with for you as the developer, but also for the editorial team working with the site. You can create custom fields with WYSIWYG functionality, radio or check boxes, and so on. It's especially handy when you're building something for a client. This is how custom fields should work in WordPress out of the box.

You might also want to check out the other plugins from the same developer: More Taxonomies (`wordpress.org/extend/plugins/more-taxonomies/`) lets you add new taxonomies to WordPress in a snitch, and More Types (`wordpress.org/extend/plugins/more-types/`) lets you add new post types. Great stuff, all.

Another option for nicer custom fields is WP-Custom (`wordpress.org/extend/plugins/wp-custom/`), although More Fields is the better choice, in my opinion.

- **Advertising Manager** (`wordpress.org/extend/plugins/advertising-manager/`): Advertising Manager helps you with managing your ads, not to mention including them in your posts. The system recognizes and supports several ad networks, including the limitations they bring (the maximum three Adsense ad units per page comes to mind). There are also widgets so that you can place your ads in any widgetized area, which should be enough to get a lot of users to try this one out. It is a bit clunky at first, but honestly, compared to the fully fledged ad managers out there this one's a breeze to use!

  A great alternative to Advertising Manager is WP-Bannerize (`wordpress.org/extend/plugins/wp-bannerize/`), which is more than enough for most smaller sites.

- **FeedWordPress** (`wordpress.org/extend/plugins/feedwordpress/`): FeedWordPress lets you syndicate feeds into your WordPress database and publish them as posts. That sounds like an RSS scrapers dream, of course, but it can also fulfill other purposes. Among other things it can power a "planet" Web site, which exists to pull together relevant content and then expose it to the visitors.

  The plugin can be used for a lot of things. Theoretically you can transform your Word-Press install into a lifestreaming monster by sorting posts into appropriate categories and such.

  Just so you're clear, scraping other people's content is bad mojo, and may be illegal. Don't do it; write your own or obtain permission.

- **Members Only** (`wordpress.org/extend/plugins/members-only/`): Members Only restricts viewing to registered users only; everyone else will be asked to login. When logged in you can redirect the user anywhere you like, so this works perfectly with the P2 theme (`wordpress.org/extend/themes/p2`) if you need internal collaboration running on WordPress. There is even a setting for private RSS feeds.

A mixed bag of administrative plugins:

- **Woopra Analytics Plugin** (`wordpress.org/extend/plugins/woopra/`) is perfect for Woopra users, just as the Google Analytics plugins are for Analytics users.
- **Random Redirect** (`wordpress.org/extend/plugins/random-redirect/`) creates a link that will send the user to a random post on your site.
- **Post Editor Buttons** (`wordpress.org/extend/plugins/post-editor-buttons/`) is a cool little plugin that lets you add your own buttons to the HTML part of the write post editor.
- **TinyMCE Advanced** (`wordpress.org/extend/plugins/tinymce-advanced/`) adds more features to the visual editor in WordPress.
- **Viper's Video Quicktags** (`wordpress.org/extend/plugins/vipers-video-quicktags/`) makes it easier to add videos from a number of sites, as well as to upload your own.

- **Custom Post Type UI** (`wordpress.org/extend/plugins/custom-post-type-ui/`) lets you create custom post types and your own taxonomies in admin, without writing any code.

- **Revision Control** (`wordpress.org/extend/plugins/revision-control/`) limits the number of post revisions WordPress can save in the database.

- **Widget Context** (`wordpress.org/extend/plugins/widget-context/`) lets you set rules for where each widget should be shown (perhaps as an alternative to having a ton of sidebars?).

- **WP-Mail SMTP** (`wordpress.org/extend/plugins/wp-mail-smtp/`) is the solution should you not want to use your host's mail servers for your WordPress e-mailing needs. It works great with Google Apps, too.

- **Editorial Calendar** (`wordpress.org/extend/plugins/editorial-calendar/`) makes it easier to manage content with a drag-and-drop interface.

- **Members** (`wordpress.org/extend/plugins/members/`) offers more control over which users can do what, what content should be shown to whom, and so on. It's a pretty cool tool, worth checking out.

SPAM AND COMMENT MANAGEMENT PLUGINS

Battling spam is important, and managing the comments in itself is important too. The following plugins will hopefully help.

- **Akismet** (`wordpress.org/extend/plugins/akismet/`): Akismet is joined at the hip with WordPress and is one of those plugins that tackles the ever-present issue of comment spam. To use it you'll need an API key from `wordpress.com`, which means you'll have to be a user there. There are also some commercial licenses available; see `akismet.com` for more. You may also want to complement it with other spam-stopping plugins, or at least try out a few others if you find that a lot of spam is getting through.

- **WP-SpamFree Anti-Spam** (`wordpress.org/extend/plugins/wp-spamfree/`): WP-SpamFree Anti-Spam differs from both Akismet at TypePad AntiSpam because it doesn't rely on a central service but rather battles the spam bots with a mix of JavaScript and cookies. It may sound like a trivial solution to this problem, but a lot of sites swear by it and it does seem to filter out a lot of spam, especially the trackback kind that other plugins miss. There's also a contact form included in the plugin, as a bonus, with spam protection of course.

  If you're spending a lot of time fiddling with spam of any kind, you may want to give this plugin a go. It works perfectly well alongside Akismet, for example, so there's really no reason not to give it a try if you need some help combating the spambots.

- **TypePad AntiSpam** (`antispam.typepad.com`): TypePad AntiSpam is Six Apart's answer to the Akismet plugin, and it works in a similar way. Just like with Akismet, it works against a server that logs and analyzes all spam, including the comments you mark as spam, and hence it "learns" all the time. Both the plugin and the necessary API key for your TypePad profile are free, so should Akismet fail for you, this is worth a shot.

- **Really Simple CAPTCHA** (`wordpress.org/extend/plugins/really-simple-captcha/`): CAPTCHA is one of those annoying "fill out what it says in the box to prove that you are human" things, and while you can argue that they aren't really user-friendly, sometimes you need to adopt desperate measures to stop spammers and other exploiters. This plugin really isn't about just slapping a CAPTCHA on your comments, for example, but rather it is meant to be utilized when you need a really simple CAPTCHA check. Works well enough in most cases.

- **Get Recent Comments** (`wordpress.org/extend/plugins/get-recent-comments/`): The recent comments widget that ships with WordPress isn't exactly exciting, and besides it tends to fill up with trackbacks. The Get Recent Comments Plugin is an excellent replacement, with adjustable layout, Gravatar support, cached output, order options, no internal pingbacks, and a lot more. If you're going to display the most recent comments, this is an excellent solution.

- **Disqus Comment System** (`wordpress.org/extend/plugins/disqus-comment-system/`): The leading hosted comment service is Disqus (`disqus.com`) and it is easy enough to get it running on your WordPress site using a plugin. If you're running Disqus you may also be interested in the (unofficial) Disqus Widget plugin (`wordpress.org/extend/plugins/disqus-widget/`), which shows off statistics for your Disqus comments.

- **IntenseDebate Comments** (`wordpress.org/extend/plugins/intensedebate/`): Two hosted comments solutions are competing for serving your reader's opinions, and IntenseDebate (`www.intensedebate.com`) is the one owned by Automattic. If you want to use IntenseDebate for your hosted comments, this is your tool.

- **CommentLuv** (`wordpress.org/extend/plugins/commentluv/`): CommentLuv is a plugin that checks the applied URL for an RSS feed, and shows the latest update with the commenter's comment. It also connects to the ComLuv Web site (`comluv.com`) for more features such as link tracking. Luckily, the whole thing is pretty customizable because the default solution isn't very pretty, including bug buttons and such.

- **BackType Connect** (`wordpress.org/extend/plugins/backtype-connect/`): The BackType Connect plugin checks the social Web for talk that is related to your blog posts, and publishes it as comments on your post. So if your mammoth article garnered a lot a buzz on Twitter, this will show up on your post as well. Pretty cool, but it can also be really messy when mixing both traditional comments and comments from microblogging systems due to the 140 character limit. Use with care and make sure that your readership is savvy enough to understand what's going on.

And a few more, short and sweet ones:

- **Cookie for Comments** (`wordpress.org/extend/plugins/cookies-for-comments/`) is a viable option when you're hit with a lot of comment spam, using cookies to make it harder for those nasty spambots to get through.

- **WP-Hashcash** (`wordpress.org/extend/plugins/wp-hashcash/`) is another spam-fighting plugin that you should try if you're overrun by comment spam.

- **ReplyMe** (`wordpress.org/extend/plugins/replyme/`) will e-mail the comment author when someone replies to him or her directly. It will only work if you have threaded comments enabled, obviously.

SOCIAL NETWORKING PLUGINS

The social Web is a concept, and you've got a ton of profiles to the left and right. Each social bookmarking tool has its own submit link, and while you can just add them all to your theme (which we'll get to in Chapter 11), you can also rely on a plugin. It's all connected these days, after all. So why not add a little bit of the social Web to your site? Show off your Twitter and let your visitors submit your content to Digg. You can do most of that directly in your theme with some custom code (usually found on the various social networking sites' tools pages), but if you want to take a shortcut or add some extra social Web flair, these plugins may help.

- **Lifestream** (`wordpress.org/extend/plugins/lifestream/`): The Lifestream plugin easily adds lifestreaming features to your WordPress site. Just install it and tell it what online accounts and RSS feeds it should fetch data from, and then you can include it using a shortcode on a Page, for example. You can also customize each element thanks to the addition of CSS classes, and there is built-in support for several of the largest social media properties out there, although just about anything with an RSS feed will work. And, of course, it is ready for localization as well as being constantly updated, which makes it an interesting option for those of you wanting to lifestream from within WordPress.

- **Twitter Tools** (`wordpress.org/extend/plugins/twitter-tools/`): Twitter Tools connects your WordPress blog with Twitter, and lets you send tweets from the blog to your account. A simple settings page makes this a breeze to set up, and you can even control how the tweets you've sent should be tagged and handled on your own site. This means that you can have an asides category and send everything posted in it to Twitter, or the other way around.

- **ShareThis** (`wordpress.org/extend/plugins/share-this/`): Sending posts to social bookmarking sites is popular, and this tool adds that functionality to every post on a site. ShareThis is more than just a plugin, it is a service that hosts your submit form, which means that you can get stats and everything if you sign up for an account.

  The only thing to keep in mind here is that using any third-party element means relying on that party's ability to serve the data. In other words, if the ShareThis server is slow or even unavailable, then so is some or all of your sharing functionality.

- **Add to Any: Share/Bookmark/E-mail Button** (`wordpress.org/extend/plugins/add-to-any/`): This plugin integrates the hosted `AddToAny.com` sharing button. You may also want to look at the Subscribe button as well, if you like this service: `wordpress.org/extend/plugins/add-to-any-subscribe/`.

More social stuff:

- **Wickett Twitter Widget** (`wordpress.org/extend/plugins/wickett-twitter-widget/`) is a simple widget that shows your tweets.
- **Twitter for WordPress** (`wordpress.org/extend/plugins/twitter-for-wordpress/`) is another widget used to show off your tweets.
- **Sociable** (`wordpress.org/extend/plugins/sociable/`) is a popular social bookmarking plugin that adds links to your site.

- **Tweet Old Post** (`wordpress.org/extend/plugins/tweet-old-post/`) will tweet random old posts at the interval you set. This might be a great way to get some more traction to your archive content if you have diehard Twitter followers.
- **Simple Social Bookmarks** (`wordpress.org/extend/plugins/simple-social-bookmarks/`) is another social bookmarking option featuring over 200 networks.
- **SexyBookmarks** (`wordpress.org/extend/plugins/sexybookmarks/`) is a popular plugin to show off social sharing icons in a visually appealing way.

SUBSCRIPTION AND MOBILE PLUGINS

Most smartphones have had RSS support for quite some time, and a few high end "regular" mobile phones as well. The natural next step is that we now consume more and more content through mobile devices, with customized versions of your site for the latest mobile phone from Apple, Google, or whatever the current craze.

- **Align RSS Images** (`wordpress.org/extend/plugins/align-rss-images/`): Images floating to the left and right on your site may be pretty to look at right there, but for RSS subscribers that same image will be in the midst of everything. You can just skip floating images, but that's a shame. Better to use Align RSS Images to parse the WordPress default align code (being alignleft and alignright) and swap for HTML equivalents to make things look good. No settings needed, just install it and forget about it.
- **RSS Footer** (`wordpress.org/extend/plugins/rss-footer/`): RSS Footer adds a line at the beginning or at the end of every item in your RSS feed. This means that you can insert a copyright notice to make things harder on the scrapers, or promote your site or other products to readers that prefer the feed to the original site. Very handy and easily customized.
- **Disable RSS** (`wordpress.org/extend/plugins/disable-rss/`): This plugin does just what its name says: it disables the RSS feeds from a WordPress install. This can come in handy in static sites where RSS doesn't fulfill any purpose whatsoever.
- **Subscribe2** (`wordpress.org/extend/plugins/subscribe2/`): Subscribe2 is a really powerful plugin. It lets your users subscribe to your updates and hence get notifications via e-mail as per the settings you have. Perhaps you want to send a digest on a per-post basis, daily, or weekly. You can also send an e-mail to registered users, much like a traditional newsletter, if you will. The settings are easy enough to manage, as are the e-mail templates, so you can get started early on. As always, when it comes to sending e-mails, all hosts may not play nicely, so you should pay attention and do some tests to make sure that everything is being sent the way it was supposed to. Also, there is always the risk of being branded as a spammer in the eyes of ISPs, so use with caution.
- **MobilePress** (`wordpress.org/extend/plugins/mobilepress/`): MobilePress is a cool plugin that serves a mobile theme rather than your regular one when the user is visiting from a mobile device. You can tell the plugin in which cases to serve the mobile theme and when not to, and there's even a theme interface similar to the standard one in WordPress so that you can create a mobile theme that fits your brand.

More mobile plugins:

- **WordPress Mobile Edition** (`wordpress.org/extend/plugins/wordpress-mobile-edition/`) is another plugin that gives your site a mobile interface when the visitor is using a mobile device.

- **WordPress Mobile Pack** (`wordpress.org/extend/plugins/wordpress-mobile-pack/`) is yet another solution for mobile visitors.

- **WPtouch** (`wordpress.org/extend/plugins/wptouch/`) adapts your site to mobile touch devices such as the iPhone or Android phones. There's a pro version if you need more than just the basic functionality.

SEO AND SEARCH PLUGINS

SEO stands for search engine optimization, and the whole idea is to get people to find your content. Luckily you don't need to hire an SEO expert to get ahead in the game, there are plugins that will help you get started.

- **All in One SEO Pack** (`wordpress.org/extend/plugins/all-in-one-seo-pack/`): This plugin adds more settings for your posts so that they'll be better optimized for search engines. A lot of people swear by it, and there's no doubt that it will help, even if you just leave it doing its thing automatically. To really push it though, you should fine-tune each post all the time.

- **Google XML Sitemaps** (`wordpress.org/extend/plugins/google-sitemap-generator/`): Google XML Sitemaps will create a compliant XML sitemap for your WordPress install, and then update it whenever you publish something new, or edit something old. This will help search engines crawl your content, which is a good thing. The plugin will even attempt to tell them that your sitemap is updated.

- **Better Search** (`wordpress.org/extend/plugins/better-search/`): The built-in search functionality in WordPress is lacking, to say the least, which is why many users turn to plugins or Google Custom Search Engine (`google.com/cse/`). Better Search tries to change things by tuning the search, as well as adding popular searches and heatmaps. Since it automatically replaces the built-in search, it is easy enough to give it a go.

- **Search Unleashed** (`wordpress.org/extend/plugins/search-unleashed/`): Search Unleashed adds a bunch of settings and options for WordPress search functionality, such as keyword highlighting and extendable search engines. It also highlights incoming traffic search queries from sites like Google, so if someone searches for "Apples" on Google and visits your site as a result, Search Unleashed will highlight "Apples." The plugin is localized and you can even give priority to various parts of posts and Pages, as well as getting all those shortcodes properly searched should you rely on that. And best of all, no database changes! Check it out; this is one of the better search plugins out there.

- **HeadSpace2 SEO** (`wordpress.org/extend/plugins/headspace2/`): One of the more user-friendly SEO plugins out there is called HeadSpace2 SEO. It features great setup pages, and does more than just tweak the metadata and descriptions. You can, for

201

example, have it manage your Google Analytics settings, which is nice. Whether this is a better choice than any of the other SEO options out there or not probably depends on what you want to achieve and how you go about it, but it is certainly the most user-friendly one.

- **Robots Meta** (`wordpress.org/extend/plugins/robots-meta/`): Having a robots.txt for the search engines to crawl is a good thing, and Robots Meta helps you set one up by giving you simple settings for categories and other types of archives. Handy for SEO knowledgeable people, for sure.

- **Global Translator** (`wordpress.org/extend/plugins/global-translator/`): Global Translator adds flags to your site using a widget, and then the user can get the site translated into their language. That is, if you enabled it and the translation engine used (Google Translate, Babelfish, and so on) supports it. Caching and permalinks for better SEO are among the features.

And a few more:

- **Search Everything** (`wordpress.org/extend/plugins/search-everything/`) is another search plugin with keyword highlighting and heavily expanded search parameters.

- **GD Press Tools** (`wordpress.org/extend/plugins/gd-press-tools/`) is not for the faint of heart. The plugin adds a lot of customizing to everything from meta tags to custom fields and cron, so use with caution.

- **Breadcrumb Trail** (`wordpress.org/extend/plugins/breadcrumb-trail/`) is a breadcrumb script that lets you insert a breadcrumb link by adding the plugin's template tag. Similar to Yoast Breadcrumbs (`wordpress.org/extend/plugins/breadcrumbs/`).

CODE AND OUTPUT PLUGINS

There are literally thousands of plugins to choose from in this category, and while a lot of them overlap, and quite a few fulfill almost no purpose whatsoever, there are some that don't fit in anywhere in the preceding sections but are still worth mentioning. Most of those are related to custom code, or are just small quirky things that can spice up a site by outputting the content differently. In other words, this is quite a mix.

- **SyntaxHighlighter Evolved** (`wordpress.org/extend/plugins/syntax highlighter/`): If you ever need to post chunks of programming code in your posts and on your Pages, from simple HTML to massive chunks of PHP, you know that the built-in parsing will get you in trouble. Sure, there are pastebins and the like, but why not solve this problem by adding the SyntaxHighlighter Evolved plugin, which not only takes care of your precious code, but also highlights it accordingly? It is styleable as well, so you can make the code boxes fit your content. Very neat. There are a bunch of other plugins that do similar things, but this one always performs.

- **Blog Time** (`coffee2code.com/wp-plugins/blog-time/`): Blog Time outputs the time of the server in timestamp mode, either via a widget or the custom blog_time() template tag. It's not a clock, it's just the timestamp, which can be pretty handy sometimes.

- **WP-Cumulus** (`wordpress.org/extend/plugins/wp-cumulus/`): Tired of your slack 2D tag cloud? Get one in 3D with WP-Cumulus and its rotating Flash rendition of the tag cloud. Flashy and fun, if nothing else, but I wouldn't recommend using it as the main navigation tool.

- **wp-Typography** (`wordpress.org/extend/plugins/wp-typography/`): The wp-Typography plugin will improve your typography, obviously, which means that it will fix things such as not line-breaking unit values, give you prettier quote marks, dashes, and things like that.

- **Widget Logic** (`wordpress.org/extend/plugins/widget-logic/`): This plugin is as simple as it is brilliant. It adds one tiny little field to every widget, and that field takes conditional tags. That means that you can add checks like is_single() to any widget, which makes it really simple to make a site dynamic.

- **WP Super Cache** (`wordpress.org/extend/plugins/wp-super-cache/`): This is the must-have plugin for any WordPress site experiencing a lot of traffic, but not wanting to go all haywire with the hardware. It lets you set up caching of your site, which means that it will serve static files rather than query the database all the time. If you plan on hitting the frontpage on Digg with your techblog and are on a share-hosting account, WP Super Cache will keep you online. It's a must-have, and better maintained than its predecessor, WP-Cache . The only caveat with WP Super Cache is that it will cache dynamic output as well, which means that your most recent comments may not actually *be* the most recent ones anymore. You can handle that by controlling what should and shouldn't be cached.

  There's also W3 Total Cache (`wordpress.org/extend/plugins/w3-total-cache/`), a great alternative to WP Super Cache. Try them both and figure out which one works best in your setup.

- **Query Posts** (`wordpress.org/extend/plugins/query-posts/`): Query Posts is a really cool widget that lets you build your very own WordPress loop in the sidebar, without even having to know any PHP! It can be a very handy way to get custom output in the sidebar, or any other widgetized area. It integrates nicely with the Get the Image plugin (`wordpress.org/extend/plugins/get-the-image/`), which lets you grab an image from the post's content, a custom field, or even an attachment.

Short and sweet:

- **WP-DBManager** (`wordpress.org/extend/plugins/wp-dbmanager/`) helps to keep your database up to speed, with repairs as well as backing up.

- **Exec-PHP** (`wordpress.org/extend/plugins/exec-php/`) lets you execute PHP code in posts, Pages, and text widgets. Make sure you don't let anyone who doesn't know what they're doing loose with this tool!

- **WP-PageNavi** (`wordpress.org/extend/plugins/wp-pagenavi/`) enhances the page navigation feature. It includes several styling settings, but you need to add the plugin's template tag to your theme files for it to work.

A FINAL CAVEAT: DO YOU REALLY NEED THAT PLUGIN?

It's easy to get carried away with plugins and additional functionality overall when working with WordPress. There is so much you can add, so many possibilities, and with the plugin install a mere click away now that you can do it from your admin interface, it's even harder to resist.

But resist you should. For every feature and every plugin you add, you'll bloat your install some more. Plugins can really slow down your site. It's not just the puny files sitting in the plugins folder; the problem is what they do to your database, and the number of access requests and extra queries performed when you use them.

Don't get me wrong, plugins are nice. Some of the coolest WordPress sites just wouldn't be possible without plugins, and the extensive nature of the platform is one of the reasons it is so powerful and widely used. The fact that there's a whole chapter just talking about what plugins you should look closer at, and teasing you with what you can do with them, certainly counts for something!

Just don't go overboard, that's all I'm saying. Use plugins when you need them, but keep it as simple and as clean as you possibly can.

IV

ADDITIONAL FEATURES AND FUNCTIONALITY

10 WORDPRESS AS A CMS

CMS IS SHORT for *content management system* — simply put, a way to manage content. You use a CMS to write, edit, and manage your work online, usually by storing content in a database or in files. This is a lot more convenient than editing files or updating the database directly, which was the way the Web used to be managed.

Although WordPress started life as a blogging platform, it has over time become a powerful and versatile CMS in its own right. This chapter tackles the challenges you face and the decisions you need to make when you want to use WordPress as a more traditional CMS, powering non-blog sites with the system. It is not only possible to use WordPress in this way, it is also a great solution that saves time and money.

IS WORDPRESS THE RIGHT CHOICE FOR YOUR CMS?

By now you've gathered that WordPress is useful for much more than just blogging (if not, just wait until Chapter 15). Basically, you can do just about anything that involves managing written content, along with other media such as images, sound, and video. I often tell newspaper and magazine publishers that there is no newspaper or magazine site that I couldn't rebuild in WordPress. Those sites are usually powered by expensive licensed systems, and while it was unlikely that anyone would make that claim a couple of years ago, today it is taken seriously. Larger publishing companies are already putting WordPress to good use for their editorial group blogs and others are powering opinion sections using the system.

Picking the right CMS is important, since your system should excel at what you want it to do. WordPress is the right choice if you want a CMS that is:

- Open source and free
- Fast and easy to use
- Easily extendable
- Convenient for designing and developing plugins
- Excellent with text
- Search engine friendly
- Good enough with images

Basically, if your site is an editorial one with primarily text content, you'll be safe with choosing WordPress. (Although as Matt Mullenweg of WordPress fame has shown on `http://ma.tt`, WordPress can also handle image-heavy sites.)

So when should you consider using an alternative to WordPress? Arguments for the potential advantages of other CMSs include:

- **Community features:** Previously, other systems offered better access to community features such as forums, but the release of BuddyPress (`http://buddypress.org`), and the easy integration with forum software such as bbPress (`http://bbpress.org`), have really overcome this deficiency.
- **Modular structure:** Some of the heavier CMSs (such as Drupal) have a more modular structure, which means you can create pretty much anything you want, wherever you want. This is usually at the expense of usability, so you need to compare features and workflow before deciding on which route you should take.
- **Product support:** Another common criticisms against open source CMS alternatives like WordPress is that commercial products offer support as a part of the package, making it worthwhile to pay for a CMS. The counterargument to this is that the money allocated to licensing could be spent on a consultant and/or developer when needed, and not just be the cause of a big hole in the coffers. You can take those licensing fees and build your adaptations, should you not find the solution available already. And after that, it is all free.

WordPress is a great CMS option, especially if you're building an editorial site. Whether you think it is right for your project or not, you should always sit back and figure out what you actually need first. Then, find the ideal CMS and consider how you would use it for this particular project.

WORDPRESS CMS CHECKLIST

So you're considering using WordPress as a CMS for a project? That's when the following checklist comes in handy. You need to think about these things first to avoid running into unwanted surprises along the way.

The first questions

- Do you really need a CMS for this project? Sometimes hacking HTML is the way to go, after all.
- Is WordPress the correct CMS for your project? It may be great, but sometimes other things would work better to meet your needs.

The WordPress admin interface

- What additional functionality do you need for the admin interface?
- Should you use plugins to cut down on functionality? The admin interface can be pretty overwhelming to less experienced users.
- If you're going to employ user archives, consider what usernames to give everyone involved.
- Do you need features for menu editing, and custom backgrounds as well as custom headers?
- Does it matter that the admin interface is branded WordPress? If yes, you need to give it some new style, and don't forget the login form.

Categories and tagging

- What is your strategy with categories and tags? Do you need to add further taxonomies, like separate tag groups or hierarchical categories to make the site work?
- Which categories should you include, and do you need to do custom category coding and/or templates?
- How should tags be used, and how will you educate the users in the praxis you've chosen?

Pages and posts

- Do you need custom fields?
- Do you need to create Page templates to manage tasks on your site? If so, make sure you've got those Pages created from the start.
- How should Pages relate to each other? What should be a top-level Page, and what should be a sub-Page? Make sure you know the hierarchy, and how you will present the various sections.

- How will you present the posts? Do they need any specific treatment to fit in?
- Will you use the new Post Formats for custom formatting of posts?
- Do you need additional kinds of content that are separated from posts and Pages? In that case, make sure you have a plan for your custom post types.
- What will be on the front page? A static page, latest news updates, or something else?

Additional considerations

- Figure out your permalink structure right away, and stick to it. You may need plugins to tune it the way you want.
- Do you need specific shortcode to speed up the publishing and avoid unnecessary HTML code in the posts (see the "Custom Shortcode" section later in this chapter for more info)?
- Do you need any features that are not built in to WordPress? Can you use plugins to achieve the necessary functionality? Will such plugins cause problems with upgrades in the future?
- If your project requires localization, are the language features you need available? There are plenty of language files for WordPress, but what about themes and plugins? Will you need to do additional work there?

TRIMMING WORDPRESS TO THE ESSENTIALS

When you work for clients or other people within your organization, you'll have to think a little bit differently than if you were going to be the primary user yourself. Remember: you're a savvy user, but that may not be the case for everybody else. That's why you need to trim WordPress to the essentials, and make sure that there aren't too many options to confuse the user.

The first and foremost trimming action you can perform is to limit the user privileges. As mentioned in the discussion of security in Chapter 1, not all users need full admin accounts. Most of the time, the Editor account role will be enough, and sometimes you may want to go below that. For every step down the user level ladder you take, fewer options are displayed for the user, and that is a good thing.

It goes without saying that you should make sure there are no unnecessary plugins activated, since these not only potentially slow things down, they also clutter the admin interface with option pages and related elements. So keep it clean.

TWEAKING THE ADMIN INTERFACE

You can make the WordPress admin interface appear in tune with your needs by using one of the CMS plugins available. There are several, but WP-CMS Post Control (`http://wordpress.org/extend/plugins/wp-cms-post-control/`) is a good choice. With this plugin, you can hide unnecessary elements for your users, disable autosave (which can be a nuisance), control which image uploader should be used, and a bunch of other things. It can really make the WordPress interface a little easier and less scary for new users. I especially like the message box option, which can contain information for the user on how to proceed, and links to more help.

There are also several plugins that let you hide parts of the admin interface. You may want to consider them if you will be responsible for running a site at your company, or for a client, for a long time. But beware if it is a one-time gig! As you know, new WordPress versions roll out all the time, and that means that plugins may stop working, or need to be upgraded. While that is easy enough in WordPress, it also means that you have to educate the client about how to do it if you're not providing ongoing support.

Still, to use WordPress as a CMS makes a lot more sense if you hide the stuff you don't need. The competition may not be doing it, but if you're using WordPress to power a semi-static corporate website, it certainly sounds like a good idea to remove all the stuff the users don't need to see. Just make sure you've got the upgrades covered when they roll out.

YOUR OWN ADMIN THEME

Did you know that you can create your own WordPress admin theme? Unfortunately, it isn't nearly as impressive as the traditional themes, but still, you can change the look and feel and that may be important.

You can hack wp-admin.css in the wp-admin folder, which is where all the admin styling goes, but a much cleaner, not to mention upgrade-safe solution is to create your own Word-Press admin theme as a plugin. It really isn't all that complicated to build. You use the `admin_head()` action hook to attach your very own stylesheet, and then just override the stuff you don't like in wp-admin.css. You'll recognize this bit:

```php
<?php
/*
Plugin Name: Smashing Admin Theme
Plugin URI: http://tdhedengren.com/wordpress/smashing-admin-theme/
Description: This is the Smashing Admin Theme, disguised as a plugin. Activate
to make your admin smashing!
Author: Thord Daniel Hedengren
Version: 1.0
Author URI: http://tdhedengren.com
*/

function smashing_admin() {
    $url = get_settings('siteurl');
    $url = $url . '/wp-content/plugins/smashing-admin/wp-admin.css';
    echo '<link rel="stylesheet" type="text/css" href="' . $url . '" />';
}

add_action('admin_head', 'smashing_admin');

?>
```

The first part is obviously the now familiar plugin header, that lets WordPress know that, hey, this is a plugin and I should show it off in the plugins page. I'm calling this admin theme the Smashing Admin Theme, so it makes sense to name the function `smashing_admin()`.

You'll put the plugin in its own folder, smashing-admin, which the users will drop in wp-content/plugins/, so first you load the `$url` variable with the siteurl value, using `get_settings()`. Then you update it by getting the siteurl value and add the path of your own wp-admin.css stylesheet, located within the smashing-admin plugin folder (/wp-content/plugins/smashing-admin/wp-admin.css to be precise). Finally, you echo it.

To get this echoed stylesheet link into admin, you use `add_action()` to attach the `smashing_admin()` function to the `admin_head` action hook. And there you have it, one stylesheet loaded in admin. Now all that's left is to pick the original wp-admin.css to pieces by altering the stuff you like. Just edit the wp-admin.css stylesheet in your plugin folder.

You can just as easily add actual content to the top or bottom of the WordPress admin. Just use `add_action()` and attach it to `admin_head` or `admin_footer`, and you've got the control you need.

What about the login screen? You can modify it as well, but the easiest solution is to use one of the numerous plugins available. See the admin plugins list in Chapter 9 for more possibilities.

UNBLOGGING WORDPRESS

Much of the functionality built into WordPress may be overkill when you're using it as a CMS to power simple websites. A company website built around static pages containing product information might not need comments or trackbacks, and the only kind of fluid content might be a news or press clippings section. It just makes sense; some functionality just isn't needed, and neither is the blog lingo.

So when you need to build the kind of site that just doesn't require all the bling and the functionality, you won't want to include all that in your theme. The following sections outline a few changes you should make when using WordPress as a CMS for an unbloggish site.

Template Files

You can stick to just one template file, index.php, for all your listing and search needs, but you can chop this up into several templates if you want to. If you don't need commenting functionality, then comments.php is completely unnecessary. Page templates, on the other hand, are very useful, and you'll most likely end up having a static front page using one of these.

Also, remember to remove any `get_comments()` calls from the template files. Yes, you can just note that you won't accept comments in admin, but that means that you'd have to change the "Comments are closed" output in comments.php, which would look pretty bad. So better to just remove `get_comments()` from any template tags where you don't need it.

Lingo

There's a lot of bloggish lingo within WordPress by default; "categories" and "tags" are used in the permalinks, for example. You can change these on a URL level in the permalink settings. Maybe you want to go with "news" or "updates" instead of the default "category," and perhaps "view" or "topic" rather than the default "tag." Actually, a good way to create a news section for a static corporate site is to use Pages for any serious content, like company information and product descriptions, whereas you'll use the one category, called News with the slug "news," for the news posts. That way, you can set up your permalinks so that /news/ will be the category listings, or the News section in this case, and then you let all the posts (which of course are just news items) get the /news/post-slug/ permalink by applying the /%category%/%postname%/ permalink structure in the settings. Really handy, and no need to build a custom news section or anything.

You would want more control over the content if you need more than one newsy section though, in which case Page templates listing the latest posts from the category in question is a nice enough solution, as opposed to just linking the category archives. You would go about it by creating a Page per section, and then having a Page template for each of these sections. Every Page template would contain a custom loop fetching the necessary posts. It all boils down to what you need to do and how flexible you want the site to be.

This inevitably leads into what you can do with static Pages and how what used to be blog posts can fill the needs of a more traditional website.

THE PERFECT SETUP FOR A SIMPLE STATIC WEBSITE

Using static Pages and categories as a news model is truly a great tool whenever you need to roll out a typical old-school website quickly. Maybe it is a product presentation, a corporate website, or something entirely different that just won't work with the blog format. That's when this setup is so useful.

Pages (as in WordPress Pages) were originally meant to be used for static content. The fact that you can create one Page template (recall that template files for Pages are individual) for each Page should you want to means that they can really look like anything. You can break your design completely, since you don't even have to call the same header or footer file, you can have different markup and you can exclude everything WordPress-related and display something entirely different instead, should you want to. It is a really powerful tool that can just as easily contain multiple loops or syndicated RSS content from other sites. Each Page template is a blank slate, and it is your primary weapon when using WordPress as a CMS; this is where you can make the site truly step away from the blog heritage that the system carries.

And don't get me started on the front page! Since you can set WordPress to display a static Page as a front page (under Settings in admin), and pick any other Page (keep it empty, mind you) for your post listings should you need that, you can really do anything. You can even put in one of those nasty Flash preloader thingies with autoplaying sound (but you really shouldn't). The point is that a Page template, along with the front page setting, is just as much a clean slate as a blank PHP or HTML file would be outside WordPress, but with all the benefits of the system!

On the other side of things, you've got traditional blog posts. These need to belong to a category and each of them will be more or less the same, visually. Sure, if you want to you can play around a lot with these too, but on a semi-static site Pages are a much better idea.

> *Naturally, it is a whole different ball game if you're going to handle tons of content, but that's usually not what you're talking about when "WordPress as a CMS" gets mentioned.*

Pages for static content, posts for newsy stuff. This is a great model for most corporate websites using WordPress as a CMS, with Pages for all those product descriptions, and posts for news, announcements, and press clippings. Assuming I've already worked out the design, here is the process I'll follow:

1. I decide what will be a Page and what will not. Usually, everything except news and announcements are Pages. I create these Pages and make sure they get the right slug. This includes making sure that the basic permalink structure is there, which means I'll make sure the post and category URLs look good. Chances are I'll use a plugin to further control this, but it all depends on the needs of the site.

2. I start creating the Page templates. Chances are the company profile Page will have other design needs than the product Pages, so I'll want to put emphasis on different things, and construct any possible submenus and information boxes in ways that fit the style.

3. I create the categories needed, one for each newsy section. This is usually just one category, called News or Announcements, but sometimes I need both, or even more. In some cases I really just want just one category — Announcements, for example — and then I opt for sorting within it using tags, one for News, one for Press Releases, one for Products, one for Announcements, and so on. Naturally, I need to make sure the category listings as well as the single post view looks good.

4. I tie it all together by creating a menu (using the menu feature for flexibility for the client, but I do tend to populate it myself to get them started) which links to both the various Pages, and the categories involved.

That's it, the elements of a static simple website using WordPress as a CMS. You can take this concept as far as you like really, since it is WordPress and you can build upon it as much as you like.

DOING MORE THAN THE BASICS

Sometimes you need more than the static site I just described. For example, you might need to add additional post types; perhaps you need a product listing, and have to create a custom post type for products with its own taxonomies and everything.

Some websites obviously need more attention: the more advanced the site, the more tweaks and adaptations are needed to make it fit. Sometimes this means you'll have to write custom loops or use Page templates, and at other times you may want more flexibility without touching the code for every little update. That's when widgets come in, not only because a lot of cool features come as plugins that are widget-ready, but also because widgets offer drag-and-drop functionality which non-techy users will surely appreciate.

The following sections discuss how you can add this kind of functionality to a pretty basic WordPress CMS setup without too much hassle.

USES FOR CUSTOM POST TYPES AND TAXONOMIES IN A WORDPRESS CMS

Custom post types is the best thing to happen to WordPress since tagging came along. I already covered the technique in Chapter 6, so this section is more about how you can put it to really good use when using WordPress as a CMS.

There are often great benefits of having more than just posts and Pages to play with. Thanks to custom post types, you can create whatever type of post- or Page-like content you like without having to mix it with your regular posts and Pages. A few examples off the top of my head:

- **Products.** Create a post type called Products and let posts residing in it be products, with descriptions, tagging, and everything.
- **Persons.** Why not create a directory of people, one person per post in this post type?
- **Portfolio.** Perhaps you have a portfolio part of your site residing in a category. No need for that anymore; should you want to separate it from the rest of the content flow, just create the post type!
- **Manual.** Need to put up a static manual? No need to mix it with your Pages anymore, just create a new post type to keep it apart.

The list goes on and on. What's really great is that your custom post types each get their own dedicated menu item on the left side of the WordPress admin interface, just like Posts or Pages. That makes it really easy for the end user to find and use them, compared to solutions sporting custom fields or similar methods.

The same advantage goes for custom taxonomies, also covered previously. With these you can have a separate tag group for properly tagging your products, for example. This is a great way to further control how things are sorted and found on your site. WordPress offers a great mix of default tools, such as posts and Pages alongside categories and tags, along with the ones you can create yourself such as custom post types and additional taxonomies. It takes some thought to find the right toolset out of all these possibilities, but it's worth it.

PUTTING WIDGETS TO GOOD USE IN A CMS

Widgets and widget areas are your friends when rolling out WordPress as a CMS. They are perhaps not as important for the small and static company websites primarily discussed so far,

215

but can be very useful for the larger ones. Take a look around online; there are numerous sites that push out mixed functionality, especially on their front pages, and display teaser images when it is suitable. You can do a lot of this with widgets.

Using Basic Widget Areas

The most straightforward usage is to litter your site with widget areas wherever you may want to output something all of a sudden; just make sure that the area doesn't output anything by default so that it will remain invisible (as in not containing anything) whenever you haven't populated it with a widget. However, a better practice is to think your widget areas through, and put the areas where you know you'll need them, not where you think you may need them two years down the road. After all, you will have redesigned the site by then anyway.

So you've got your widget areas in. Now, how to use them? Besides the obvious answer of drag-and-drop widgets on the Appearance → Themes page in WordPress admin, can add widgets that do whatever you need. The ones that ship with WordPress are simple and somewhat crude; the Pages widget (listing your Pages) won't even let you display just the Pages, it forces an h2 title out there, which you may not want. You want control over how your content will display, so if you're moving down this route, be sure to look at the many plugins that offer widget support; there are several available that will list just the Pages with adding that h2 heading, for example.

The most useful widget is by far the text widget. It accepts HTML code, which means that putting text and images in it is a breeze. This is good, because if you want to show off that special promotion (or pimp your Facebook fan page) just below the menu in the header, you can just put the necessary HTML code in a text widget and drop it there for the duration of the campaign, and then just remove it, and the area will disappear until you add new content. There are some great plugins that will help you in Chapter 9.

Making Widgets a Little More Dynamic

Why not just put empty widget areas where the various elements on the site could go? It will do the job, but you'll have to cram them in wherever they will fit, and you will have to take the rest of the design and content into account. You will have to do that either way, of course, but there is an alternative: Replace parts of the content with a widget area.

If you're running a magazine-ish site, you may have an opportunity to roll out big so-called *roadblocks*, ads that take over a lot more of the site than just common banners and leader-boards. Roadblocks usually run for a shorter amount of time, and you get paid a lot for them, compared to ads.

Or, take another approach: say you're an Apple blogger and you want to cover the Apple WWDC or MacWorld in a timely manner, making sure that your readers won't miss it. How? Plaster the site in promotional graphics of course!

Both these examples will typically work poorly if you just add content into widget areas positioned around the site's normal elements. They will, however, work perfectly well if you replace parts of the site's content, meaning any element really, with a widget area. This effect is pretty easy to get working, thanks to the fact that widget areas can come preloaded with content.

The following code is for a widget area called Teaser, and it should come preloaded with the content you want in that particular spot on a day-to-day basis:

```php
<?php
    if ( is_active_sidebar('Teaser') ) {
        dynamic_sidebar('Teaser');
    } else { ?>
        [The normal content would go here. Links, headlines, whatever. . . ]
<?php }; ?>
```

Just put it in there; it can be anything, really. A headline section, a poll, must-read lists, loops, links, images — you name it. Anything.

However, when you drop a widget in the Teaser widget area within the WordPress admin interface, the default content won't show; it will be replaced with the widget you dropped thanks to the `is_active_sidebar()` check. So dropping a text widget with your big fat promo image for the Apple event, or your new e-book, or whatever, will replace the original content. When you remove the image from the Teaser widget area, the default content will return by default.

Pretty nifty, huh? And actually pretty simple to maintain as well; if something goes wrong, you can just remove the widget you put there, and you'll always revert to default.

Another great use of widgets is navigational menus, which make sure users can add menu items themselves without having to rely on the theme designer.

MANAGING MENUS

Menus need to look good and be easy to maintain, that's true for just about every website. When you're using WordPress as a CMS, this is perhaps even more important. Thanks to the great menu feature in WordPress discussed in Chapter 6, it's easy to create the kinds of menus you need. Given their importance, you'll want to give the menus some thought.

There are two primary ways to create menus. First is the menu area, which uses `wp_nav_menu()` to output a predetermined menu area. Using `wp_nav_menu()` limits you to menus, as opposed to the second solution, widget areas, but it also let's you name the menu area appropriately. This makes it easier for the end user when working with the menu.

The second way you can add menus is by using widget areas. You can use the menu widget to insert any created menu anywhere you can drop the widget. This can sometimes be handy, but offers less control than the alternative solution.

Either way, the important thing here is that you utilize the menu feature, since it makes it a whole lot easier for the site administrator to change the menu(s) on the site. If the menu feature is enabled in your theme you can check it out under Appearance → Menu as seen in Figure 10-1.

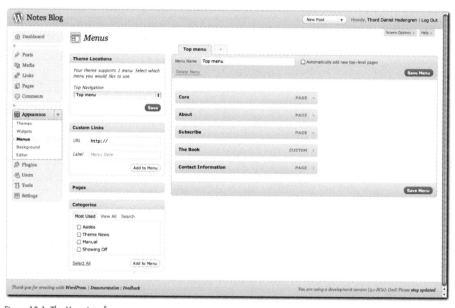

Figure 10-1: The Menu interface

CUSTOM SHORTCODES

Shortcode is tagged code that you can input in your posts to output something specific. The [gallery] tag is shortcode. You can create your own shortcode, which can come in handy when using WordPress, particularly when you're doing non-bloggish things with it.

ADDING SHORTCODE WITH FUNCTIONS.PHP

You can add shortcode functionality through a plugin, or by using functions.php. The following example uses functions.php to add shortcode.

1. Start by creating a simple shortcode tag that outputs some simple text; you'll put it to more interesting use later.

2. Next, you need a function that does what you want, written within the PHP tags of functions.php, of course:

```
function text_example() {
    return 'Why, this text was just outputted using the shortcode tag you
  created! Smashing.';
}
```

3. Now you need to assign `text_example()` to a shortcode. You do that with the `add_shortcode()` function:

```
add_shortcode('textftw', 'text_example');
```

This creates the `[textftw]` shortcode, and loads it with the contents of the `text_example()` function. So `[textftw]` in your blog post will output in your post, "Why, this text was just outputted using the shortcode tag you created! Smashing."

Simple enough. Now do something useful with it, like making a shortcode for promoting your RSS feed.

4. Starting with the function, this time you'll use it to output some HTML code as well, which gives you control of how the promotion appears:

```
function rss_promotion() {
    return '<div class="rsspromot">Never miss a beat - <a href="http://
  notesblog.com/feed/">subscribe to the RSS feed!</a></div>';
}
```

5. Next you need to create the shortcode, and add the `rss_promotion()` function content to it:

```
add_shortcode('rsspromo', 'rss_promotion');
```

6. Now you've got the `[rsspromo]` shortcode that outputs the `div` container from the `rss_promotion()` function. All you have to do to wrap this up is to add some styling to the style.css stylesheet. Maybe something like this:

```
div.rsspromo {
    background: #eee;
    Border: 1px solid #bbb;
    color: #444;
    font-size: 16px;
    font-style: italic;
}
div.rsspromo a { font-weight:bold; font-style:normal; }
```

You can use whatever styling fits your design.

Now you can add an RSS promotion box anywhere you like, using the `[rsspromo]` shortcode. Another idea using the same approach would be to add e-mail subscription forms. And why not load a function with your default ad code? That way you can easily change it should you get a better deal/click ratio somewhere else.

SPIFFING UP TEXT WITH PULLQUOTES

The next example features pull quote functionality. It adds the `[pull]` shortcode, which takes one attribute: `float`. Here's the code in functions.php:

```
function pullquote( $atts, $content = null ) {
    extract(shortcode_atts(array(
        'float' => '$align',
    ), $atts));
   return '<blockquote class="pullquote ' . $float . '">' . $content . '</
 blockquote>';
}
add_shortcode('pull', 'pullquote');
```

This is similar to the previous example, except that you're extracting the `shortcode_atts()` array, and the `$content = null` part which tells you that you need to close this shortcode. You'll also call that in your return statement to get the stuff in between the opening and closing shortcode tags. In other words, it is `[shortcode]$content[/shortcode]`, and whatever else you cram in there.

That is where the attributes come in, in this case just `float`. The idea is that when using the `[pull]` shortcode, the user sets `float` to either `alignleft` or `alignright`, like this:

```
[pull float="alignright"]My text[/pull]
```

Seasoned theme designers know that both `alignleft` and `alignright` are standard classes for positioning used in WordPress, so your theme should have those already. You'll use them to position the pull quote.

In other words, you return the code, being a block quote with the class pull quote, and whatever value the user has given the `float` attribute, and output it. The use `[pull float="alignright"]My text[/pull]`, will output this in code:

```
<blockquote class="pullquote alignright">My text</blockquote>
```

This is handy for people not wanting to hack the HTML code. Of course, if you want more attributes you can just add them to the array, and then include them where you wanted them.

SHORTCODE TIDBITS

You may be wondering if nested shortcode works. It does, and you can put one shortcode tag inside another as long as you open and close them properly, just like HTML. For instance, this will work:

```
[shortcode-1]
    [shortcode-2]
    [/shortcode-2]
[/shortcode-1]
```

But the following would probably break and give you funky results:

```
[shortcode-1]
    [shortcode-2]
[/shortcode-1]
    [/shortcode-2]
```

However, for the first snippet to work you have to allow shortcode within your shortcode by using `do_shortcode()`. So if you wanted to allow shortcode in the `[pull]` tag, from the previous example, you'd have to put `$content` within `do_shortcode()`, like this:

```
function pullquote( $atts, $content = null ) {
    extract(shortcode_atts(array(
        'float' => '$align',
    ), $atts));
   return '<blockquote class="pullquote ' . $float . '">' . do_shortcode($content) .
 '</blockquote>';
}
add_shortcode('pull', 'pullquote');
```

Otherwise, any shortcode placed between `[pull]` and `[/pull]` wouldn't be properly parsed.

Remember, shortcode only works within content, not in headers or even excerpts. It is tied to the `the_content()` template tag. However, you can make it work by using the `do_short-code()` function and adding a filter. It may be a good idea to at least add shortcode support to widget areas, if you intend to do impressive stuff with them. After all, that text widget can be mighty handy.

The following code in your functions.php file will add shortcode support to the default text widget:

```
add_filter('widget_text', 'do_shortcode');
```

It applies the `do_shortcode()` function to the `widget_text()` function as a filter (with `add_filter()` obviously). Simple, just the way I like it!

The shortcode API is actually pretty extensive. You can read up on it in the WordPress Codex at `http://codex.wordpress.org/Shortcode_API` if you want more information.

Using shortcodes is a great way to let users add both features and functionality to their content. However, sometimes you need to go outside the obvious design elements (be they widgets or loop hacks) and the content itself, especially if the website in question needs to promote other services. Integration of non-WordPress content is tackled in the next section.

INTEGRATING NON-WORDPRESS CONTENT

Sometimes you need to get non-WordPress content into your WordPress site. This can be tricky, because not all publishing platforms play along nicely. At best, the content you need to expose within your WordPress site can either be exported in a widget-like fashion (not the

221

plugin kind, the JavaScript sort), included in whole with PHP, or perhaps even displayed in an iframe if all else fails.

These days an RSS feed can be a savior if you're looking at text content especially, but also when it comes to video and images. If the outside content is material from the image service Flickr, for example, you can fetch the RSS feed either with a separate plugin (there are Flickr plugins along with RSS variants), or with the built-in WordPress functionality for displaying feeds.

This is the basic `fetch_RSS` code that can be used with WordPress. In this case, you're calling `http://notesblog.com/feed/` and displaying the last five posts from it in an unlimited list. You would put this code in a template file in your theme, possibly a sidebar, or a Page template perhaps.

```
<h2>Latest from Notes Blog</h2>
<?php // Get RSS Feed(s)
include_once(ABSPATH . WPINC . '/rss.php');
$rss = fetch_rss('http://notesblog.com/feed/');
$maxitems = 5;
$items = array_slice($rss->items, 0, $maxitems);
?>

<ul>
<?php if (empty($items)) echo '<li>Oops, nothing here!</li>';
else
foreach ( $items as $item ) : ?>
    <li><a href='<?php echo $item['link']; ?>' title='<?php echo $item['title'];
  ?>'>
    <?php echo $item['title']; ?>
    </a></li>
<?php endforeach; ?>
</ul>
```

So you can use this whenever you need to display content that is available in a RSS feed, (or any of the other available plugins, of course).

Either way, when you've figured out how to display the content you want within your Word-Press site, chances are you'll be creating a Page with its own template containing this code. Putting the code in the template files is my advice. It is the easiest way, and the technique I recommend before reverting to ExecPHP or similar plugins that let you put PHP code within posts and Pages, as they can really break things.

At other times, the solution may involve making a plugin that acts as the middle ground. I've done this in the past, when I ran my own CMS and wanted to move to WordPress, but had this huge database of games along with a lot of data. Text and images were easy enough to import into the WordPress databases, but flexible taxonomies and native tagging support didn't exist back then, so I had to be creative with the games database. The solution was to write a plugin that read that part and displayed it using shortcodes. It was a lot more hassle than just displaying something from an RSS feed, but sometimes you just can't get the content into WordPress itself without extending it further.

Finally, if all else fails, just fake it. Make the page look like your WordPress theme, but have it outside of the actual theme. I know, that's not as fun, but sometimes systems just clash, and while you can usually sort it out it may just not be worth the time.

DON'T FORGET TO INCLUDE A MANUAL

For people experienced with Web-based systems, WordPress may seem like a breeze to use. The problem is, not everyone sees it that way. In fact, people not used to Web-based systems may find WordPress daunting, despite being perfectly comfortable with word processors and other common desktop software. There are user-oriented manuals built into WordPress, but will they be enough?

While the `wordpress.org` website and the `wordpress.tv` screencast-fest may be helpful references for your users, you're probably better off creating a small how-to guide as to how WordPress works. This is especially important if you're using WordPress as a CMS for a static website rather than blogging, if you point your users of such websites to the Codex, they'll just be confused.

If you're a WordPress developer and/or designer and you do a lot of WordPress sites, I advise you to put together a starter kit that describes the most common tasks of the day-to-day usage. This kit, which can be anything from a simple document to a printable booklet, should be easily updated as new versions of WordPress come along. It should also be constructed in such a manner that you can add to it whatever custom functionality is used for the client sites. Maybe you have a category for video that acts differently from the other ones, or perhaps there's the ever-present issue with custom fields and their usability. Add plugin usage, widgets, and possible settings that you've devised for your client, and you can save yourself a lot of questions if you deliver a simple "Getting Started" manual with your design.

A FINAL WORD ON USING WORDPRESS AS A CMS

It is a common misconception that WordPress isn't a fitting choice as a CMS solutions for various projects. Obviously, it is not always the perfect choice — no publishing platform will ever be — but the ease with which you can roll out a site with WordPress is a strong factor in its favor. Add a simple user interface and great expandability thanks to plugins and themes, and you've got a fairly solid case right there.

One of the pros that come with using WordPress as a CMS is how well it is equipped for search engines. With nicely written code, and perhaps with the help of a plugin or two (you'll find some suggestions in Chapter 9) you'll have no trouble ranking in the search engines, assuming you've got the proper content for it, of course. That, alongside the social Web, is how a lot of traffic is driven these days. So the next chapter shows you how you can integrate the social Web into your WordPress sites.

11 INTEGRATING THE SOCIAL WEB

THERE IS NO doubt that the social Web is important these days, with Facebook and Twitter being the most prominent examples. When used correctly, services like these can be excellent platforms to promote content, collect stories, or encourage communication. It is only natural that most sites today have some sort of integration with popular social Web services, even if it's only a simple "share on Facebook" or "send to Twitter" button or link.

Before digging into the various techniques used to display and connect to the social Web, it is important not to forget the most obvious integration tool offered: RSS feeds. For the simplest solution, you can use the RSS widget that ships with WordPress, and it easily lets you show off content from an RSS feed. And today, any social Web service, app, community, or whatever has an RSS feed for you to play with, which means that a lot of the integration of these services you may want can be done using RSS. From showing off your latest tweet to mashing up a lifestream, it's all about RSS most of the time.

So when you want to flash your latest finished book saved to www.anobii.com, consider the RSS feed (or their widget) before you start looking for plugins or hacking your own solutions. Chances are the service you want to show off your latest actions/saved items/whatever from already transmits this data with RSS.

Enough of that, it's time to get your hands dirty!

INTEGRATING FACEBOOK INTO YOUR SITE

Let's start with Facebook, since this not only is the largest social network as I'm writing this but also because it is by far the easiest to integrate on a site, at least on its most basic level. Facebook has excellent tools to help you integrate its features into your site; just check out the Social Plugins page at `http://developers.facebook.com/docs/reference/plugins/` for a lot of alternatives (see Figure 11-1).

Figure 11-1: Facebook has great tools for adding related features to your site

Most often, you want to promote two things on your site when it comes to Facebook: having people "like" your content, and your Facebook fan page.

THE LIKE BUTTON

The Facebook Like button is incredibly easy to integrate. Just go to this page and build your own: `http://developers.facebook.com/docs/reference/plugins/like`.

Don't worry about the "URL to Like" field as I'll show you how to swap it for `the_ permalink()` template tag anyway.

Clicking Get Code will get you two code snippets; one is for XFBML users, and one is a simple iframe. Let's start with the latter since it is almost cut and paste:

```
<iframe src="http://www.facebook.com/plugins/like.php?href=http%3A%2F%2F
google.com&amp;layout=standard&amp;show_faces=true&amp;width=450&amp;action=
 like&amp;
colorscheme=light&amp;height=80" scrolling="no" frameborder="0"
style="border:none; overflow:hidden; width:450px;
height:80px;" allowTransparency="true"></iframe>
```

See the `href=` part? That's where you want `the_permalink()` instead of the rewrite of `http://google.com` (which I put in). Like this:

```
<iframe src="http://www.facebook.com/plugins/like.php?href=<?php the_permalink();
    ?>
&amp;layout=standard&amp;show_faces=true&amp;width=450&amp;action=like&amp;
colorscheme=light&amp;height=80" scrolling="no" frameborder="0"
style="border:none; overflow:hidden; width:450px; height:80px;"
allowTransparency="true"></iframe>
```

Just put this code snippet in your various theme templates (such as single.php) where you want to let people "like" things and you're ready to go.

But what about that XFBML thingy? That code is smaller and a lot more versatile, but it requires quite a bit more, namely Facebook's JavaScript SDK. If the Like button is all you need, I'd say it's something of an overkill to load this one, but if you're doing other Facebook things on your site then by all means check it out. Either way, all details on how to load the JavaScript SDK so that you can use the XFBML code instead are available here: `http://developers.facebook.com/docs/reference/javascript/`.

Obviously you need to change the code here as well. Here's the same code as the iframe snippet above, but for XFBML:

```
<script src="http://connect.facebook.net/en_US/all.js#xfbml=1"></script><fb:like
href="http://google.com" show_faces="true" width="450"></fb:like>
```

Just replace `http://google.com` with `the_permalink()` and you're good to go:

```
<script src="http://connect.facebook.net/en_US/all.js#xfbml=1"></script><fb:like
href="<?php the_permalink(); ?>" show_faces="true" width="450"></fb:like>
```

PROFILE WIDGETS

If you want to promote your Facebook fan page, or perhaps your personal page, there are really simple widgets for that as well. There are simple badges, available at `http://www.facebook.com/badges/`, but chances are you want something cooler. Maybe you want to show off your activity feed, or just have people fan you (that is to say, your Facebook page) on your very own site? Then check out the social widgets Facebook offers at `http://developers.facebook.com/plugins`.

Let's say you want to put a Like box for your Facebook page on your website. Facebook is consistent, because the Like box builder page works just like the Like button above, but without the need to put in any extra code like `the_permalink()`. Just style it anyway you like, copy the code and paste it in a text widget or wherever you want in your theme files.

227

INTEGRATING TWITTER

There is certainly no doubt that the rise of Twitter has changed things. These days everyone and their cat tweets, at least among the techie crowd, and the momentum doesn't seem to be slowing down. So while 140 characters is quite a limitation to someone used to punching out 3,000-character blog posts, it can still be quite a tool for online publishers.

If you or your brand are on Twitter, it is likely you'll want to promote the Twitter account on your site. That is easily done with graphics, of course, but you can take it even further. It works the other way as well: by promoting your content with tweets you can reach an audience that may only know you on Twitter. And that's just scratching the surface; there are a ton of cool mashups and services built around Twitter and its API that you may want to mimic or at least get a piece of.

First things first: building a cool new Twitter app isn't what this book is about. However, it would most likely be a good idea to take the Twitter promotion one step further than just a small "Follow me on Twitter" graphic, right?

ADDING TWITTER BUTTONS AND WIDGETS

These days it is easy both to show off your tweets, thanks to the Twitter widget, and promote a story on Twitter using the official Tweet button. You can get the latest tweets, search results, have your tweets marked as favorites, and so on, all using a simple widget that you build and style on Twitter's site: `http://twitter.com/about/resources/widgets`. What you get, after having styled the widget the way you want, is something like this:

```
<script src="http://widgets.twimg.com/j/2/widget.js"></script>
<script>
new TWTR.Widget({
    version: 2,
    type: 'profile',
    rpp: 4,
    interval: 6000,
    width: 250,
    height: 300,
    theme: {
        shell: {
        background: '#333333',
        color: '#ffffff'
        },
    tweets: {
        background: '#000000',
        color: '#ffffff',
        links: '#4aed05'
        }
```

```
        },
        features: {
            scrollbar: false,
            loop: false,
            live: false,
            hashtags: true,
            timestamp: true,
            avatars: false,
            behavior: 'all'
        }
    }).render().setUser('tdhedengren').start();
</script>
```

Paste this in your theme's files, or better yet, in a text widget, and you're good to go. If you want to change something, the easiest way is to just go back to Twitter and redo the whole thing, although a somewhat savvy user can analyze this code and make changes there directly.

Getting a Tweet button is equally simple. Just go to `http://twitter.com/about/resources/tweetbutton` and pick the look for your button, and add any Twitter account you might want to mention (see Figure 11-2). Again, you'll get a simple code snippet that you can put in your theme's single.php template, for easy twittering of your posts:

```
<a href="http://twitter.com/share" class="twitter-share-button"
data-count="horizontal" data-via="tdhedengren">Tweet</a>
<script type="text/javascript" src="http://platform.twitter.com/widgets.js">
</script>
```

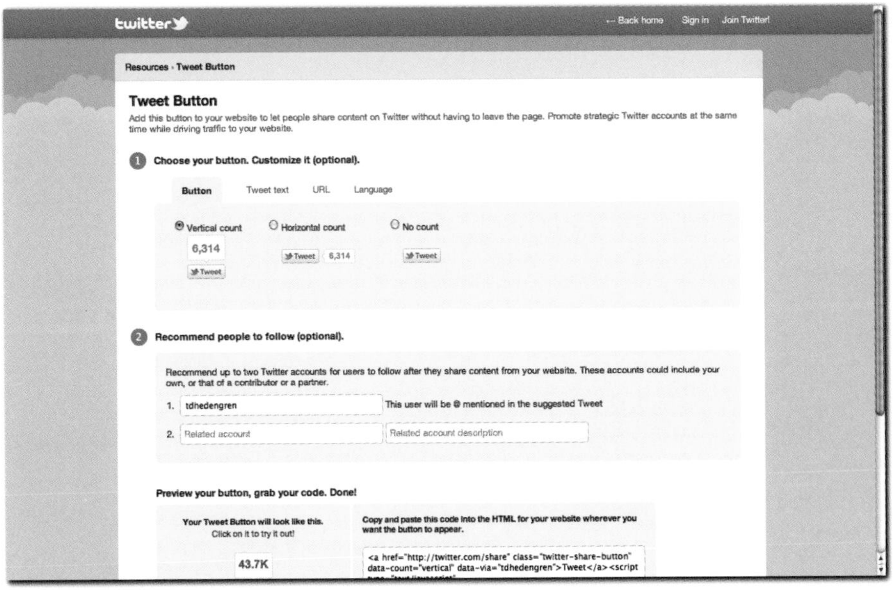

Figure 11-2: It's easy to get the code for your own Tweet button

If you want more control than this, check out the Tweet button API at `http://dev.twitter.com/pages/tweet_button`.

USING THE API METHOD TO SHOW OFF YOUR TWEETS

One of the best and most stylistic ways to show off your Twitter updates is to display the latest tweet. I'm sure there are a ton of plugins that can do that, but the most straightforward way to do it is to use the Twitter API (see the reference at `http://dev.twitter.com`) and some JavaScript.

This is me, returning the latest tweet from my user account (`http://twitter.com/tdhedengren` if you're curious), relying on two JavaScripts supplied by Twitter:

```
<div id="mytweet">
    <div id="twitter_update_list"></div>
    <script type="text/javascript"
      src="http://twitter.com/javascripts/blogger.js"></script>
    <script type="text/javascript"
      src="http://twitter.com/statuses/user_timeline/tdhedengren.json?
      count=1&callback=twitterCallback2"></script>
</div>
```

First, the outer `div#mytweet`, is not required, but since you may want some additional control it is a good idea to add it. The `div#twitter_update_list`, with nothing in it (at first glance), on the other hand, is necessary. It is inside this one that the blogger.js and the JSON script are returning the status updates requested (in this case, mine).

In this line you'll find my username, `tdhedengren`, added as if it were an actual file on the twitter.com server:

```
<script type="text/javascript"
    src="http://twitter.com/statuses/user_timeline/tdhedengren.json?
    count=1&callback=twitterCallback2"></script>
```

That tells Twitter to fetch the updates from my username. Naturally, `count=1` means that just one tweet should be fetched, and you can change that to, say, five if you'd like five tweets. Finally there's the `callback=twitterCallback2`, which is necessary since you're using JSON here and Twitter wants you to.

What you'll get it a bulleted list inside the `div#twitter_update_list`, so style it accordingly. Figure 11-3 shows how it could look with a bit of CSS added.

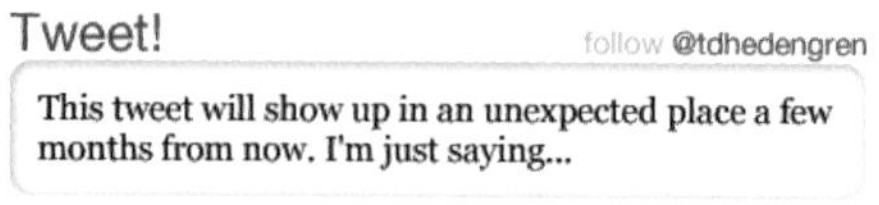

You can fetch the user RSS feed instead, but that one contains a lot of rubbish, not to

Tweet!   follow @tdhedengren

> This tweet will show up in an unexpected place a few months from now. I'm just saying...

Figure 11-3: A simple box showing off the latest tweet can get you new followers on Twitter.

mention the username in front of everything, from the tweet title to the actual content. Naturally, you can cut that away with some PHP, but then you're hacking away in such a sense that it may be more prudent to use one of the available plugins.

Full documentation on this method (along with information on other settings and methods that may suit you better) is available in the Twitter Search API documentation at `http://dev.twitter.com/doc/get/search`.

TWITTER SITE EXTENSIONS

There are numerous widgets, plugins, services, and applications surrounding Twitter. The fairly open ecosystem around the microblogging service makes it easy to build on, and the ever-increasing buzz around the brand isn't exactly slowing things down. That's why you've got TweetMeme (`http://tweetmeme.com`) tracking the hottest stories on Twitter, as well as Twitterfeed (`http://twitterfeed.com`) that lets you post automatic links to your Twitter account using an RSS feed. The following sections provide a few handy links to services and URL shorteners that might come in handy.

You won't find any Twitter plugins here either: they are all in Chapter 9.

Site Enhancers

Some Twitter-related services stand out more than others. The following three add functionality to your site by using Twitter.

- **TweetMeme** (`http://tweetmeme.com`) tracks what's hot on Twitter, and borrows a lot from Digg while doing so.
- **Tweetboard** (`http://tweetboard.com`) adds a Twitter conversation to your site with threaded replies and everything.
- **Twitterfeed** (`http://twitterfeed.com`) publishes links from any RSS feed to your Twitter account, so that you won't have to. There are competing services that do this as well, but this is the original one with OpenID login and everything.

URL Shorteners

The 140-character limit means that long URLs just won't fit into your tweets. Enter the URL shorteners, a necessary evil according to some, and a great tool according to others. You can roll your own of course (see Chapter 9 for cool plugins) but if you can't or don't want to, these shorteners are great options. Remember, you may want to pick one and stick to it so that people get used to seeing you use it. It might also be worth keeping in mind that Twitter uses the `t.co` URL shortener by default. On top of that, WordPress can actually shorten the URLs for you. When logged in and looking at a single post or page, look for the Shortlink link in the admin bar, as shown in Figure 11-4 (assuming you haven't disabled the admin bar and are running 3.1 or later).

Figure 11-4: The Shortlink link in the admin bar is only visible on single posts or pages when logged in

Here are those URL shorteners:

- **t.co** (`http://t.co`) is the official Twitter URL shortener, which you get to by using the official Twitter buttons and apps, listed here for reference only.
- **TinyURL** (`http://tinyurl.com`) is the original URL shortener used by Twitter before `t.co` entered the fray, but it doesn't offer much compared to the competition.
- **Bit.ly** (`http://bit.ly`) not only shortens your URL but offers statistics as well.
- **goo.gl** (`http://goo.gl`) is Google's very own URL shortener.

Of course, sometimes you want to do more than just flaunt your tweets. Maybe you want to show off everything you do online on your site? That's called lifestreaming, and we'll look at that next.

LIFESTREAMING WITH WORDPRESS

Lifestreaming is a term commonly used to describe the mashing up of everything you do online. (A bit presumptuous, perhaps, to assume that your life is online, but there you go.) Usually your lifestream involves links to your blog posts, status updates on Facebook, tweets on Twitter, photos from Flickr, books you read from LibraryThing, videos from YouTube, and so on. Basically, the more the better, with everything mashed together in a chronological list of sorts.

The mashing together of your online life usually relies on RSS, and so, theoretically, you can use WordPress for lifestreaming. You do it either by creating your theme in such a way that it uses the built-in SimplePie RSS parser to mash up and then output everything, or using one of the RSS scraping plugins to feed your WordPress database with the content as posts.

SETTING UP A LIFESTREAM

While you can just pull in all those RSS feeds yourself using SimplePie and the multifeed feature mentioned in Chapter 14, lifestreaming is one of those situations where I feel plugins are the best solution. While it is possible to create a fully functional lifestream using SimplePie functionality, you might have a hard time making it load snappily.

In my mind there are three possible setups — discussed in the following sections — for someone who wants to lifestream with WordPress.

Use the Built-in RSS Parser

If you pull in all your content from the various RSS feeds generated by your accounts across the Web, you'll have a hard time managing the feeds. You can mash them up, and perhaps cache the content in either files (which SimplePie supports), or in the database (which isn't officially supported but possible), and then serve it in your theme. This is a stiff project to get working, but it is definitely possible. You can read more about this in Chapter 14.

A slightly less daunting solution relying on the built-in RSS parser is to have a set of boxes containing different kinds of content, grouped by relevance or however you like. It may not be the typical chronological list of updates, but it will serve you just fine in most cases.

Use a Lifestreaming Plugin

There are a couple of lifestreaming plugins available, with the most aggressively heralded one being WP-Lifestream (`http://wordpress.org/extend/plugins/lifestream/`). It works well enough, Figure 11-5 shows it in action on `tdh.me/stream/`, and lets you set up what sources you want to fetch feeds from, and then you can include the lifestream in your sidebar or on a Page, for example. This is by far the easiest way to get started with lifestreaming using WordPress, but it may not offer you the customizations you crave. Also, there are other issues regarding load times, which I'll get to in a bit.

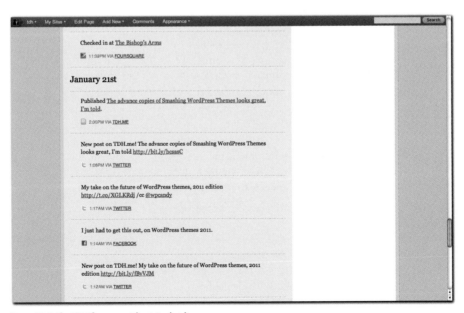

Figure 11-5: The WP-Lifestream with minimal styling

The WP-Lifestream plugin saves the fetched content to the database. Not all lifestreaming plugins do that, but I think it is a good idea to do so. After all, without saving the content (and hence maintaining an archive of your activities online) you might as well just show the content as it is of this moment, right? Make sure your lifestreaming plugin of choice has the features you need, and be extra wary on this one.

Feed the WordPress Database

The third solution is to feed the WordPress database with content from RSS feeds using scraping plugins. The idea here is to actually create a WordPress post, preferably sorted into a suitable category and perhaps even tagged (although that will probably be hard), and then display it in your theme using the normal methods. This would theoretically mean that you can have a Flickr category containing everything from Flickr, a Twitter category that saves all your tweets, and so on. The fact that everything is stored as normal posts makes it easy to manage, which is a good thing.

The FeedWordPress (`http://wordpress.org/extend/plugins/feedwordpress/`) plugin is one of several scraping plugins that can fetch RSS feeds and save them in your WordPress install. Using a solution like this may seem a little extreme, but it is definitely possible, and with some nifty theming you can get a site with blog and lifestreaming sections and a great database for search and categorization.

ABOUT THOSE CRONJOBS

The problem with fetching RSS feeds (and anything that comes from outside the server, really) is that it takes time. PHP needs to ask the target server for the feed, then the server has to send it, and then your server needs to receive it, and PHP has to wrap everything up by doing something with the fetched content. Compare that to querying the database and outputting the data, and you'll see the problem.

Now imagine you have 10 online identities that you want to include in your lifestream. When a visitor comes to see what you're up to online, PHP needs to query them all, receive all the content, and then output it. And that's assuming nothing lags behind, causing the script to break (which would be poor programming) or delay until an answer, even if it is a negative one, has been received. Then you'll understand that a lifestream page can take a lot of time to load.

That's why you cache content, and any decent solution will have support for caching. However, the fetching and caching has to be initiated by someone. In its purest form it means that even if the content is cached, one poor visitor every 30 minutes (or whatever limit is set) will have to wait for everything to be downloaded, cached, and then outputted for it to work. You can do this with SimplePie, and most lifestreaming plugins will have some form of caching solution. Both files (text files basically) and database solutions can be used.

There are better solutions. One is the built-in WP-Cron feature that is something of a pseudo-cronjob called by some plugins. Another, preferable solution, is a cronjob. This is basically timed instances run by the server independently, which means that no visitor will have to sit and wait for all those RSS feeds to be loaded. The only thing that will be served is the saved (cached) content, and that's the only thing that is updated as well. How you set up your cronjob depends on your host. Most likely you have a control panel where you can make changes to your site. Look for cronjob settings there. Diehard Linux fans will obviously use the terminal, but that's pretty far from the scope of this book. For the rest of us, the host's built-in control panel solutions will do.

If you plan on running a lot of RSS feeds, which comes with the territory with lifestreaming, you need to look into caching, which should be supported by your solution from the start, and how to run the content fetching scripts without slowing down the site. Again, most decent plugins support this, and so does SimplePie if you want to dive into that. The best solution is a cronjob, so talk to your Web host about that, and make sure whatever plugin or service you want to use supports it.

GETTING YOUR CONTENT OUT VIA SOCIAL WEB SUBMIT BUTTONS

The social Web is certainly a big factor to take into consideration when working with editorial content today. While search engines can trickle in visitors over a long period of time, hitting the front page of Digg will boost your statistics dramatically in the short term. If your content is technically oriented, the social Web offers a number of services to submit the story to so you can get the word out to the right audience, but whatever your content you should look around in your niche and see if there is a social site that makes a good match. After all, you all want more visitors, right?

There's a lot to be said about what content works where in the social Web, and every time it boils down to writing good, interesting, and easily accessible content, and submitting it to the right site. Then it's up to the users to vote it up or neglect it completely, which may in fact be up to how many friends you've got that can give the story the head start it needs.

So, yes, it is a popularity contest, and yes, you can easily participate by extending your site toward it.

USING PLUGINS

The easiest way to make your site ready for the social Web is to use one of the numerous plugins available (see Chapter 9 for suggestions). These typically add links or buttons to the end of each post, where the visitor can vote up the story in question, or submit it to a service if it hasn't been submitted yet.

Adding a plugin to manage these things for you is easy and certainly tempting, but there are some things you should consider before jumping the gun:

- **Which social Web services can the plugin handle?** Make sure the ones for your particular niche are there, and that you don't clutter your site with the ones that never work for you. In other words, don't ask people to submit your site to Digg if you're writing about gardening in Norwegian; that just won't work.

- **Does the plugin look good with your design or can you customize it to?** If not, you should probably look for another one.
- **Does the plugin look the same everywhere?** If it does, chances are the visitors are so used to seeing it that they just don't register it anymore. It's just that block of icons between the post and the comments on every other blog out there, and that's no good since you want your visitors to interact.
- **Is the plugin actually hosted elsewhere?** There are third-party plugins that load everything from an external server. This will slow down your site, so make sure you're okay with that before using such a plugin.

Most plugins, unfortunately, add clutter in the form of buttons or icons that just won't work with every site. Some are limited to a set number of services, while others tempt you by adding too many. Make it classy and don't overdo the number of social bookmarking services; that won't make it more appealing to vote. In fact, maybe just one or two "Please vote for my story" buttons will work better for you than filling the screen with them.

HACKING YOUR OWN SUBMIT LINKS

You don't need to rely on plugins to add social bookmarking submit buttons. Most sites offer their own buttons that you can embed, but you have to tackle this manually.

Personally, I'm a fan of adding simple submit links to the single post view, preferably in a way that isn't overly obtrusive to the user and doesn't clutter the design. Better to promote the stories that do look like they can go somewhere by themselves, with additional graphics and/ or updated stories asking for help. A few sitting links, however, isn't too much in most cases, as long as you keep them relevant.

The following lines show the code to add sitting links to the most commonly used sites. You submit the permalink of the post in question to the service, so when someone clicks the link they'll go to the submit page.

```
<a href="http://delicious.com/post?url=<?php the_permalink() ?>&title=<?php
the_title(); ?>">
    Save on Del.icio.us
</a>

<a href="http://digg.com/submit?phase=2&url=<?php the_permalink() ?>">
    Post to Digg
</a>

<a href="http://friendfeed.com/?url=<?php the_permalink() ?>&title=<?php
the_title() ?>">
    Share on FriendFeed
</a>
```

```
<a href="http://www.mixx.com/" onclick="window.location=
'http://www.mixx.com/submit?page_url='+window.location; return false;">
    Post to Mixx
</a>

<a href="http://reddit.com/submit?url=<?php the_permalink() ?>&title=<?php
the_title(); ?>">
    Post to Reddit
</a>

<a href="http://www.stumbleupon.com/submit?url=<?php the_permalink();
?>&title=<?php the_title(); ?>">
    Post to Stumbleupon
</a>
```

For the most up-to-date code, along with graphics, logos, icons, and so forth, visit each site individually. It is easy enough to add similar links to new sites; most sites have similar share links that can be built around `the_permalink()` and `the_title()`.

You'll notice that Twitter and Facebook aren't in this list. That's because they have their own buttons for this, the Twitter Tweet button, and the Facebook Like button, covered previously. You should use them instead. Figure 11-6 shows a set of submit links on blogherald.com.

Figure 11-6: The social bookmarking submit links, along with some other stuff from blogherald.com

And remember to use these on a per-post basis! Otherwise you'll just send your category or front page to Digg. In fact, a nice place to put these links would be between the content and the comments. It makes sense to submit a link to your great content after reading it and before moving onward to the comments. Learn more about pimping your comments in the next section.

USING A HOSTED COMMENT SOLUTION

With the addition of threaded comments in the WordPress core and the excellent CSS styling options that are now available, as well as the ever-present Gravatar (`http://gravatar.com`) support, you might wonder how it is possible to enhance the comments. Simple: either by filling them with additional functionality using plugins, or by moving them from WordPress altogether. The former solution can mean anything from user grading of the comments to fetching the buzz from Twitter, while the latter means that you'll rely on a third-party service for managing your comments.

See Chapter 9 for a whole bunch of plugins that make your in-house comments hotter, and a few that help you manage logins and the like. This section will deal with the alternative.

Hosted comment solutions mean that you leave the complete comment solution to a third party service, not relying on the WordPress comment functionality at all. There are two major players in this arena, Disqus (`http://disqus.com`) and IntenseDebate (`http://www.intensedebate.com`). The former has seniority, but the latter is owned by Automattic, which makes it a tempting choice to anyone loving WordPress. Both systems have their pros and cons function-wise, and both are being actively developed, although most would say that Disqus has the upper hand.

To start using either Disqus or IntenseDebate, you simply download a plugin for WordPress and take it from there. Getting started with either Disqus or IntenseDebate is a breeze, although localization has proven to be something of an issue for some, as well as customizing of the styling.

> *Incidentally, you can add these services to static sites as well, giving any site a commenting functionality. That's pretty cool.*

There are some great advantages to using a hosted comment solution. First, spamming is taken care of on a wider scale. Both comment systems also offer various login methods, including using Twitter and Facebook credentials, reply by e-mail, and RSS feeds, as well as social web integration and e-mail notifications. The scope of features you'll get out of the box from Disqus or IntenseDebate is something you'd have to supercharge your WordPress comments with plugins to achieve. Finally, it is often said that sites using these systems results in more comments, and that doesn't seem to be just the PR talk of the companies themselves.

My main gripe with the concept of hosted comments, however, is the fact that you're basically giving content to someone else to maintain. That means that if your comment service of choice breaks down or goes out of business, your comments will break in a worst case scenario, or revert to WordPress default otherwise. The fact that comments degrade some-what gracefully back to WordPress default when there's an outage at the hosted comment solution is obviously a good thing, but it might confuse readers. Other possible issues include downtime and added clutter since chances are that the comment solution won't fit seamlessly with your smashing design. Also, problems experienced by the commenting system's host will hit your site as well. That's not good.

With those caveats in mind, if you are to use a service like this, which one should you pick? I've used Disqus for more projects than IntenseDebate (including my own blog `http://tdh.me`, as you can see in Figure 11-7) and find that it works well, but you should take them both for spin and make up your own mind.

Figure 11-7: Some social sharing buttons in action, as well as the Disqus commenting form, found on http://tdh.me

USING UNIFIED LOGINS

The idea of a unified login system is a great one. Think about it: wouldn't one login for everything be great? Not a ton of passwords to mess around with, and no risk of the "one password for too many sites" security hazard. (Except, of course, for the fact that you can access all those sites with one password anyway.) The idea, however, is that the few providers of these Master Accounts would be so secure that the only risk of users being compromised would be human error, and on your side of things at that. Compared to the risk of some minor site being hacked and your "one password fits all" master password being out there, it sounds pretty good.

That's why OpenID (`http://www.openid.net`) is interesting, and that's why the giants like Yahoo!, Google, and Microsoft are interested in this. For the same reason Facebook has developed Facebook Connect (`http://developers.facebook.com/docs/guides/web`), a unified login using your Facebook account. The Sign in with Twitter (`http://dev.twitter.com/pages/sign_in_with_twitter`) solution is something similar, and the list goes on.

You may wonder why you should even consider using your own sign-in procedure if you can lean on those giants. Most WordPress sites don't have their own sign-in procedures for anyone other than the actual writers and administrators, at least not for commenting. It is usually enough to leave a name and an e-mail address. However, if you want sign-ins, one of the unified solutions is worth considering. I would like to point to OpenID, but the truth is that Facebook Connect is way more user-friendly (right now), and Facebook is also an OpenID member.

Soon you'll be using your Google and Live.com accounts to sign in across the Web, alongside Facebook and Twitter, all perhaps being connected through the OpenID Foundation. Or not. Either way, the thing is you should consider a unified login for your site if you need login functionality for your users. There are plugins that solve this for you (you'll find them in Chapter 9), but don't let that stop you from pursuing other options. Read up on the services themselves and make up your mind regarding any potential user registrations in the future.

THE IMPORTANCE OF THE SOCIAL WEB

Today the social Web and all the content we publish on services like Twitter and Facebook are an integral part of the online lives of a lot of people. We interact with each other, choose who to follow or friend, and essentially subscribe to content by "liking" Facebook fan pages and following certain accounts or lists on Twitter. It is only natural that the social Web is a part of our sites as well, and that we want to promote the content we publish to both our followings on the various social Web services we use, and the ones our visitors might be using.

It is pretty simple, really. In the social Web you choose who to follow, and chances are that you trust the ones you follow more than you trust the average person. So when a friend on Facebook posts a link, you're more inclined to click it than to follow a random link you come across. Think about it, you're more likely to see a movie recommended by a friend, than one that's just advertised.

This has made social Web elements, such as like and tweet buttons and the various bookmarking options available, a reality in our designs. When done right it looks good, but when incorporated poorly it adds clutter and can make sites perform poorly. With that in mind, the next chapter helps you play around with some design elements to make sure your sites look as good as possible.

12 DESIGN TRICKERY

THIS CHAPTER IS all about making your WordPress theme more interesting, and giving it that extra functionality that makes it pop. Some of the techniques covered here are directly tied to WordPress and the kind of data you can get out of it, while others are adaptations of other techniques and solutions that can come in handy for your projects. This chapter shows you a variety of cool tricks: how to use tag based design, make the menu do your bidding, include both stylesheets and JavaScript libraries the proper way, make your 404s help the lost visitor, and work with ads within the loop.

In other words, get ready for some WordPress design trickery.

ADDING MORE CONTROL OVER YOUR POSTS

WordPress offers various methods for adding more control over your posts. This section covers three such methods: tag-based design, custom fields, and adding your own taxonomies.

TAG-BASED DESIGN

The most common setup for a WordPress site revolves around categories and Pages. The former gives individual control of post listings and can be queried by conditional tags such as `in_category()`, which means that you can make them all behave differently. This in turn means that a category archive can easily become a section on a site in a most natural way, and posts belonging to that category can get adequate styling if you want them to. At the very least, this can be a specific set of colors for the category, or perhaps an icon or other kind of graphic, but if you take it further it could be a completely different style of content presentation.

Tags, on the other hand, are less fixed and generally work best if used to describe only individual posts. That means that they may seem redundant for more static (or other less Web 2.0-bloggish) sites. However, you can still put them to good use should you want to. Tags offer three primary ways of achieving special interactions. The first way is the most obvious: the ability to control the tag archive pages. You may remember that tag.php in your theme can control the display of tags, but you can also use tag-X.php where X is the slug of the particular tag. That means it differs a bit from category-Y.php where Y is the category ID and not the slug. It means that you can have your very own properly styled post listing by tag, just like you can with categories. In theory this means that your tag archives can become sections on your site in the same way as categories.

The second way to control the content based on tags is the conditional tag `is_tag()`. It works more or less just like `is_category()` and you just pass the tag slug to identify a specific tag, like this:

```php
<?php is_tag('pirates'); ?>
```

Naturally, you need some conditions as well. This kind of usage usually covers it when it comes to categories, since most well planned WordPress theme designs are built around using as few categories as possible. Tags, however, are different so you may want to check for several tags at the same time using an array:

```php
<?php is_tag(array('pirates', 'ninjas', 'mushrooms')); ?>
```

That will return `true` whenever the tags `pirates`, `ninjas`, or `mushrooms` are used.

The final way to put tagging to good use is utilizing the fact that `post_class()` returns every tag as a class to post div. That means that you can have a lot of potential classes for more in-depth styling.

This, for example, is a post with the ID 129, which you can tell from the `id="post-129"`, as well as the fact that it even has the class `post-129`:

```
<div id="post-129" class="post-129 post hentry category-news tag-pirates
   tag-ninjas tag-mushrooms">
     <!-- The actual post stuff would come here -->
</div>
```

You get a bunch of automatic classes, and finally you get one class per category and one class per tag. In this case, the category used has the slug `news`, so `post_class()` adds the `category-news` class. The same goes for the tags: you've got your `pirates`, `ninjas`, and `mushrooms` tags on the post, and they get added with the prefix `tag-` so that you can see them for what they are. Hence you get `tag-pirates`, `tag-ninjas`, and `tag-mushrooms`.

The brilliance of this is that it gives you even tighter control of your content. If you want to give some posts more emphasis than others, but don't want to tie them to a particular category, then a suitable tag is an excellent solution. Common usage would be featured posts, or perhaps sponsor dittos. Say you want to push out a "Thanks to our sponsors" message among the content, but don't want the readers to mistake it as an actual post. Then you'd just tag it with something appropriate like `sponsor`, and add some CSS to your stylesheet making every post with the class `tag-sponsor` look different, using a different font, color, background, border, or image to show that it is something outside the regular content.

As with categories, you can build your sites around tags. My philosophy is that you should be really, really, really careful with adding categories; save them for the main sections. Then you can make things happen on a more per-post basis using tags and CSS styling in particular.

USING CUSTOM FIELDS

Say you don't want to use tag-based design. Perhaps you want to push out ads in your content as sponsored posts, and style them differently so that you don't risk fooling the readers, but don't want an ads-only tag to show up in tag clouds. You can just exclude that particular tag from the tag clouds, like this (the excluded tag being `sponsor`):

```
<?php wp_tag_cloud('exclude=sponsor'); ?>
```

However, maybe this particular solution just won't do it for you, and you really don't want to use tags in that particular way because of other ways you use them, but want the same type of result. A category isn't an option either, because you want to control which section of the site the ad posts show up in. That's when you turn to custom fields. The following example creates a custom field called `Poststyle`; you just add it once, on any post, and then save a value for it. This example uses `ad` to keep things apart. (If you don't remember how custom fields work, revisit Chapter 4 for a refresher.)

Put the class you want in the value for the key `Poststyle`. You can easily get that by checking for the `Poststyle` key on a per-post basis and echoing it. Remember, that last `true` parameter is to make sure that just one value is echoed should more be added. That won't do in this case; you just want the one value that you'll use as a style for the particular post. This in turn means that when you give `Poststyle` the value `ad`, you want that added as a class so that you can style it accordingly. (It also means that you can do even more stuff by adding other classes, but that's a different story.)

The code to echo this is as follows:

```php
<?php $specialstyle = get_post_meta($post->ID, 'Poststyle', true); echo $specialstyle; ?>
```

How do you add that to the list of classes outputted by `post_class()`? This is the code for outputting the ID and classes for the post `div`:

```php
<div id="post-<?php the_ID(); ?>" <?php post_class(); ?>>
```

You can just add it to the ID, like this:

```php
<div id="post-<?php the_ID(); ?> <?php $specialstyle = get_post_meta($post->ID, 'Poststyle', true); echo $specialstyle; ?>" <?php post_class(); ?>>
```

That would add `#ad` to the post should you give `Poststyle` the value `ad`, but it isn't all that pretty doing it in the ID after all, so let's get it into the `post_class()` template tag instead.

The good thing is that `post_class()` can take parameters, meaning that if you want to add a class — `turtles`, for example — you can do so like this:

```php
<?php post_class('turtles'); ?>
```

That would make `post_class()` add `turtles` to the CSS classes outputted, which is what you want to do, but you want to squeeze your custom field value for `Poststyle` in there instead. This means you have to pass the preceding PHP code to `post_class()`, which luckily is pretty straightforward. However, you can't use it straight out, so you need to alter it a bit. This is the code to use:

```php
<?php $specialstyle = get_post_meta($post->ID, 'Poststyle', true); ?>
```

The echo part is removed, since `post_class()` will return what you pass to it. And adding it is actually as easy as just removing the PHP declarations from the code, and putting it within `post_class()`:

```php
<div id="post-<?php the_ID(); ?>" <?php post_class( $specialstyle = get_post_meta($post->ID, 'Poststyle', true) ); ?>>
```

This will add the value of the `Poststyle` custom field as a class to the post div, just like the `turtles` parameter did.

ADDING YOUR OWN TAXONOMY

Another way you can get more control over your posts is by adding a custom taxonomy. With this method, you can do conditional checks using `taxonomy_exists()`, which returns `true` should the taxonomy in question be available. (Keep in mind that you need to create your custom taxonomy first, as described in Chapter 6.)

Much like any other conditional tag, this method lets you do a conditional check to see whether a certain taxonomy is present; if so, you do something, and if not you do something else. Unfortunately your custom taxonomies won't attach to `post_class()` with custom styles, so you'll have to do that yourself if you want to. You could choose to echo your custom taxonomies with your post `divs` or use them in a similar fashion if you prefer to style your posts that way, mimicking the way tags are added with `post_class()` as described earlier.

Read more on `taxonomy_exists()` in the Codex at `http://codex.wordpress.org/Function_Reference/taxonomy_exists`.

Controlling how posts appear, by using tags, custom fields, or taxonomies, is a great way to add more visual appeal to your site, as well as to highlight important content. Making the various elements in a design stand out on their own is important, assuming they fit together in the end. The next section addresses another important part of any design: the menu.

IMPROVING THE MENU

The menu is one of the most important parts of a design. It needs to include enough content to help the visitor dig deeper into a site, but not so much that it becomes cluttered and hard to use. You really need to get the menu right since it is so prominent for the user. That's why there are so many visual approaches used to make menus more interesting, sometimes for the worse since a lot of them tend to ignore utility in favor of a "cool" design.

That being said, a useful and intuitive menu (see Figure 12-1) can also be spiffy looking, and trying out different approaches to how the menu is used is always a good idea. Just don't forget that easy navigation is the main point.

Figure 12-1: A simple menu

The kind of menu you opt for when using WordPress depends a lot on what kind of site you're working on. Some WordPress sites are built around Pages (static sites in particular), while others are more free-flowing and really could do just with a tag cloud and a search field. In the middle you've got the most common usage with categories (consisting of posts obviously) for sections and Pages for static informa-tion (the boring "About" stuff), and tagging is just a way of describing the post's content better. Whichever it is, you should definitely build the menu using the menu feature that you no doubt remember from previous chapters. That way populating the menu won't be a problem, and it'll be easy enough to update it. It doesn't solve things like making everything fit, but it does let you mix categories with Pages with posts with links with whatever.

As if that weren't enough, you still need to decide how the menu should look, what orienta-tion it should have, and if it needs additional bling to make it interesting. One popular technique is called sliding doors. The next section explains how to implement that method on a WordPress menu.

SLIDING DOORS

The sliding doors CSS technique is a simple yet effective way of using graphics as the back-ground in a horizontal menu, without having to set a fixed width. The idea is to add graphics as a background to your menu items, making them flexible enough to handle any length of text within. The following code is the basis of your menu:

```
<ul id="navigation">
    <li><a href="menu-item-1">First Item</a></li>
    <li><a href="menu-item-2">Second Menu Item</a></li>
    <li><a href="menu-item-3">Third One</a></li>
    <li><a href="menu-item-4">Number Four</a></li>
    <li><a href="menu-item-5">Fifth!</a></li>
</ul>
```

Basically it's the typical output from most of the WordPress template tags that list categories and Pages, an unlimited list that is the proper usage for menus whenever remotely possible. What is a menu if not a list, after all?

Say you want to use a button with rounded corners like the one shown in Figure 12-2 for your menu items; that's pretty and modern, right? Problem is, just applying it to the back-ground of each menu item would require the actual menu item to be of a fixed width, and since you don't want to create a graphic for each of them but rather have the menu item text rendered by the browser with all the freedom that provides, it means that you have to be creative.

Figure 12-2: A button background image with rounded corners

The solution is to chop up the image into three parts.

First you've got the left-hand side, being the rounded corners on that side. Second, there's everything that is in the middle, which will be the background of your menu link. And the final part is the right-hand side's rounded corners. See Figure 12-3.

You want to put the middle part in as the background of the link, and since I'm lazy and won't dwell on this subject too long we'll go for a one-colored middle. Then you want the left side's rounded corners to go to the left of the link, and the right side's rounded corners to the right, leaving the colored background to fill out the gap between.

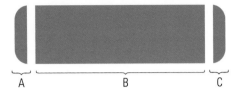

Figure 12-3: How to chop a button

How would you do this in HTML? Easy, just add a span inside each link, like this:

```
<ul id="navigation">
    <li><a href="menu-item-1"><span>First Item</span></a></li>
    <li><a href="menu-item-2"><span>Second Menu Item</span></a></li>
    <li><a href="menu-item-3"><span>Third One</span></a></li>
    <li><a href="menu-item-4"><span>Number Four</span></a></li>
    <li><a href="menu-item-5"><span>Fifth!</span></a></li>
</ul>
```

And then you'd just add the images in the proper way using CSS. The link would get the left-hand side's rounded corners fixed to the left, and then it would fill out with the color of choice, and then you'd apply the right-hand side corners to the span but fixed to the right. What you get in effect is a button that can have any width you want, since the actual link background is a filler after the left-hand side's corners are displayed.

Or, to make it even clearer, here's some dummy CSS that you'd want to alter before usage, but it still explains how it works.

```
ul#navigation li {
    float:left;
    padding: 5px;
    list-style:none;
}
ul#navigation a:link, ul#navigation a:visited {
    display:block;
}
ul#navigation a:hover, ul#navigation a:active {
    background: #888 url(corners-left.gif) no-repeat left;
    float:left;
}
ul#navigation a span {
    float:left;
    display:block;
}
ul#navigation a:hover span {
    float:left;
    display:block;
    background: url(corners-right.jpg) no-repeat right;
}
```

How would you make this work with `wp_nav_menu()`, the template tag for proper output of menus? Easy, just add the necessary span HTML with the help of the `before` and `after` parameters, like this:

```php
<?php wp_nav_menu('before=<span>&after=</span>'); ?>
```

This would add the necessary span tag to each link in the menu, hence enabling sliding door usage.

You could apply this method to other template tags as well, such as `wp_list_categories()` for the sites where you need to list the categories in this fashion. It's a bit trickier, but if you run the whole `wp_list_categories()` through PHP, using `preg_replace` (PHP manual entry: `http://se2.php.net/preg_replace`), you can alter the output of `wp_list_categories()`. This code is a bit more technical; it searches for some expressions (in this case the `li` and `a` tags) and then adds an opening and closing span tag around each link. On the WordPress side of things, it is important to pass a `false` (that is, zero) to the `echo` parameter to make sure that the `wp_list_categories()` tag doesn't output the content (that's what you do with the echo before `preg_replace()`, after all), and it is probably a good idea to pass nothing to the `title_li` parameter, hence not getting a heading for the category list, as well as pass 1 to `depth` to make sure you only get top-level categories.

Here's the code:

```php
<?php echo preg_replace('@\<li([^>]*)>\<a([^>]*)>(.*?)\<\/a>@i',
'<li$1><a$2><span>$3</span></a>', wp_list_categories('title_li=&echo=0&depth=1'));
?>
```

What about `wp_list_bookmarks()` then? Here it is in action, showing only the links category Important, which has the ID of 15. Naturally, you'd also add the necessary span code, and remove the heading:

```php
<?php wp_list_bookmarks('category=15&title_li&link_before=<span>&link_after=
</span>'); ?>
```

THINKING ABOUT HOVER-BASED MENUS

The more content you've got, the more you want to cram into the menu. After all, the purpose of a menu is to help your visitors navigate the site, so it is easy to be tempted to just add and then add some more to the menu. Horizontal menus are popular, but width is a limitation when it comes to expanding these. The solution is usually a hover effect that will drop down a submenu, as shown in Figure 12-4, so that the visitors get easy access to the sections under each menu item.

With the advent of touch-based devices such as smartphones and tablets, however, you should be careful about relying on hover-based design. Because menus are such an integral part of a site, I recommend that you avoid building them around hover. After all, there is no way to hover on a touch screen, since it is either "press" (meaning that you're touching it, comparable to a click with a mouse-based interface) or not. You can't hover on a touch screen, so a menu relying on hover effects won't work as intended on tablets. There are already millions of tablets on the market, and everyone's expecting this market to explode.

So should you never do hover-based menus then? Although I recommend caution, I still think there's room for them. If you've got decent fallbacks, for example making the top menu item clickable and making sure it is easy to reach the lower items from the target page, then you're pretty much in the clear. It's not as

Figure 12-4: The hover menu of the Twenty Ten theme isn't at all iPad friendly

snappy and easy to navigate as it will be with a mouse pointer, but at least it works. Keep this in mind when deciding what kind of menus to use on your future projects.

Now we'll take a sharp turn, from spicing up how the posts and menus are displayed to adding ads within the loop.

PLACING ADS WITHIN THE LOOP

A common question I get is how to insert ads — particularly Google AdSense ads — within the loop. Usually, bloggers want to run an ad after the first, second, or third post, and then continue with the loop as if nothing happened.

One way of doing this is to split the loop in two, first querying for a couple of posts (say two), and then displaying the ad. After that there's a second loop with a post offset corresponding to the number of posts queried in the first loop; hence it looks like one big thing.

A better way, perhaps, is to just count the number of posts and then output the ad when a certain number has been reached. You can do this with PHP by adding to a variable every time the loop runs, which it does for each post that is to be outputted.

Here's the common way of displaying an ad after the first post, stripped of all the post output code:

```
<?php if (have_posts()) : $postcount = 0;
while (have_posts()) : the_post();
$postcount++;
```

```
    if ($postcount < 2) : ?>
        <!-- Post output -->
        <!-- Ad code goes here -->
<?php else : ?>
        <!-- Post output -->
<?php endif;
endwhile;
endif; ?>
```

This code is a basic loop, with some counting added to the mix. No doubt you recognize the first `if (have_posts()` line, but the one below that is new. You give `$postcount` the value 0, and then add +1 to the value every time the loop loops. This is done in the `while (have_posts()) : the_post()` line, which means that the first thing you do after that is add +1 to the `$postcount` value, and you do that with ++, which means just that, add +1.

After that it is pretty straightforward. If the `$postcount` value is less than 2, the code will output the post and the ad code, and if not it will move on to the else post output, which is your standard one.

What if you want to insert the ad after each of the first two posts? In that case, just change the `if` query for the `$postcount` value from 2 to 3 instead, which would mean that the ad output would happen on posts one and two in the loop:

```
<?php if ($postcount < 3) : ?>
```

Beware of the Ad Rules

Inserting ads between posts may sound like a great idea. After all, it is a pretty unobtrusive practice and hence it isn't bound to annoy people greatly. It can, of course, but it is a lot better than putting ads in the actual content, which you also can do with some nifty hackery.

However, while it may seem like a great idea to spread out the ads between the posts, you need to observe the rules of the ad network you're using. Google AdSense, widely used, has a limit on how many ads per page you can show, and if you break that limit you're bound to get in trouble, and perhaps get your account suspended. Bad news for most people, but even worse for people earning a living on ad revenue.

So while I encourage you to spread out your ads across the site (it is, after all, a lot nicer than having them concentrated to the top of the page) I also feel obliged to remind you to check the ad network's rules for any limitations.

And be careful! Automatic outputs like this one can be dangerous stuff, and a mistake somewhere may land you with a lot of ads all over the place. Neither you nor your readers, nor the ad network, will like that, I'm sure.

Another thing you should be careful with is using 404 page not found error outputs with ads. Sure, you can display ads on these pages, but they won't perform well if they are contextual by nature, and I doubt advertisers paying for ad views would appreciate being on an error page.

CREATING 404S THAT HELP THE VISITOR

Creating useful 404 error pages is important. These are the pages that will show whenever someone reaches a page within your site that doesn't exist, and although you may have everything covered in your end, people linking to you may not, so you need these. The theme template file to manage the 404 Page Not Found errors is aptly named 404.php, and you can do just about anything you want with it since it is served from WordPress.

This section won't go into detail on how to build your own 404.php template file (that was covered in Chapter 4). I will, however, tell you what I think a good 404 error page should offer the visitor:

- **It should be obvious that the page is not there.** In other words, tell the visitor that the page they were looking for doesn't exist, and do it in such a way that there is no risk of misunderstanding.
- **Offer alternative routes.** Since the most likely source of hitting a 404 error page in a WordPress setup is a faulty link from elsewhere, you should offer a different route to the content the visitor was looking for. Encourage searching in particular.
- **Open up your site.** The visitor may not care enough to search for the content that sparked the 404 error, but maybe you can snag him or her anyway. Add links to your categories and offer a very brief intro on what they are all about. Turn your 404 error into a sales pitch for your site.
- **Show the latest content.** It is easy to display a list of links showing the latest updates. Maybe something there will appeal to the visitor.
- **Use humor.** A bit of light-hearted humor can be a way to make the visitor less annoyed by the fact that the content they wanted to see isn't there.
- **Offer a means of error reporting.** Let the visitor get in touch with you to tell you of the missing content; that sends a positive message as well as helping you find any particular faults in your site.

A useful 404 page says a lot about a site, so spend some time making yours a good one.

USING JAVASCRIPT LIBRARIES WITH WORDPRESS

JavaScript can be a great tool, thanks especially to excellent libraries like jQuery, MooTools, Scriptaculous, and so on. A ton of these libraries are available, making it easy to add transitions and similar visual bling, as well as more useful stuff. Most cool services online today rely on JavaScript, and the WordPress admin interface isn't particularly fun to work with if you turn off JavaScript in your Web browser.

You can bring JavaScript functionality to your WordPress sites as well, whether you're just adding some visual appeal to your theme with smooth animations or similar, or adding some actual new functionality thanks to your brilliant coding. What you need to think about is how you do it, and that is where `wp_enqueue_script()` comes in. With this tag, you can load any of the many JavaScript libraries that ship with WordPress, or you can just attach your own.

The usage is simple. Add a JavaScript to the hook where it is needed, using `wp_enqueue_script()`. If you want to load a JavaScript as late as possible, since it probably won't be needed before the user does something special anyway, you can use `wp_enqueue_script()` and attach it to the `wp_footer` hook, like this (using jQuery as an example):

```
function load_my_scripts() {
    wp_enqueue_script('jquery');
}
add_action('wp_footer', 'load_my_scripts');
```

This will load the version of jQuery shipped with WordPress. You can find other JavaScript libraries to load this way in the wp-includes/js/ folder. The use of `wp_enqueue_script()` also makes it easy to load the scripts only when you need them, with some clever use of conditional tags. If you just want the script on the home page, use `is_home()`, and so on.

You can do a ton of things with JavaScript, and it all depends on the site as well as your own preferences. Some people are more at home in Prototype than in jQuery, and others prefer MooTools or something entirely different. That's why `wp_enqueue_script()` can load anything. You should use it, and you should in particular make sure that you don't slow down your site with JavaScripts if you don't need them, or let them load too early. After all, what's the point of waiting for a JavaScript when there isn't a page to utilize it on?

I urge you to read up on `wp_enqueue_script()` in the Codex, where you'll also find information on the various JavaScript libraries that ship with WordPress, and how you can pass elements such as dependencies and how you deregister JavaScript libraries and replace them with your own. Start with the Codex page (`http://codex.wordpress.org/ Function_Reference/wp_enqueue_script`) and then move on to the JavaScript library itself.

There are a lot of JavaScripts out there that you can use, not to mention extensions to the popular libraries mentioned. Be sure to read up on them, though, not only to keep your site clean but also to make sure that they work in all the Web browsers you want to support. Barring that, if the extra functionality, flair, or bling does it for your site, it can be a great way to make it more visually appealing.

MAKING WORDPRESS YOUR OWN

Sometimes you'll find yourself in a position where you want to make WordPress carry your brand a bit further than usual. More often than not, this occurs when you're using plugins or features that let the visitors become registered users, with settings and privileges on the administrative side of things. Or, in plain English: they can access the WordPress admin interface.

This means two things. First, visitors get to log in, and that means that they'll use the Word-Press login form, shown in Figure 12-5. The default login form doesn't look the least bit like the carefully designed site you're sporting, so naturally you'll want to do something about that. Second, they get into the WordPress admin interface, and that looks every bit like WordPress and nothing at all like Your Super Brand™. Who would want that?

Unfortunately, WordPress doesn't offer the same theming possibilities for the administrative side of things as it does for your site's front end, but there are quite a few things you can do. It all depends on how important it is that the WordPress parts look as little like WordPress as possible, and how much time you want to spend making the changes.

Figure 12-5: The default login form

A CUSTOM LOGIN FORM

If you need to tweak one thing when it comes to WordPress admin stuff, it is probably the login form. This totally screams WordPress, which in itself is pretty annoying, especially if your site does something totally different from the typical WordPress blog.

You can, of course, just hack the login form by altering the core files in WordPress, but that would mean that you may end up breaking something crucial, and also that you will have to do it all over again with every update, since the update will overwrite your hack. A much better choice is to use a plugin. You may have already found a few possibilities in Chapter 9. They are good, so try them out.

However, you may want to keep the login form in line with the theme, since it is a design matter after all, and that means that you want the custom stuff with the theme files. Luckily, you can do that by hooking on to the `login_head` action hook, and applying some extra stylesheet goodness. This means that you can make the login form look just about any way you'd like, as long as you don't need to change the actual layout of the thing. So a black background and your grungy logo is not a problem at all; you just need a bit of CSS.

First, however, you need to create the function to hook onto the `login_head` action hook. You should recognize this type of code from Chapter 6, which covers action hooks in-depth. Keep in mind that you should make it easy to build child themes upon your theme, and these child themes may want a custom login of their own. That's why I use the `stylesheet_directory` parameter in the `get_bloginfo()` tag, and not `template_directory`, which is a lot more commonly used. Here's the code:

```
// Custom login stylesheet
function nbcustom_login() {
    $nbCustomLoginUrl = get_bloginfo('stylesheet_directory').'/noteslogin.css';
    wp_register_style( 'nbCustomLoginStyle', $nbCustomLoginUrl );
    wp_enqueue_style( 'nbCustomLoginStyle' );
}
add_action('wp_head', 'nbcustom_login', 1);
```

This code is simple enough; the only thing it does is add the contents of the `nbcustom_login()` function to the `login_head` hook. And that is, of course, the `wp_enqueue_style()` (which works very much like `wp_enqueue_script()`) containing a stylesheet located in a folder called `custom` in the theme's directory. You can read up on `wp_enqueue_style()` in the Codex at `http://codex.wordpress.org/Function_Reference/wp_enqueue_style`.

The rest is up to you: just hack away at the new included stylesheet (located in custom/login.css in this example). The login page is easy enough to figure out. Some of the elements you may want to change are the background color (using the body tag), the WordPress logo, which resides in the `h1` tag, and the whole login box itself, which is in `div#login`. Happy modifying!

ADMIN THEMES

Theming the WordPress admin is, unfortunately, a slightly tricky affair. First, the only way to do it without hacking or overwriting the core files (which you never want to do) is by using a plugin. Basically, you create a plugin that hooks on to the `admin_head` action and applies your own stylesheet, much like you did in the login form example previously:

```
function smashing_admin() {
    echo '<link rel="stylesheet" href="' . WP_PLUGIN_URL . '/smashing.css"
      type="text/css" media="screen" />';
}
add_action('admin_head', 'smashing_admin');
```

You know the drill: you include the smashing-admin.css stylesheet directly inside the plugin directory, using something like `http://domain.com/wp-content/plugins/smashing-admin-plugin/smashing.css` in this case. After that, you have to change the behavior of the tons of elements within the WordPress admin interface. It is not something for the faint of heart. And, of course, don't forget to install and activate the plugin!

You may also want to add something to the admin footer. If so, just hook on to `admin_footer` with whatever you want, in a similar way.

There are some pretty impressive admin themes out there, including those mentioned in Chapter 9, but you should be under no illusions. Making the admin interface look the way you want will most likely be hard work. That being said, sometimes all you need is make small changes, like swapping colors and such, and that shouldn't be too much of a problem to do this way.

POLISHING YOUR WORDPRESS SITE

Learning the various tricks of the trade when it comes to WordPress is important to lift your site from a mere WordPress theme (no matter how great) to something more complete. Any good site will benefit from the polishing these tricks provide, so you should experiment with techniques and see what you can do with your site.

While controlling the look and feel of your posts and getting the menu right are all important things, there are limitless possibilities for your site. Excellent blogs such as Smashing Magazine (`http://www.smashingmagazine.com/`) and A List Apart (`http://www.alistapart.com/`) will help you find even more interesting techniques for your site. Some you can employ right away, others needs a more hands on approach. Experiment away!

13

FUN WITH IMAGES

IT'S SAID A picture is worth a thousand words; an image can tell a story a lot faster than text can. It is no secret that images and text work extremely well together. Other than just spicing things up, an image can help tell a story and (literally) illustrate a point.

If you are using images in your site, it's important to give some thought to how you plan to incorporate galleries and illustrations. This chapter is about displaying images in a WordPress site, beyond the traditional inclusion of illustrative points or inspiring scenery in your posts and pages. It is more about galleries, presentation, and photo-sharing services, not to mention the small matter of actually setting up WordPress image management in a way that makes sense.

WORKING WITH IMAGE GALLERIES

WordPress has included support for the [gallery] shortcode for a long time, with all the possibilities it brings.

If you're working in the visual editor you won't see the gallery button; you'll just see a big box telling you that it is an image area. You can switch to HTML view for a more refined representation.

What [gallery] really does is output uploaded images in a clickable thumbnail grid. Then you can let your visitors see a larger version of the image, either in your theme's design, or the original file itself. The former is called the *attachment page*, since that's what images are — attachments to blog posts. This built-in functionality should cover most of your needs if you run a text-based site that sometimes publishes images.

To fine-tune it even further, the first stop after installing WordPress and picking the theme of your choice should be the Media page under Settings in the admin interface. Here you can control the circumstances under which the various images are scaled. Each image you upload is saved in up to four different versions, designed for your needs across the site.

Figure 13-1 shows the WordPress Media settings page, which outlines the various sizes your images can be:

- **The thumbnail** is a cropped version of an image meant to symbolize the image in question. You can set it to be cropped to exact sizes, which means that it won't actually show the whole image all the time. It's a small image meant to be clickable. Default size is 150x150 pixels, but you can change that to fit your theme.
- **The medium image** is the full image downsized, with width and height proportional to the original image you uploaded. You can set a maximum width and height that dictate how the image should be scaled. This is also the image used in the attachment pages.
- **The large image** is also your full image but downsized proportionally.
- **The original image** is also available, untouched.

There's one caveat: no image version will be created if it is in fact larger than the original image. So if your large image is set to 800 pixels width and height, but the image you're uploading is smaller than that, it won't be created nor will it be available to include or link to in WordPress. There's just no point.

So what about it then? Why bring this up?

Simple. The thumbnail should be in a size that fits your width and the number of columns you expect to use normally in your image galleries created with the [gallery] shortcode. Make it a nice size for your site.

Figure 13-1: The WordPress Media settings page

Meanwhile, it is my belief that the medium image should be the exact same as the maximum width your design can manage. In other words, if the max width is 580 pixels, set the max width of the medium image to 580 pixels, to ensure that you can include it in your posts whenever you like. Since the medium image is the one used in attachment pages, it is a good idea to make it fit well there. Granted, you're in something of a pickle if your attachment pages are constructed in such a way that they can manage a larger image than your traditional blog posts, but if that is the case you'll just have to create custom images for your posts. The important thing is to make the attachment page look good.

Finally, the large image is good for linking a larger variant. One can argue that perhaps the large image should be the one in the attachment page, and it is probably possible to make it so, but by default that's not the case and hence you can't rely on it. The large image is usually only interesting if you're uploading a high-resolution photo and don't want to link the original version since it is 15 megabytes and ridiculously large for Web view, and the large one is substantially smaller and fitted to the screen.

STYLING THE GALLERY

Making the galleries included with the [gallery] shortcode look good is easy, assuming you've configured your thumbnails according to the number of columns you'll be using. This is something you can choose when you're including the gallery, so you need to pay attention to that.

Actually styling the gallery is also pretty simple. The whole thing resides in a `div` with a number of identifying classes to use, one of which is actually called `gallery`. As is the norm in WordPress, there are unique IDs and classes as well, but you'll probably settle with `div. gallery` for your CSS needs.

Moving on, each item in the gallery is enclosed in a `dl.gallery-item`, which in turn contains `dt.gallery-icon`, which has the linked thumbnail image, and possibly also a `dd.gallery-caption` if a caption is provided for the image in question. You get this for as many images you've chosen to display in a row, then it all breaks down to a new row quite unceremoniously with a `br` tag with `style="clear:both"`, and it begins again.

That means that, for the thumbnail gallery listings, you need to style the following (listed hierarchically):

```
div.gallery {}
    dl.gallery-item {}
        dt.gallery-icon {}
        dd.gallery-caption {}
```

This is the code used by Notes Blog, with a subtle font color and size for the captions, and some white space in between because that's always pleasant to the eye. Naturally your design may be a lot flashier than this, adding background images, borders, and so on.

```
div.gallery { margin-bottom: 14px; }
    img.attachment-thumbnail { border:0; }
        dd.gallery-caption { margin-top: 8px; font-size: 12px; color: #777;
            font-style: italic; }
```

Now, that's just one half of it. While you can configure your gallery thumbnails to link to the actual image, you can always choose to link to the attachment page. That's the one showing the image in your theme's design, which probably means that it will revert to either single.php or index.php since most themes lack the attachment.php template file, and very few have template files for video.php, image.php, and so on.

To get your theme to be image-friendly, you really should add a link back to the post containing the actual gallery, and you should add Previous/Next links so the user can browse the gallery from image to image.

Start with the Previous link. The following code, which you might recognize from Notes Blog, fetches the post's parent (the actual post the attachment is attached to) and links it. Nothing fancy. You can't use `the_permalink()`, of course, since that would indicate the attachment itself, while `the_title()` naturally is the image title. You probably want to make sure that your attachment template outputs that too:

```
<p class="attachmentnav">
    &larr; <?php _e('Back to', 'notesblog');?>
    <a href="<?php echo get_permalink($post->post_parent) ?>" title="<?php echo
    get_the_title($post->post_parent) ?>" rev="attachment">
        <?php echo get_the_title($post->post_parent) ?>
    </a>
</p>
```

Speaking of outputs, the description you can fill out when uploading or editing an image is in fact outputted by the_content(), which means that you can add decent attachment support to your single.php or index.php template easily enough. Just use the is_attachment() conditional tag to check for it and output accordingly, and you'll be fine.

Back to business: add those Previous and Next links for navigation within the gallery, in attachment image view. This is done with previous_image_link() and next_image_link(), both of which by default will output the thumbnail, linked, to the other target image. Here you're using div's to float the Previous and Next links to the left and right:

```
<div class="left"><?php next_image_link(); ?></div>
<div class="right"><?php previous_image_link(); ?></div>
```

While the thumbnail output may be cool if tailored to the task, you may want to use text instead. Just pass nothing to the image size parameters (yes, it takes other sizes as well) and it will output the image post title, being the name you gave it, instead. Or you can add another parameter to pass a custom text link, like this:

```
<div class="left"><?php next_image_link('', 'Next Image'); ?></div>
<div class="right"><?php previous_image_link('', 'Previous Image'); ?></div>
```

That's about what you need to know to work with galleries on a WordPress site. The next natural step, after getting it to work with your theme, is pimping the whole affair using plugins.

BETTER BROWSING WITH LIGHTBOX

A Lightbox effect is a common name for an overlay that displays an image on top of a site, without opening a popup (see Figure 13-2). You need to close the image to access the actual site again, which may sound like a bad idea, but compare it to having to open a new page to view the image in full size and you get the picture. Most decently designed Lightbox solutions have accessible browse buttons as well.

261

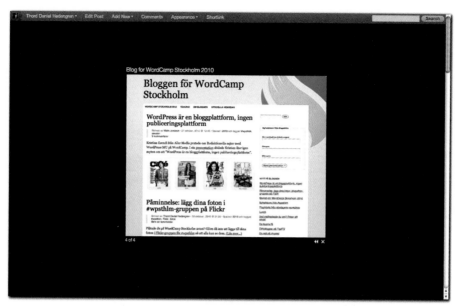

Figure 13-2: Lightbox effect in action

This is pulled off with JavaScript and some design trickery, and there are a ton of possible solutions waiting for you. Which solution you choose all depends on how much visual bling you want, and what sorts of effects suit you and your site. I do think you should go with one that comes as a WordPress plugin though, because that means that you won't have to add any classes to your images manually to make sure the Lightbox solution recognizes the link as a Lightbox one. Consult Chapter 9 for some excellent Lightbox plugins, if you don't have a favorite already. The plugins do this for you, and suddenly your image gallery won't have to open those attachment pages at all, and your visitors can browse your photos with ease.

However, there are drawbacks, the most obvious one being what happens if the visitor has turned off JavaScript, or if someone clicks the thumbnail link before the Lightbox script is fully loaded. The result is an opening of the image as a whole, outside of the design, just as if the link pointed to the image itself only (which it usually does, but then the script puts it right in the effects it adds). It isn't too pretty when that happens, especially if the visitor expects that nice overlay effect and the easy Previous/Next links it probably sports, but then again it is a fully functional solution as well, thanks to the Web browser's back button.

Why wouldn't you use a Lightbox solution? One main concern is smaller devices. How good does something like this look on a seven-inch low-resolution screen? Is it really useful then? The same can, in all fairness's sake, be said about attachment pages, but it is a bit easier to style those on a per-user agent basis. You should make sure that the Lightbox script doesn't override any such solutions.

Finally, if you make your money on page views, don't go the Lightbox route unless you think it will bring in more readers. After all, having people load a new page, and hence a new set of ads, whenever they want to view the next image in a gallery can be good business in itself!

USING OUTSIDE SCRIPTS AND SYSTEMS

Finally, a few words about using gallery solutions from outside of WordPress, such as stand-alone gallery software. There are several gallery scripts available, some of which are fully fledged systems in themselves, while others just crunch images to various sizes and output content in physical folders on your server as HTML.

I recommend that you should think very carefully about using external image galleries, such as Gallery2, before doing so. The foremost concern behind this is flexibility. WordPress can be extended with numerous plugins, and if your images are a part of WordPress they can sometimes benefit. However, if you're running your images in an outside script and just showing them in your theme one way or the other, you won't benefit. And what happens if that outside script suddenly stops working, or starts clashing with your WordPress install?

The same really goes for plugins that move the gallery functionality from the WordPress core to their own setup. This may mean that they can add new features, better sorting, or whatever, but it also means that whenever the plugin isn't being maintained anymore and it stops working because of defunct WordPress functionality or other conflicts, you'll be on your own in a way that wouldn't have happened otherwise. And besides, instead of the flashy gallery functionality that the plugin you were considering offered, why not look for something that adds that to the core image gallery features instead?

That said, sometimes you need more, and then you'll have to move outside of WordPress core features, either by relying on plugins or to external systems and/or services. Just make sure you know what you're doing, and make sure you know what to do if you need to move back, or to something else. Conversion and importing tools can certainly help you to feel more secure in such cases.

RANDOMIZING IMAGE ELEMENTS

Setting up your site to randomly display your images and other elements can spice it up and make it feel more alive. In the blogosphere having a random header image is popular, as well as having random posts promoted. After all, elements that change a bit between visits (without disrupting visitors' ability to navigate) are generally seen as more interesting than a static display.

The most basic way of randomizing is using PHP and any of the randomizing functions it offers, such as `rand()` and `mt_rand()`, for example. There are also several JavaScript solutions you can utilize. Solutions for both of these techniques are readily available online so you shouldn't waste time on hacking your own unless you really need to.

It doesn't stop there, however. Several plugins can help as well, a few of which are discussed in Chapter 9. Randomized content, especially images, has been done so many times it is almost ridiculously easy to get going. That is, unless you want to display random images from posts you've uploaded. For some reason this is a bit harder.

DISPLAYING RANDOM IMAGES FROM YOUR GALLERIES

An even cooler type of random image content would come from your galleries: the images you've uploaded to WordPress. Those are attachments, and you can get to them by doing a little bit of get_post() hacking in an additional loop. The idea is to show the thumbnail of any attachment that is an image, and link it to that very image. Since you'll have properly styled your gallery (as you learned about in an earlier section) you know that the visitor can continue clicking and enjoying your photos or whatever from there, so it sounds like a good way to catch the readers, right?

This code shows how to do it, in this case outputting everything in an unlimited list since it seems appropriate:

```php
<ul class="random-attachments">
    <?php $new_query = new WP_Query('&showposts=4'); ?>
    <?php while ($new_query->have_posts()) : $new_query->the_post(); ?>
    $args = array(
        'post_type' => 'attachment',
        'numberposts' => 1,
        'orderby' => rand,
        'status' => 'publish',
        'post_mime_type' => 'image',
        'parent' => $post->ID
    );
    $attachments = get_posts($args);
    if ($attachments) {
        foreach ($attachments as $attachment) {
    echo '<li>';
    echo wp_get_attachment_link($attachment->ID, 'thumbnail', true, '');
    echo '</li>';
        }
    }
    ?>
<?php endwhile; ?>
</ul>
```

The first two lines are just to get the new WordPress loop started and limit the number of posts to loop out. Next comes an array belonging to the $args function. This is fairly common usage in WordPress; it makes it easier to pass all the parameters and store them in a function. The parameters belong to get_posts(), which will control what you'll actually output. We'll get to that in a little bit.

The $args array should be pretty self-explanatory, sorting by the attachment post type, showing just one attachment per post (otherwise you'd get several images rather than just one), randomizing the ordering, using only published posts, and limiting things to the 'image' MIME type. (That could just as well have been 'video', for example, so it can come in handy.) Finally, you attach the parent post's ID for good measure; it really isn't needed, but can come in handy in other cases so is left in here for info.

So you've got all that information in the array stored in `$args`, now to load `get_posts()` with it. This is done with the following line:

```
$attachments = get_posts($args);
```

Now the whole `get_posts()` with all the parameters from `$args` is stored in `$attachments`, which you'll use in the `foreach` loop. There you'll find the following line, which is what controls how the attachments are outputted:

```
echo wp_get_attachment_link($attachment->ID, 'thumbnail', true, '');
```

The `wp_get_attachment_link()` template tag outputs the relevant attachment by default. Here you're giving it the ID from the `foreach`, then you tell it that it should display the thumbnail rather than the original size (which is the default). The `true` passed after that says whether or not to link the output to the attachment page, and since that is kind of the point this needs to be passed. Finally, the last parameter is whether or not to display a media icon, which defaults to `false`, so you don't need to pass that.

Putting that little code snippet in the sidebar will get you an unlimited list of randomized thumbnail images linked to their respective attachment page.

MORE RANDOM IMAGE OPTIONS

Not good enough for you? Then you should turn to the wonderful world of photo-sharing sites and their various widgets and embed codes, as well as to the plethora of plugins available (see the section "Making the Most of Image-Sharing Services" later in this chapter for more detail). A combination is usually a pretty good recipe for nice image blocks showing off your latest works of art (or just snapped vacation photos), so dig deep into that for more random image goodness. You'll find a bunch of plugins and suggestions in Chapter 9 if you haven't seen that already.

A word of advice, though: beware of clutter, and beware of long load times.

Adding third-party services always adds to the load time, and it doesn't get any better if an image, which may or may not be properly compressed for the Web, is served. I know it's tempting to put in a cool Flash widget from some photo sharing site, or an Ajax-y plugin that shows off all your best photos in a never-ending slideshow, but you should be careful.

Another consideration is whether you really need the image block. Just because you've got access to a stream of images doesn't mean you have to use or display it. Will the visitor be interested? If not, forget about it and use that valuable screen real estate to show something else.

265

Creative Uses of Featured and Header Images

Two special types of images can be used even more creatively in your projects: the header image and featured image. As you know, the header image is often used as a traditional blog header, but there's nothing in the feature that limits you to that. The featured image is a per post option of setting a specific image as the one that symbolizes the post, most commonly used to headline images or related purposes.

But you could do other things with these types of images as well! Here are some ideas to get you started.

- **Use a header image as a seasonal message.** In almost bloggish fashion you can use the header image feature to display seasonal greetings and other things to your visitors.
- **Use a header image for additional branding.** As a more traditional take on the idea above, use the header image for additional branding, highlighting a product, a convention, a service, a person, or something else.
- **Use a featured image as a background.** Who said you had to have your featured image as a traditional headline image? Use it to set a background for your post instead, further branding it.
- **Use a featured image as the header.** Did you know that the Twenty Ten theme will swap the custom header for the featured image (if there is one) when you're reading a post? This concept could be refined even further, giving your post a header of its own, perhaps as a site in the site?

266

MAKING THE MOST OF IMAGE-SHARING SERVICES

For sites running on limited hardware or shared hosting accounts, it may be crucial to save on both space and bandwidth, and what better way than to host the videos on YouTube and the images on Flickr? The same actually applies to larger sites not generating much money, but those tend to be able to afford custom solutions like stored data in the cloud or static files on servers.

Serving the images from any of the photo-sharing sites out there is a sure way to keep both bandwidth and storage down, especially if the site in question is running a lot of photos. A good example would be a videogame site, pumping screenshots typically over 700 KB in size each, plus larger screens and HD resolutions add the need to share them in that resolution as well. Say you shoot out two screenshot galleries every day, each containing 10 images. That's 140 images every week, or 560 per month. At around 700 KB each, that adds up for sure; to over 380 MB per month actually. You don't need to be a mathematician to understand that such a site will require a lot of megabytes in bandwidth, as well as storage, over the long run.

That's why photo-sharing sites are interesting. Pumping images in to Flickr means that you needn't worry about those things, as Flickr will cover your bandwidth. It may be a bit of a stretch to have the big videogame sites running their screenshot library on Flickr, but the same mathematics apply for a photographer's site, for example.

There is money to be saved here, by "doing a YouTube" with images as well. After all, few sites host their own videos these days. Instead they rely on embedding videos from services like YouTube or Vimeo, so why not do the same with images?

Naturally there are drawbacks, most importantly the fact that if your image host goes out of business you'll lose all your images. You can sort that out as long as you have backups, of course, but you'd need to put them in again manually. On the other hand, these services are rarely small players, and if you stick to the big ones it isn't likely they'll go away. If you can rely on YouTube you should be able to rely on the likes of Flickr.

Another issue is loading time. If your image host is struggling to serve the images for some reason, your site will suffer for it. In the long run I believe that images are more of what I like to call "direct content" than video, and that's why I tend to store and serve them locally whenever I can. If I really need to serve them from someplace else to keep a site up, I'd look into file servers and cloud solutions before relying solely on a third-party service.

However, that doesn't mean that I don't think about going the third-party route, and as a dedicated Flickr user I sometimes use it as an image host. It is convenient and saves time as well as bandwidth and space. Despite all I've said so far, those are hard facts to argue with.

POSTING FROM FLICKR

Flickr (`http://flickr.com`) is probably the most popular photo-sharing site out there. It lets you upload photos for free, up to a limit, and if you want to upload more photos you can purchase a pro account. It also works very well with blogs, and you can even share your Flickr photos (and those of others) directly to your blog. This is done in your account settings. WordPress is just one of many types of blogs that Flickr can let you share photos to. Follow these steps to share photos on your blog using Flickr:

1. Sign in to Flickr and go to the Your Account page.
2. Click the Sharing & Extending tab, and then click the edit link to the right of Your Blogs (see Figure 13-3).
3. Add your WordPress blog by filling out the details (see Figure 13-4). You need to activate publishing by XML-RPC in your blog's admin interface, under Settings → Writing. The address you'll fill in on Flickr is the URL to xmlrpc.php, which resides in the root of your WordPress install.
4. Go through the guide and be sure to pick (and possibly edit) a default layout for the posts you'll publish from Flickr.

That's it! Now you can send photos from Flickr directly to your blog. Find a photo you want to send, click the Share This link in the top right when viewing it, and then choose your blog under the Blog It tab. Unfortunately, you can't share all photos from Flickr this way; it all depends on the content owner's license as some licenses don't allow sharing.

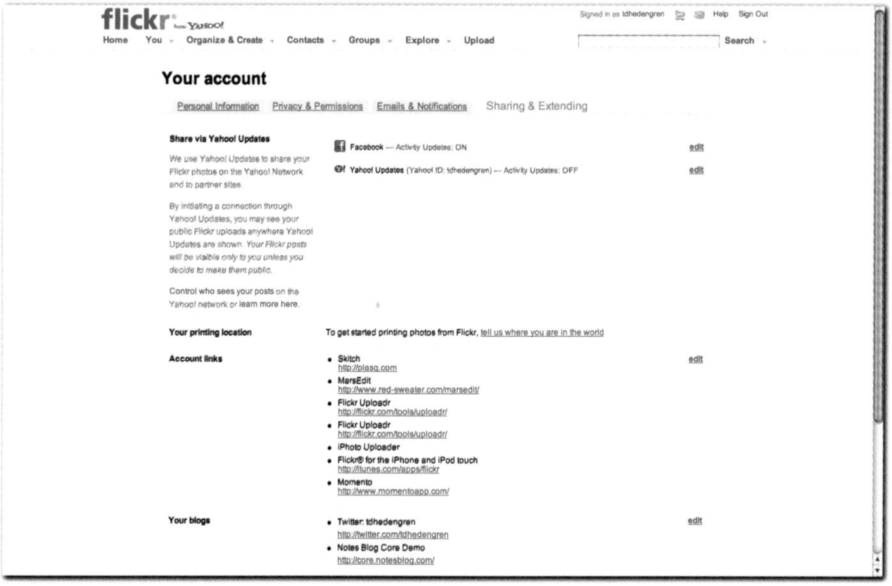

Figure 13-3: The edit link is to the right of the blogs listed

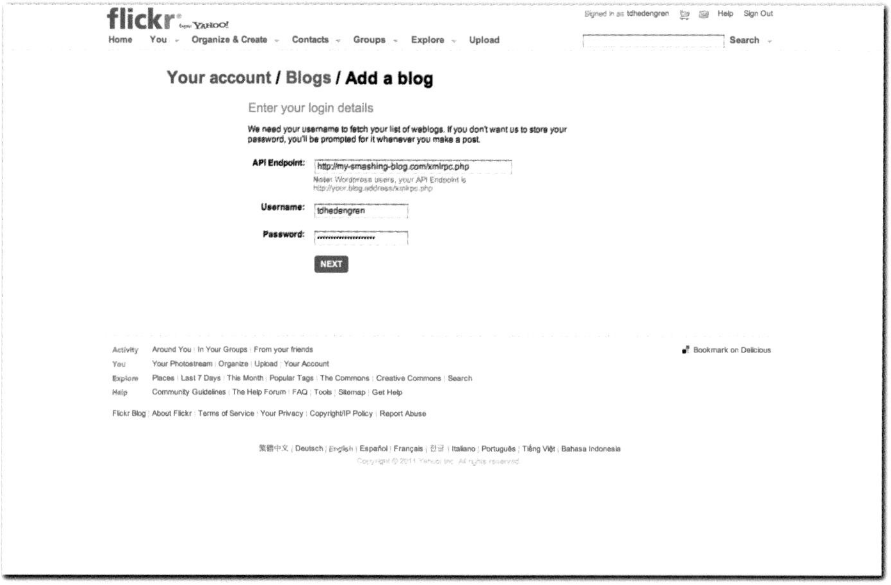

Figure 13-4: Add your WordPress blog's details

Flickr is a commonly used tool not only for posting images, but also for saving traffic. By serving the images from Flickr you won't strain your own server. Of course, it works both ways, because if Flickr should go down (or out of business), your images will go down with it, so make sure you've got backups of everything.

USING THE FLICKR SLIDESHOW

If you're a dedicated Flickr user you may be interested in embedding a Flickr slideshow. Basically it is a small Flash widget that you can put wherever you want on your site; you can even alter its size. You can get a slideshow of anything grouped on Flickr, be it a full user's photostream or a set of photos. Naturally, the slideshow will only include public photos.

Adding the slideshow is easy. Just find the set or photostream you want to embed and click the Slideshow link at the top right (see Figure 13-5), next to the Share This link. If the Share This link is present, you can slideshow the content; if it's not, you can't — simple as that.

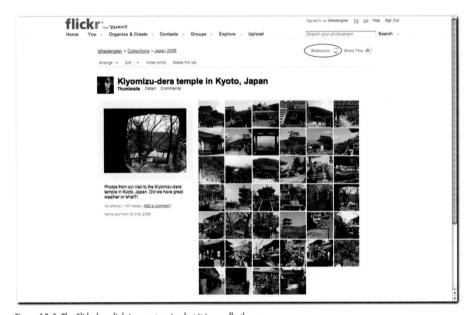

Figure 13-5: The Slideshow link is easy to miss, but it is usually there

The slideshow begins (see Figure 13-6). Click Share at the top right, and then click the Customize HTML link below the embed code. This will bring up a new window where you can set the desired width and height, or pick a predefined width and height. Copy the embed code and paste it wherever you want.

269

Figure 13-6: Grab the embed code from the custom page rather than directly from the Slideshow to get more options

So when is using a Flickr a slideshow useful? Sites can use it for coverage when they need to lean on Flickr's weight to get the message (and traffic!) across, but otherwise I'd say you're better off creating cool galleries instead. However, the slideshow does indeed fulfill a purpose as an extension to everything else, as in putting a box in the side column showing off your latest exploits and such.

Other than that, the Flickr slideshow is more of a novelty. To really put Flickr to good use, other than to serve static images, you have to dig a bit deeper. There is an API to play with (www.flickr.com/services/api/) and the numerous plugins available can sometimes take things to a different level, depending on what you need from the service.

BEWARE THE CLUTTER

Images are great to spice up a site, especially when you can utilize services like Flickr and get nifty little widgets that show off your latest photos, or display your images in other ways. Your visitors will enjoy the living elements you've added, and they all add value to the experience. At least that is the ideal usage; in the real world, a lot of this type of usage means clutter and breaking of the design.

My point is that you need to make sure you put these tools to good use, whether it is a random image element or your latest updates from Flickr. They need to make sense, just like every other element in a good design.

14 EXTRA FUNCTIONALITY

YOU CAN DO a ton of things with WordPress. This chapter is all about showing off some of the cool functionality you may want to use in a project or on a site. You'll take a look at tabbed boxes, login forms, doing stuff with RSS feeds, making your WordPress print friendly, and more. Many of the elements described here can be used in myriad ways; since every site is different, your solution may very well differ a lot from the ideas presented here.

For each element described, I also explain when it is a good idea to use the technique, and when you should forget about it. Between the plugin expandability and the various features you can put in your theme, there are a ton of options and it is way too easy to clutter a site with things it just doesn't need. You should question every addition, even if it is hard to resist adding some cool features sometimes.

TABBED BOXES

Tabbed boxes are a great way to save some of that all-important screen real estate. On blogs and somewhat dynamic and living sites, tabbed boxes can be used to show off popular posts, recently commented posts, and similar elements that can be grouped together in a natural way. The key is to make sure that tabbed content that isn't shown by default doesn't always have to be visible. In fact, that's the key thing with tabbed boxes right there: make sure you don't hide something crucial in a tab.

Technically, tabbed boxes aren't very hard to create or manage. Some of them may not even look like boxes with tabs on them; it is more a type of functionality than anything else.

SMART USAGE

Creating the actual tabbed box functionality is easy enough, and there are a ton of scripts available out there if you don't want to do it yourself. The code in the following example is simple enough for most cases, but it would also work well with some bling. After all, if you've decided to use a tabbed box, why not make it look really good and fit your design?

The following code relies on the Prototype JavaScript library, so you need to load that with `wp_enqueue_script()`. See the JavaScript section in Chapter 12 for more instructions. In this example, assume that Prototype is loaded. Here is the part that needs to go in the head section in header.php:

```
<script>
// Function to view tab
function viewTab(tabId) {
    // Get all child elements of "contents-container"
    var elements = $('contents-container').childElements();
    // Loop through them all
    for (var i=0, end=elements.length; i<end; i++) {
        // Is clicked tab
        if (tabId == elements[i].id) {
            // - Show element
            elements[i].show();
            // - Make sure css is correct for tab
            $('tab-'+ elements[i].id).addClassName('active-tab');
        }
        // Is not the clicked tab
        else {
            // - Hide
            elements[i].hide();
            // - Make sure css is correct for tab
            $('tab-'+ elements[i].id).removeClassName('active-tab');
        }
    }
}
</script>
```

You may want to put that in its own file.

Moving on, here's the basic markup for the actual tabbed box:

```
<ul id="tabs">
    <li id="tab-content-recent" class="active-tab">
        <a href="javascript:viewTab('content-recent');">Recent</a>
    </li>
    <li id="tab-content-popular">
        <a href="javascript:viewTab('content-popular');">Popular</a>
    </li>
    <li id="tab-content-comments">
        <a href="javascript:viewTab('content-comments');">Comments</a>
    </li>
</ul>
<div id="contents-container">
    <div id="content-recent">
        Content for Recent tab.
    </div>
    <div id="content-popular" style="display: none;">
        Content for Popular tab.
    </div>
    <div id="content-comments" style="display: none;">
        Content for Comments tab.
    </div>
</div>
```

You'll need to style this to look like the sort of tabbed box you want, which may not at all be a tabbed box but something entirely different. The key is that the links in the list items open a `div` container with the contents for the tab (or whatever) in question.

You could stop here, by putting the necessary code for Recent and Popular posts, as well as the latest comments, in the corresponding `div`. No big deal.

However, if you want to make it a little bit easier to manage, you can create a widget area for each tab's containing `div`, giving you the freedom to easily swap faulty functionality for a new plugin of your choice. If you want to do it that way, you need to widgetize a bit.

First there is the register part that goes in functions.php:

```
register_sidebar(array('name'=>'Recent Posts'));
register_sidebar(array('name'=>'Popular Posts'));
register_sidebar(array('name'=>'Recent Comments'));
```

Then there are the actual widget areas, which of course go in each containing `div`, respectively:

```
<ul id="tabs">
    <li id="tab-content-recent" class="active-tab">
        <a href="javascript:viewTab('content-recent');">Recent</a>
    </li>
    <li id="tab-content-popular">
        <a href="javascript:viewTab('content-popular');">Popular</a>
    </li>
    <li id="tab-content-comments">
        <a href="javascript:viewTab('content-comments');">Comments</a>
    </li>
</ul>
<div id="contents-container">
    <div id="content-recent">
        <!-- Recent tab widget area -->
        <?php dynamic_sidebar('Recent Posts'); ?>
    </div>
    <div id="content-popular" style="display: none;">
        <!-- Popular tab widget area -->
        <?php dynamic_sidebar('Popular Posts'); ?>
    </div>
    <div id="content-comments" style="display: none;">
        <!-- Comments tab widget area -->
        <?php dynamic_sidebar('Recent Comments'); ?>
    </div>
</div>
```

Now you can just drop the contents for each tab in the widget area of your choice from within the WordPress admin interface, just like you would with your footer or sidebar widgets.

Figure 14-1 shows how a tabbed box can look with a few minor alterations to the preceding code.

TO TAB OR NOT TO TAB

So should you use a tabbed box or not? It all boils down to the kind of site and content you're dealing with. Most importantly, you need to make sure that the usage is intuitive and obvious for every possible kind of user. The content you hide away in tabs can't be crucial, since the visitor may not be the clicking kind. Also, content in tabs can be

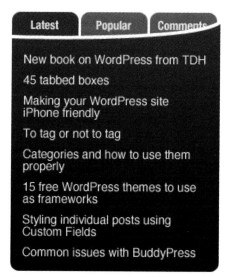

Figure 14-1: Tabbed boxes can help with organization and navigation

entirely missed when you get an accidental visitor, who scans the site briefly and then decides whether to stay and explore or move on elsewhere. You can't hide away your best stuff in tabs, just like you shouldn't make a menu or search box too obnoxious to actually use.

That being said, for a lot of sites tabbed boxes can make sense. It's all about how much space you want to free up for listings of content, activity, and other things. Is there, for example, any real reason to show your blogroll all the time? Why not put all links in one tabbed box, having a tab for your social Web profiles, another for friends' Web sites, and so on. That takes a lot less space, and anyone looking to delve deeper into your online presence or the friends and partners of a site can easily resort to using a tabbed box. The same user would also most likely appreciate the tabbed box whenever it isn't the focus of attention, since it save space and makes your site a lot easier to deal with.

Overall, you should be careful with tabbed boxes, and the same goes with tabbed menus. It is one extra click, and that can be annoying for the visitor. That being said, it's not so nice to clutter a site with lists and functions that are rarely used either, so use your best judgment.

DISPLAYING RSS FEEDS

RSS feeds are really useful not only for subscribing to updates using a feed reader, but also for displaying content from partners, or other projects you may be publishing online. You're probably already acquainted with the RSS feed widget that ships with WordPress; it can display updates from just about any working RSS feed.

When you want to work with feeds on your site you're not limited to just that widget, or even any of the available plugins. You can, in fact, tap into the feed parser directly and hence do more custom stuff with the output from the feed. If you want to output the description you can do so, just as you can add HTML code around the various elements to get more control, and so on. If you want to do more advanced stuff with content from an RSS feed you either need to rely on a plugin, or code it yourself using the built-in functionality (which, incidentally, often is what the plugin you may be considering relies on in the first place!).

One thing worth thinking about, however, is that displaying RSS feeds can slow down your site. If you're fetching the latest updates from several sites (or even just one) you'll find that your site sometimes lags behind. That's because the feed is being queried from your server, to the feed host's server, and the PHP needs to get all the data and parse it to be able to produce the output you want. This is true both for hardcoded RSS fetching, as well as if you were putting a ton of RSS widgets on your site. If you rely on a lot of feed content you should look into caching solutions to make your site as snappy as possible. In fact, ideally you'd let the server run a cronjob at regular intervals and cache the content for you to output whenever needed. There is some support for caching, but you're on your own when it comes to scheduling the content fetching. Most likely that would mean that you would have to develop your own plugin, or find one that does this already.

So, yeah, feeds are great and really useful, but if you browse the blogosphere (in particular) and pay close attention to what it is that slows down sites, you'll find that feed fetching is one of the culprits, along with other functionality that nabs content (be it badges or ads) from external services. Bottom line: make sure your site isn't too bogged down by RSS feed content.

THE BUILT-IN PARSER

WordPress includes built-in support for outputting RSS feed content on your site. You can use the feed widget (covered a bit later), but most likely you want more control than that. Luckily this is pretty easy to achieve, thanks to the addition of SimplePie in the core. That's right, there's a new feed parser in WordPress as of 2.8, which means that although your old `wp_rss()` calls may still work, they are outdated and should be changed to something more up-to-date, namely, `fetch_feed()`.

This may seem a bit daunting when you first delve into the SimplePie documentation. However, it isn't that complicated after all. Here's a simple inclusion of the latest headlines, linked, from my lifestream over at `http://stream.tdh.me`:

```
<ul>
<li><h2>Lifestream</h2></li>
<?php $feed = fetch_feed('http://stream.tdh.me');
    foreach ($feed->get_items() as $item){
        printf('<li><a href="%s">%s</a></li>', $item->get_permalink(),
           $item->get_title());
    }
?>
</ul>
```

By including the feed like this, I'm opening it up for SimplePie functions. I'm basically looping the feed here and printing it, fetching the data as I go along. In this case, I'm just pulling the permalink and the title of every post. You can expand on that by adding the description and a date:

```
<ul>
<li><h2>Lifestream</h2></li>
<?php $feed = fetch_feed('http://stream.tdh.me');
    printf($feed->get_title());
    foreach ($feed->get_items() as $item){
        printf('<li><a href="%s">%s</a></li>', $item->get_permalink(),
           $item->get_title());
        printf('<p>%s</p>', $item->get_description());
        printf('<p><small>%s</small></p>', $item->get_date('j F Y at g:i a'));
    }
?>
</ul>
```

SimplePie is worthy of a book on its own. What you need to know is available in the SimplePie documentation, which unfortunately isn't entirely compatible with WordPress since it is a stand-alone RSS parser, really. That being said, you should take a look here: `http://simplepie.org/wiki/reference/`.

We'll return to SimplePie in a little bit. But first, some words about the built-in widget solution.

WHEN TO USE THE WIDGET SOLUTION

So when would you want to use the default built-in RSS widget? The answer is simple: never! It may sound a bit harsh, especially since what the widget really does is the same as you did in the preceding section with `fetch_feed()`. That's right, the widget calls SimplePie in the same way.

The problem is, it also slaps on a feed header, linked to the feed URL and everything. That's not really such a good idea, now is it? If you want to display the latest updates from your blog, a news site, Twitter, or whatever, you don't want to link the actual RSS feed at the top of the listing! You may want to link the site itself, but not the feed. I'm hoping this is something that will be changed in WordPress in the future, but it's been around for some time now.

So should you never use a feed widget? That's taking a bit far, because others have realized this problem and released plugins that remedy the situation. Refer to Chapter 9 for some cool RSS plugins that may achieve what you're after.

In fact, hacking the RSS parsing code yourself should be avoided unless you need to do really funky stuff. It is better to add a widget area and then add an appropriate feed widget. That means you can easily add stuff around it too, but naturally you have a lot more control if you code the whole thing yourself. As is generally the case, pick the solution that fits your project.

MULTIPLE FEEDS WITH SIMPLEPIE

With the addition of SimplePie you get the power of multiple feeds, and I'm not talking about the capability to display several feed blocks on the same page. No, I mean the capability to take a bunch of feeds and then mash them together and present the content. In SimplePie, this functionality is often referred to as *multifeeds* (a useful thing to know when looking for solutions in the SimplePie documentation).

In the next example, I put SimplePie to a quick test by taking two feeds and listing them depending on date, but limiting the output to just show ten items:

277

```
<ul>
<Li><h2>Interesting Headlines</h2></li>
<?php $feed = fetch_feed( array('http://rss1.smashingmagazine.com/feed/',
'http://feeds.digg.com/digg/topic/apple/popular.rss'));
    $feed->enable_order_by_date(true);
    foreach ($feed->get_items(0, 10) as $item){
        printf('<li><a href="%s">%s</a></li>', $item->get_permalink(),
          $item->get_title());
        printf('<p><small>%s</small></p>', $item->get_date('j F Y at g:i a'));
    }
?>
</ul>
```

You're defining the two feeds in an array within `fetch_feed()` rather than just putting the single feed URL in there as you did when you just wanted a single feed output. You can add several more feeds to this in the same spirit if you want to. After that, an `order_by_date` setting is added, acquired from the SimplePie documentation:

```
$feed->enable_order_by_date(true);
```

This could just as well have been in the single feed example, but if you just output a single feed you can probably rely on the fact that the latest item will come at the top, so it would be a bit redundant.

After that there's the `foreach` loop again, starting at the first item (the 0) and moving onward to the tenth (the 10), after which the loop is over and hence you get ten items.

Again, SimplePie is huge, but this is a start at least. At the time of writing, the help section in the WordPress Codex is pretty scarcely populated given that `fetch_feed()` was added in version 2.8, but I'm sure it will be completed with more examples as time goes on. Meanwhile, turn to the SimplePie documentation for an extensive look to what you can do with this RSS parser.

SENDING E-MAIL WITH WORDPRESS

If you want to have WordPress send e-mails for you, you can use the `wp_mail()` function. This can be anything from a verification for some action that you want to confirm went through (or didn't) on your site, to building a full "My blog has been updated!" notification list.

The `wp_mail()` function is easy enough to use. This code snippet would, assuming you activate it with a function of some sort, send an e-mail to smashing@domain.com with the subject "Smashing Party!" and the content (in text format) "Thanks for the smashing party the other night. TTFN!" Figure 14-2 displays the result.

```
<?php wp_mail('smashing@domain.com', 'Smashing Party!', 'Thanks for the smashing
party the other night. TTFN!'); ?>
```

You can even attach files and send in HTML format rather than the default plain text. There's more on this in the Codex at `http://codex.wordpress.org/Function_ Reference/wp_mail`.

As always when sending e-mail from Web pages, there are a few things to observe:

- **Don't spam people.** That's bad form and evil.
- **Beware of e-mailing too much.** That can get you blacklisted.
- **Make sure your code works.** After all, an unintended hiccup can send hundreds of duplicate messages, bringing your server to its knees and getting you into all kinds of trouble.
- **Prevent exploits.** Make sure that some nasty person won't be able to spam through your e-mailing solution. It can be anything from just shooting random e-mails to the left and right, to just being a pain by pumping that submit button a thousand times.
- **Tell everything.** Users like to know what's going on, especially when there are e-mail addresses involved. In other words, be sure to explain how you will use their e-mail address and what they can expect from you. When it comes to e-mail, no surprises is a good thing.

Figure 14-2: A simple e-mail sent from WordPress

ADDING A LOGIN FORM

Sometimes it can be prudent to have the WordPress login form (Figure 14-3) a little more handy than just on its own page as it is by default (on /wp-login.php, from your WordPress install's point of view). If your site relies on user features that require logins, then naturally there is no harm in adding a login form to, say, the sidebar or the header.

Figure 14-3: A simple login form

The following example assumes you want to put the login form in the sidebar, which usually is a `ul` itself, so the code would go in a `li` of its own. However, you may want it in the header

279

instead, or someplace else, in which case you probably should put it in a `div` so you can style it accordingly. All you need for the actual login form is `wp_login_form()`.

```php
<?php if (!(current_user_can('level_0'))){ ?>
<h2>Login</h2>
<?php wp_login_form(); ?>
<p>
    Lost your password? <a href="<?php echo get_option('home'); ?>/wp-
        login.php?action=lostpassword">Recover!</a>
</p>
<?php } else { ?>
<h2>Admin</h2>
<ul>
    <li>
        <a href="<?php bloginfo('wpurl'); ?>/wp-admin/">Dashboard</a>
    </li>
    <li>
        <a href="<?php bloginfo('wpurl'); ?>/wp-admin/post-new.php">Write a
        post</a>
    </li>
    <li>
        <a href="<?php echo wp_logout_url(urlencode($_SERVER['REQUEST_URI']));
        ?>">Logout</a>
    </li>
</ul>
<?php }?>
```

What you have here is an `if` clause checking first to see if you're logged in, or rather, if you're a user of `level_0` or higher, which is the most basic WordPress user level. You may recognize it as the Subscriber role from the admin interface, which means that it can do just about nothing.

> Read up on roles in the Codex (`http://codex.wordpress.org/Roles_and_Capabilities`) and remember that there are 11 user levels; the lowest is level 0 and the highest is 10.

So the first check is to see if you're a logged-in user, basically, and if you're not the site will display the login form using `wp_login_form()`. There are some settings for the `wp_login_form()` template tags, for what labels should be called and things like that. They are straightforward enough, but you can learn more from the Codex at `http://codex.wordpress.org/Function_Reference/wp_login_form`.

Moving on, the `else` clause is what is displayed when a user is actually logged in. In this example, I output a list with a link to the Dashboard in wp-admin, along with another to the Write Post screen, and finally a logout link. This might be a bit redundant unless you have disabled the WordPress admin bar that shows up on top for logged in users. There should probably be checks to make sure you're not showing admin links to pages where the user can do nothing, like I'm doing here. After all, the Subscriber user (level 0, remember) can't write any posts, so they wouldn't be able to use a link to the Write Post screen. A check with `current_user_can()` much like the one done at first would be prudent, or a longer `if-else` logic, perhaps. Again, this is just to show the basic workings.

Remember, don't put login forms in your designs unless they serve a purpose. After all, why show off a login form and tease those nasty brute forcers to abuse your WordPress install if you don't have to. Also, there is no point in showing off a login form if the visitor can't put it to good use, as that's just poor use of screen real estate. Make the login forms count.

PRINT THAT BLOG

Sometimes readers prefer to print an article or blog entry on paper for convenience. You should make printing easy, if your site is the kind that would benefit from it.

Start with adding a simple "Print This Page" link. This is easily done with a tiny little JavaScript, no extra custom stuff or enqueuing of script libraries needed:

```
<a href="javascript:window.print()" rel="nofollow">Print This Page</a>
```

That's it; the browser will try and print the page. It's simple enough, though your site may not be all that print-friendly, especially if you have a big, fancy header and lots of columns. That's why you need to create a print stylesheet. Technically, you don't really have to add another stylesheet, but it may be a good idea to separate print-only things from the regular screen stuff.

First, create a stylesheet called print.css and look over your theme for what should or should not be included. Most likely your sidebar and footer will be unnecessary when printing, so remove them:

```
#sidebar, #footer { display:none; }
```

Gone! At least assuming that the sidebar has the ID `#sidebar`, and the footer has `#footer`, which they usually do.

Now, make sure the actual content looks decent enough on paper:

```
#content {
    width:100%;
    margin:0;
    padding:0;
    float:none;
    background: #fff;
    color: #222;
    }
a:link, a:visited { color: #000; }
```

281

Almost black text, white background, full width and no floating or weird margins or padding that will do it. I also added code to make sure that the links are black (no need for the :active or :hover pseudo-classes, obviously).

I could go on forever on stuff to put in your print stylesheet. You may want to make sure that headings look decent, and perhaps you don't want to have those 637 comments you've got on every post printed either. Just hide the elements you don't want on paper, and style the others. It is as simple as that. You may also want to set all font sizes to points (pt) rather than pixels or em, since that is talk the printer can understand. Also, speaking of printing, consider adding page-break stylings to headings, and possibly also elements like block quotes and lists. It all depends on how you want to present your site in printed form.

Right, the only thing that remains is to include the stylesheet in header.php:

```
<link type="text/css" media="print" rel="stylesheet" href="<?php
bloginfo('stylesheet_directory'); ?>/print.css" />
```

Add the stylesheet below the standard stylesheet inclusion code in the head section of the file. You may notice that I opted to use 'stylesheet_directory' rather than 'template_directory' when passing the stylesheet URL. This is purely semantic, since I imagine you'd want all your stylesheets in the same place, and hence print.css should be in the same place as style.css.

> There are several solutions for making it even easier to print your pages. One that I've found is pretty nice is Printfriendly (http://www.printfriendly.com) which lets you add buttons in a jiffy. There's also a plugin that can help out. If you want to save time, check out Printfriendly for more info, especially this page: http://www.printfriendly.com/button.

AND EVEN MORE . . .

Expanding a site with necessary functionality is a natural and obvious step in the development of a site. When it comes to WordPress, expanding a site often means that you want to show off or promote content in some way, or add possibilities for interactions, like the login form, for example.

To top this off, the next chapter shows you some more uncommon stuff that you can do with WordPress. It is not all blogs and traditional websites; after all, WordPress can do so much more. Chapter 15 is all about uncommon WordPress usage, to get your mind going with the possibilities of this fantastic publishing platform.

15 UNCOMMON WORDPRESS USAGE

YOU ALREADY KNOW that Word-Press can power blogs as well as other editorial sites. You can use it for static Web sites, newspaper or magazine-like sites, and just about anything where you are publishing text, images, or any kind of multimedia.

But why stop there? WordPress can be used for projects even further from its bloggish roots, as this chapter will show. You can build sites on top of WordPress that the developers definitely didn't have in mind from the start. Hopefully the

adaptations of the platform discussed here will help you see the full potential of the system. You'll see how WordPress can be used to create a job board or as a FAQ and/or knowledge base, how you can add a product directory, how to use WordPress for e-commerce, and a lot more. There are so many things you can do with WordPress, and hopefully this chapter will be an inspiration to you and get your brain started on what you can do with this wonderful publishing platform.

WORKING WITH USER-SUBMITTED CONTENT

Just because WordPress is great as a CMS for sites, big or small, you're not limited to using it for just that. You can have your users submit content beyond comments, and then do things with that alongside your regular content. Either you separate the user-submitted content from the rest, or you mix and match with whatever type of content you're producing yourself.

Technically you need to have your users register to submit content using WordPress' standard features. A popular theme that does that out of the box is the P2 theme, found at `http://wordpress.org/extend/themes/p2` and shown in Figure 15-1, which is inspired by Twitter and actually used for internal communication at a number of companies, Automattic included.

Figure 15-1: WPDevel, the official blog of the WordPress core development team, uses the P2 theme

To demonstrate just one of several possible ways you can work with user-submitted content, the first example in this chapter applies the concept to a job board that you could house in an existing site (with some minor tweaks), or just build as a stand-alone project.

ABOUT THE JOB BOARD

You have probably seen this kind of site already, where people and companies can post job openings or resumés. This example uses WordPress posts for storing each job offer, and for sorting them into main categories. Tags are used to pinpoint more precisely what the job is all about. You tag each post with the company that posts the opening, among other things.

So far, so good. This usage is really pretty close to what WordPress was made for, isn't it, Despite the fact that it's not a blog.

The problem comes when you want to let the parties offering jobs post their jobs themselves, so you won't have to. Granted, you can just give them each a username (and even open up the signup form), but not let them have publishing rights, but should they really be mucking about in the WordPress admin interface? I say no; that isn't a particularly clean nor user-friendly solution, since all they really want to do is to fill out a form detailing their job opening, send it in, and then have it approved by the site staff.

And that's exactly how this example works. You employ a plugin for this functionality, offering a specific page containing said job form.

In the end, what you get is a site where parties offering jobs can send them in through a form, so that they end up in WordPress as posts that the site staff will approve. Approved jobs (published posts in reality) will be sorted into categories (depending on the type of job), and tagged appropriately. You'll take as much of this data from the job submission as possible, without hacking any plugins, so anything that will not go straight in easily will have to be added manually.

The whole idea is to build this job board in a quick-and-dirty way, launch it with WordPress, and then continue to build it after launch. Time to get started.

THE CONCEPT

The actual theme code and design is less important for this project, since it will be so straight-forward. You just output the jobs in a flow of posts. You could separate them in columns or whatever if you like, but for now just a simple output will do.

In terms of template files, the example uses a specific front page loop (loop-home.php), and of course a header (header.php) and a footer (footer.php) template, respectively. And, of course, you have a stylesheet (style.css) for your specific stylings.

All listings, from category and tag listings, and things like that, can be managed from an index.php template, since it is the fallback template file for everything. You can even put the 404 error into index.php if you want to.

To get started as quickly as possible, you build this on Notes Blog, as a child theme. That's right; you won't even have to bother with the fundamental basics, just getting right into the fray. I did mention that's the beauty of child theming, right?

So what are you building? A simple job board theme that will display the latest job offerings available, as shown in Figure 15-2. It is more a concept than a finished product obviously, but should be enough to get you started.

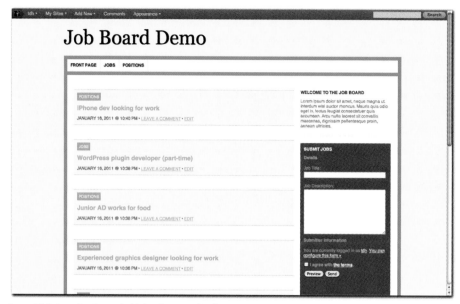

Figure 15-2: A simple Job Board added to the Notes Blog theme

The Header and Footer Templates

The default Notes Blog header.php file doesn't support custom headers as I'm writing this (although it probably will in the future), so you will most likely want to add your own header. php template file to the theme should you opt to use it. I'll leave that be here though, in the interest of saving space, and by now I'm sure you're more than capable of copy-pasting and creating your own header.php file anyway!

As for the footer, you won't alter anything there besides possibly some styles using style.css. The fact that Notes Blog footer has four widget areas by default means you can show the latest jobs there using widgetized plugins, and add graphics (using the text widget for example) for promotions. In the future you may want a more customized footer, but this will do for now.

The Front Page

To make things easy, you just create loop-home.php for the front page because that's what Notes Blog looks for first. The loop-home.php template is pretty straightforward. Add the `job-listing` parameter to `post_class()` for some custom styling. The loop doesn't output any content either, just the linked title of the actual job and some metadata that might be handy in a listing. That's basically it. This is what it looks like:

```php
<?php
    // The basic loop
    while ( have_posts() ) : the_post(); ?>

    <div id="post-<?php the_ID(); ?>" <?php post_class('job-listing'); ?>>
        <span class="meta-category-job"><?php the_category(', '); ?></span>
```

```php
            <h2 class="entry-title">
                <a href="<?php the_permalink(); ?>" title="<?php
                  the_title_attribute(); ?>" rel="bookmark">
                    <?php the_title(); ?>
                </a>
            </h2>
            <div class="job-postmeta">
                <?php the_time( __( 'F j, Y @ g:i a', 'notesblog' ) ); ?>
                <?php
                    // If the comments are open we'll need the comments template
                    if (comments_open()) { ?>
                        &bull; <span class="comments-link">
                            <?php comments_popup_link( __( 'Leave a comment',
                              'notesblog' ), __( '1 comment', 'notesblog' ),
                                __( '% comments', 'notesblog' ) ); ?>
                        </span>
                <?php } ?>
                <?php edit_post_link( __( 'Edit', 'notesblog' ), '<span
                  class="meta-sep">&bull;</span> <span class="edit-link">', '</span>'
                ); ?>
            </div>
        </div>

<?php
    // End the loop
    endwhile; ?>


<?php
    // When possible, display navigation at the top
    if ( $wp_query->max_num_pages > 1 ) : ?>
    <div id="nav-below" class="navigation">
        <div class="nav-previous">
            <?php next_posts_link( __( '<span class="meta-nav">&larr;</span>
              Older posts', 'notesblog' ) ); ?>
        </div>
        <div class="nav-next">
            <?php previous_posts_link( __( 'Newer posts <span
              class="meta-nav">&rarr;</span>', 'notesblog' ) ); ?>
        </div>
    </div>
<?php endif; ?>
```

Remember, loop-home.php will only be used when someone visits the front page of the site, so if you want other listings to look and behave the same you'll have to change those too.

Single Post View and All Those Listings

In single post view, job postings should probably be presented less like a blog post and more like an actual job offering. This isn't so different from traditional blog posts, but it is one other place where it is a good idea to debloggify the lingo. In other words, do away with everything that smells of "blog" terminology, from comments (unless you want that sort of functionality) to permalinks and category labels. Make it a page just like everything else, and then spice it up, perhaps with some elements similar to the following:

- **Related jobs** are an obvious extension to any job posting. After all, you want people to use the site.
- **Most recent updates** in each particular category can also encourage the visitor to dig deeper into the site.
- **Tags** may sound a bit bloggish in themselves, so you may consider calling them something else. Either way, showing what tags the job offering has is a way to allow the visitor to find more of the same, should a particular tag be of interest to them.
- **Contact information** is, of course, crucial for any job listing, so it should be a required field in the job postings form. Make it stand out in the listing as well; a container sporting a different background tends to do the trick.

Consult Chapter 10 for more on how to make WordPress less of a blog platform, and more like a CMS.

The same debloggifying approach applies to other listings on your site. You probably want to give the archive.php template a similar look and feel as the front page listing of jobs, for example. Just remember that archive.php is a fallback for all archives, so should you only have content other than job posts in your install you're better off working with the specific category templates. Consult Chapter 4 for more on template files and what's loaded when.

Search functionality might be a bit tricky if you're mixing job posts with traditional content. Most likely you'll want to use some conditional tags for changing the output depending on the results, but you might get away with just styling the CSS accordingly. Remember, `post_class()` outputs specific classes for each category so at minimum you could get to the specific search results that way, separating job posts from other content.

Finally, the Stylesheet

The stylesheet starts off like any other theme would, but you'll find the `'template'` reference to Notes Blog's folder since that's your template — this is a child theme after all. You're also starting off with a CSS import since the template's stylesheet will give you a good start. That is optional, however.

The rest is simple, mostly some general styling changing the Notes Blog CSS. Two things stand out. First there's the `div.job-listing` which obviously is connected to the `job-listing` parameter used with `post_class()` in loop-home.php. This way we can pinpoint the style without having to list all the categories that are job listings and should get this general treatment.

Second, under the `Hack` heading in style.css you'll find some code for the TDO Mini Forms plugin. We'll get to that in a little bit. Here's the style.css:

```
/*
Theme Name: Notes Job Board (built on Notes Blog)
Theme URI: http://notesblog.com/themes/blog/job-board/
Description: The Notes Job Board is a child theme using Notes Blog.
Version: 1.0
Tags: light, two-columns, right-sidebar, fixed-width, threaded-comments,
  sticky-post,
translation-ready, custom-background, custom-menus
Author: Thord Daniel Hedengren
Author URI: http://tdh.me/
Template: notes-blog

    Get support and services for the Notes Blog theme:
    http://notesblog.com

    Created and managed by Thord Daniel Hedengren:
    http://tdh.me

*/

@import url('../notes-blog/style.css');

div#blog { border: 10px solid #0ad; }

div#top-navigation { margin-bottom: 20px; border-color: #0ad;
  border-bottom-width: 10px; }

a:link, a:active, a:visited { color: #0cf; }
    a:hover, div#header h1 a:hover, div.homecol h1 a:hover, h2:hover { color:
  #f90; }

div.job-listing {
    padding: 10px;
    background: #effffe;
    border: 1px dotted #0ad;
    border-width: 1px 0;
    font-family: Helvetica, Arial, sans-serif;
}
    span.meta-category-job { font-size: 11px; text-transform: uppercase; }
        span.meta-category-job a {color: #fff; padding: 5px 5px 4px 5px;
            background: #f90; text-decoration: none; }
            span.meta-category-job a:hover { background: #444;; }
    div.job-listing h2 { font-size: 18px; font-weight: bold; margin: 5px 0; }
    div.job-postmeta { font-size: 12px; text-transform: uppercase; color: #666; }

div#copy { background: none; padding:0; }


/* HACK */
li#tdomf-form-1 { padding: 10px; background: #666; color: #bfbfbf;: }
    li#tdomf-form-1 a { color: #fff !important; }
```

289

```
li#tdomf-form-1 h2.widget-title { margin-bottom: 10px; color: #fff; }
li#tdomf-form-1 form input#content-title-tf, li#tdomf-form-1 form textarea
{ width: 230px !important; }
```

There you have it. You've constructed the basics of a job board! Next, you should get it some user-submitted content, or at least the functionality the board needs to receive the content.

RECEIVING THE JOBS

There are numerous ways to receive the actual content for the job listings. The easiest way would be to just have people e-mail listings to you, and you'd then put them in yourself, but that's tedious work. Better to use a plugin and have the advertisers put the data straight into a draft post that the administrators can approve.

You can use a plugin to do this, TDO Mini Forms (http://wordpress.org/extend/plugins/tdo-mini-forms/). It is by no means the only option available; another option is the excellent Gravity Forms which also features some great add-ons for premium features, but TDO Mini Forms is simple enough and also free so that you can try it out and then decide whether it will do for your needs or not.

Anyway, the only thing you're interested in at this time is a plugin that lets users, which in this case are the people either advertising for a job, or the people looking for one, to post content into WordPress that is stored in draft form in categories. So you want to build a form where you can send in the following data:

- Type of job ad (user will choose from the two categories, either Jobs Available or Looking for Work)
- Listing submitter (the post submitter will have to give a name and an e-mail, and optionally a Web page URL)
- Job post title (the intended title)
- Post text (the job post's content)
- Contact information (otherwise a job listing wouldn't do much good, now would it?)

That's it, although you may consider spam protection as well. The TDO Mini Forms plugin can handle this easily enough, but you may want to build or use other solutions.

When using TDO Mini Forms to build this solution, you can specify that the posts be saved as drafts and append the advertiser information to the post content so you won't have to create a WordPress user account for everyone posting an ad. Alternatively, you can force advertisers to register first to access the actual "post a job" page. If you do, they will use the user info from WordPress instead, and there's support for that in TDO Mini Forms. If you force advertisers to register you can easily create archives for all their posted job offerings, for example, which can be handy. It also means that you can mark some advertisers as reliable and hence bypass the administrative approval stage, publishing their ads automatically.

You can do it any way you like. The important thing is that you can get advertisers and people looking for work to post content directly into WordPress (as drafts) so you can manage the job listings easily.

FURTHER DEVELOPMENT

So where do you go from here? After all, at this stage the WordPress-powered job board is fully functional, but there's certainly room for improvement. The first things you may think of is how to charge for job listings, and how to control how long they are visible. After all, a lot of job boards out there are charging for use, and you may want that, so attaching PayPal or a similar payment service is a natural next step. Controlling how long a post is displayed can be done by running a script that automatically changes the post status from "published" to "draft," but it is probably better to just add a code snippet at the top of the post that either outputs a "this job listing is outdated" message, or even hides the job information or redirects the visitor. This can be easily done with PHP and a little use of conditional tags.

Other natural enhancements would involve more control when an advertiser submits a job listing. This may include image attachments, tagging, not to mention geographical localization. That last part can either be maintained by a custom taxonomy, or using custom fields. That way, it can easily be queried and listed for location-based job offerings. You might also want to separate the jobs from the rest of the content altogether if you're adding the job board functionality to an already active site. A custom post type for the jobs will sort that out for you easily enough; just make sure your method of collecting the jobs, such as the TDO Mini Forms in the example above, works with your own custom post types.

Sticky posts can be used to make some jobs featured, for those generous advertisers that want more exposure. You can just style the sticky posts accordingly (larger fonts, stronger colors, borders, or whatever) and let them jump to the top of the post display, which may not be so much fun in the job board example design presented here since it is based on just links in lists. Another solution would be to have a separate loop that queries just posts marked as sticky, and displays them independently. That would mean that you had full control over them, naturally.

There is no doubt that it is possible to take the job board quite a few steps further. The whole idea with this example is to show you that WordPress can be used to power such a site. Now it is up to you, or someone else, to make it grand and a killer site. Good luck!

And with that, the next section moves on to another non-bloggish concept: from job board to knowledge base. The step isn't as big as you may expect.

USING WORDPRESS AS AN FAQ-LIKE KNOWLEDGE BASE

Companies that want their very own FAQ-like knowledge base can put WordPress to good use. The concept is really quite simple, revolving around user-submitted posts as well as tagging and/or categories. Thanks to commenting there can be a conversation around an issue that a user submits, and when it is resolved the administrator can move it to the knowledge base part of the site.

Here are the key features:

- User-submitted issues using a plugin; each issue is in fact a post.
- Two main categories: The FAQ and the Knowledge Base.
- Tagging of posts (which are the issues, remember) to make keyword searching easier.
- A custom tagging taxonomy for the Knowledge Base.

The site usage flow would be as follows:

1. A user submits an issue using a form on the site. The issue is saved as a post, marked as a draft, by using a plugin.
2. An administrator publishes the issue in the FAQ category.
3. The issue can now be commented on. If an administrator answers, his comments will be highlighted, but it is possible to let anyone answer should you want that. If you turn off user comments you need to attach some way for the original submitter of the issue to ask for follow-ups without having to resubmit a new issue each time.
4. When the issue is resolved, an administrator adds the post to the Knowledge Base category.
5. All posts in the Knowledge Base category get proper tagging in the Knowledge Base Tagging custom taxonomy. This means that you can output a tag cloud (or whatever) based only on tags from within the Knowledge Base.

The point of the custom Knowledge Base Tagging taxonomy is so the users can browse issues that have been resolved to find solutions to their specific problems. It works alongside the standard tagging feature, which also includes FAQ posts and hence unresolved issues. This can also come in handy.

Finally, there's also category browsing, which means that it is really easy to create these two sections — the FAQ and the Knowledge Base — of the site.

ADDING THE FUNCTIONALITY

The actual design of the theme in the following example will be simple enough, so I'll stick to the important parts. You can build it on top of just about any theme you like. First, you need to build your new taxonomy. You can read more about that in Chapter 6; this is the code you'll be using in your functions.php file for the child theme:

```
add_action( 'init', 'kbase', 0 );

function kbase() {
    register_taxonomy( 'knowledge_base', 'post',
        array(
```

```
            'hierarchical' => false,
            'label' => 'Knowledge Base Tags',
            'query_var' => true,
            'rewrite' => true
        )
    );
}
```

That's it. Now you'll get another tag field in the WordPress admin interface to tag away on any post you like (see Figure 15-3).You will just do this on posts marked with "Knowledge Base" status, as described previously.

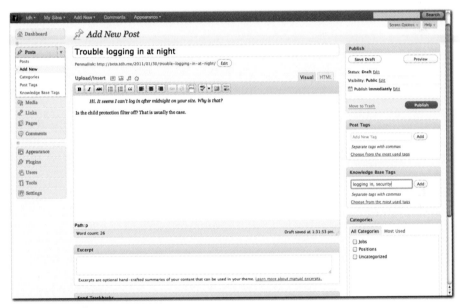

Figure 15-3: Knowledge Base tagging

With the taxonomy set up, the next step is to start receiving issues. This process was described in the job board example previously, so refer to that for various solutions. The TDO Mini Forms plugin will work for receiving issues, so you can use that, or something else if you prefer. You may want to create a home.php template for featuring the most recent submissions, additions to the Knowledge Base (which would just show the latest posts in that particular category), and also either to promote or offer the submit issue form. Personally, I'd add a huge search box as well as a tag cloud showing the hottest tags from the Knowledge Base taxonomy. The latter is done by passing the taxonomy name to wp_tag_cloud(), like this:

```php
<?php wp_tag_cloud('taxonomy=knowledge_base'); ?>
```

The taxonomy parameter reads the name, not the label, of your custom taxonomy. Style the tag cloud accordingly and you'll have a series of keywords belonging only to the Knowledge Base taxonomy, which in turn means that only issues that have been resolved will appear.

That's about it, really. By adding the submission part, along with the taxonomy, the rest is just about displaying the latest posts from each respective category, and trying to get the users to actually search for an issue before submitting it again.

FURTHER ENHANCEMENTS

While it is easy to get a FAQ/Knowledge Base site rolling on top of WordPress, there are many ways to make it better. The first step is to make sure users understand they should search and browse the site before submitting an issue, otherwise you'll likely end up with a great deal of duplication. You want your visitors to search, and that means pushing for that functionality. Unfortunately, if WordPress is weak in one area, it is search, so you may want to consider using an external service like Google Custom Search Engine (`http://google.com/cse`) or a similar variant that can be easily embedded in your site to add search functionality. There are also a bunch of plugins to enhance search, so you should play with those as well. See Chapter 9 if you don't have a favorite already.

Here are some other ideas on enhancements to this setup:

- **Registration and editing.** Let people register so that they can edit their own questions, get an author archive, and so on. You may even want to force it to make spamming a bit harder.
- **Use a custom post type.** If you need to implement this solution into an existing site, you would be well advised to use a custom post type for it instead of relying on regular posts. This method would be just as easy, as you'll see later in this chapter.
- **Grading.** Let the users grade your answers, in the comments when the post is in FAQ mode, and the actual resolution of the issue when it has moved to the Knowledge Base. In the latter case, you need a plugin that offers grading of the post rather than the comments. Chapter 9 offers some suggestions.
- **Related issues.** Expose other issues automatically by using a related posts plugin. The user may find an answer through that route.
- **Further enhance search.** With the use of JavaScript you can make it easier for users to find the answer to common issues. Use the type of search fields that ask you if you meant XYZ when you typed XPT.
- **Tweak the front page.** The better you can expose the issues, the faster the users will find them, and since that's what it's all about, you should tweak the front page as much as you possibly can.
- **Subscriptions and alerts.** Offer ways to subscribe to updates and resolved issues. There are several ways to manage this, and since WordPress has an RSS feed for just about anything, I'm sure the answer is there. Make sure your users know and understand that, so they can subscribe to things that interest them.

The knowledge base concept is another way you can use WordPress for a non-bloggy site. Another way is using WordPress to power an online store.

WORDPRESS AND E-COMMERCE

It goes without saying that WordPress can be used to sell stuff. In its simplest form you'll run a blog or traditional site with WordPress as the backend, and use your reach to sell products. You can add *affiliate links*, which basically means that whenever you link to Amazon using your affiliate URL and someone buys something, you'll get a provision. In fact, if you bought this book by following a link from any of my sites, I made a little extra. Thanks!

However, when most of us are thinking e-commerce we've got bigger things than affiliate links in mind — shopping carts, digital distribution, payment received via PayPal accounts, that sort of thing.

You can have all this for sure, and Chapter 9 includes a bunch of plugin ideas that can make such things easier to implement, from simple integrations to full shopping carts.

RUNNING A WEB SHOP ON WORDPRESS

You may be wondering if you can run a Web shop on WordPress. In short, the answer is yes; you *could* if you wanted to, and if you didn't have too many products.

The long version: it's probably not simple to implement a shopping site, but don't let that stop you since there's really no reason why it shouldn't work perfectly well if you're prepared to extend WordPress with plugins, work with custom fields, and then figure out how to connect your shopping cart with PayPal and other payment solutions.

Kind of disheartening isn't it? Relax, it's not as bad as it sounds: there are plugins out there that do most of the work for you. However, compared to the other e-commerce systems out there the available plugins are kind of bleak. It is hard to truly recommend WordPress for e-commerce other than for hobby businesses or if you're selling a small number of products.

That being said, there's nothing that's stopping you from attaching any of the various shopping cart scripts out there right into your theme. Most will probably work with minor hassle, and that would only leave you with the discomfort of figuring out how to charge for your merchandise. Luckily companies like PayPal (and many others) have made that easy, so you can certainly monetize your blog or WordPress-powered site with a shop selling your goods if you want to.

Just make sure you know what you're getting yourself into. This is sales, after all, and not the content business anymore.

SELLING DIGITAL PRODUCTS

Digital merchandise such as e-books are a completely different matter altogether. Absolutely nothing is stopping you from implementing a payment solution for a digital file, and when paid, you serve the file. In fact, it has almost nothing at all to do with WordPress since it is all about verifying that you got paid, and then directing the customer to the file in question. Adding that sort of solution to your blog is really easy if you rely on a third-party service such as E-junkie (www.e-junkie.com), for example (which will take a chunk of your processed money) to both manage payment and delivery of the files. It's just a matter of setting up a link, and then your provider will handle the rest; much like an affiliate program, but with the benefit of you getting a larger chunk of the money, it being your product and all.

You can do the same on your own as well with the necessary plugins or scripts. However, it is really hard to sidestep the fact that you need to actually charge for your products, which means handling payments. You can, theoretically, handle payments yourself as well. I advise against it, if for no other reason than the fact that people feel more secure when they recognize the party handling their money.

Digital products fit any site perfectly. While WordPress may be no Magento when it comes to e-commerce, it is fine for selling e-books, MP3s, design files, or whatever you want to make money on.

BUILDING FOR E-COMMERCE

So you've decided to use WordPress as a basis to sell products, big or small, a lot or a few, doesn't matter. Now you need to figure out how you can set it up to make it as powerful and easy to manage as possible.

While you could rely on either posts or Pages for your website, you should consider the use of custom post types. Separating the products you want to sell from the rest of the site's infrastructure might not always be necessary, but if it is, or could be in the future, then custom post types is the best solution. The next section is all about using custom post types for product-like content on just about any site.

BUILDING A PRODUCT DIRECTORY

Adding a product directory (or any kind of directory really, could just as well be real estate listings, persons, or whatever) to a WordPress site is a breeze thanks to custom post types. You want to create a new post type for your products to keep them separate from the rest of the content, whether you have just 10 products, or over 500.

The kind of information you need to store per product is obviously something unique to your offerings, so this example just shows you the basics:

- Create a custom post type called Books.
- Each individual product is actually a book of sorts, and is stored in a post-like fashion in the Books post type.
- The example includes support for categories, which in fact will be Books categories for better sorting.
- It does not support tagging (although you could).

The reason for leaving tags out is just to simplify the example. In most cases it is probably a good idea to enable tagging, since it could be used to sort by manufacturer or something like that.

Why Books, by the way? Well, I figured I might as well put this code to good use and create a Books product listing on `http://tdh.me`. It's always nice to use a live example. You can adapt this code for your own use, just like everything else in this book, and most of the stuff I write.

CREATING THE BOOKS POST TYPE

Chapter 10 covered custom post types, so if you feel uncertain what they are and how they work you should jump back and read up.

To create the Books post type, I add this code to the functions.php template file of my theme of choice:

```
register_post_type('books', array(
    'label' => __('Books'),
    'singular_label' => __('Book'),
    'public' => true,
    'show_ui' => true,
    'capability_type' => 'post',
    'hierarchical' => false,
    'taxonomies' => array('category'),
    'has_archive' => true,
    'rewrite' => array('slug' => 'books'),
    'query_var' => false,
    'supports' => array(
        'title',
        'editor',
        'author',
        'thumbnail',
        'excerpt',
        'custom-fields',
        'comments'
    )
));
```

The code is pretty straightforward, registering the post type as `'books'` and setting appropriate labels to make it look nice in the admin interface, as shown in Figure 15-4. Make the post type `public`, make it behave as a post with the `capability_type` setting, make sure it has support for categories, supports archive pages, and has a proper rewrite for nice permalinks. (That last one is the default settings but I tend to put it in anyway.) Finally, the `supports` parameter contains an array of boxes this post type will offer in the admin interface. The rest is default values; again if you need a refresher, see Chapter 10.

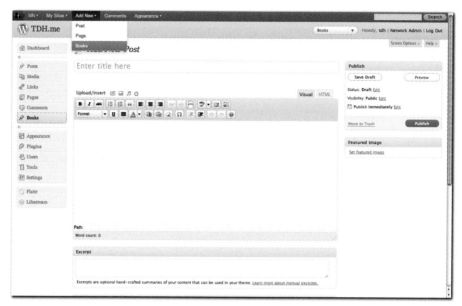

Figure 15-4: Writing a Books post

Now all I need is to add posts to the Books post type, and I have a working post type!

THE BOOKS PAGE

There are two ways to create a page containing all the products of your custom post type ('books' in this example). One way is to create a Page in WordPress, and use a Page template to add a custom loop to display the Books posts the way you want. The second method is to rely on the appropriate template file for listings. In this example I do the latter, which means I want to use archive-books.php (the archive-[post type].php file takes precedence over archive.php). I could just add a few conditional tags to archive.php or even index. php to do the same thing, but this way it's a bit cleaner.

A common issue with custom post types is the post not showing up. That's because WordPress per default won't include custom post types in the loop. If you want to output posts from a particular post type, say 'books', in a template you need to use query_posts('post_type=books') to tell WordPress to fetch it. Obviously you can add several post types together by using an array instead, so if you want 'books' and regular posts it would be:

```
query_post( 'post_type => array( 'post', 'books' ) ' )
```

Obviously you could use WP_Query as well (shown in an upcoming example) since that behaves like query_posts(). Consult the Codex for more on query_posts(): http://codex.wordpress.org/Function_Reference/query_posts.

Back to the books archive page. Since I don't have a ton of books, I want to give each book (being a post in the Books custom post type) ample space on my listings page. That means I

298

write a loop and use a custom field to show off the cover (with a fallback should there not be one yet), and then use the excerpt to catch the reader's eye. I would use the featured image feature had it not already been implemented for different purposes on the site, so a custom field with the image URL it is!

Here's my archive-books.php file:

```php
<?php get_header(); ?>

    <div id="content" class="widecolumn">
    <?php
        // The basic loop
        while ( have_posts() ) : the_post(); ?>

        <div id="post-<?php the_ID(); ?>" <?php post_class('books-archive'); ?>>
            <div class="books-cover">
                <a href="<?php the_permalink(); ?>">
                <?php
                    // Check for book cover
                    $bookscover = get_post_meta($post->ID, 'book_cover',
                        $single = true);
                    // There was one, let's output it!
                    if ($bookscover !== '') { ?>
                        <img src="<?php echo $bookscover; ?>" alt="<?php
                            the_title_attribute(); ?>" />
                <?php }
                    // No cover, show the placeholder
                    else { ?>
                        <img src="<?php bloginfo('stylesheet_directory'); ?>
                            /img/books-nocover.jpg" width="150" height="200"
                            alt="No cover available" />
                <?php }
                    // And we're done
                ?>
                </a>
            </div>
            <div class="books-content">
                <h2 class="entry-title">
                    <a href="<?php the_permalink(); ?>" title="<?php
                        the_title_attribute(); ?>" rel="bookmark">
                        <?php the_title(); ?>
                    </a>
                </h2>
                <div class="entry-summary">
                    <?php the_excerpt(); ?>
                </div>
            </div>
        </div>

    <?php
```

```php
        // End the loop
        endwhile; ?>

    <?php
        // When possible, display navigation at the top
        if ( $wp_query->max_num_pages > 1 ) : ?>
        <div id="nav-below" class="navigation">
            <div class="nav-previous">
                <?php next_posts_link( __( '<span class="meta-nav">&larr;</span>
                    Older posts', 'notesblog' ) ); ?>
            </div>
            <div class="nav-next">
                <?php previous_posts_link( __( 'Newer posts <span
                    class="meta-nav">&rarr;</span>', 'notesblog' ) ); ?>
            </div>
        </div>
    <?php endif; ?>
    </div>

<?php get_sidebar(); ?>
<?php get_footer(); ?>
```

This is a pretty ordinary loop, looking much like the one in Notes Blog (by all means back-track to Chapter 4 for a more detailed walkthrough on the code). There are just two differences worth mentioning. The first one is `post_class()`, which has gotten the parameter `books-archive`. This is used for styling; you'll see it in the stylesheet, and the only thing the parameter does is add the class `books-archive` to the output from `post_class()`.

The second thing is the check for a book cover. The code has some simple custom fields in action. First, I need to store the contents of whatever's in the key `book_cover` in `$books-cover`. Then I check if `$bookscover` contains anything, which of course means that I've stored something there — a URL for the books cover image, in fact. If `$bookscover` contains something, it will output the code, and if not, it will output a dummy image. This is a simple usage of custom fields; you could make it a lot easier on the backend by employing a plugin such as More Fields (see Chapter 9), but this will do for the example.

The styling is pretty obvious, but here it is anyway:

```css
div.books { margin: 20px 0 40px 20px; clear:both; } /* 640 px - from div.post */
div.books-archive {
    float:left;
    margin-bottom: 10px;
    padding-bottom: 10px;
    border-bottom: 1px dotted #efefef;
}
div.books-cover {
    float:left;
    width: 190px;
}
```

```
    div.books-cover img { padding: 5px; border: 1px solid #efefef; }
div.books-content {
    float: right;
    width: 440px;
}
```

This is all straightforward. It's worth noting that custom post types won't get the typical post or page classes from `post_class()`, they'll get one named after the post type instead. So in this case I've got `books` from `post_class()`, which means that I have to style that just like the post class if I want the Books posts to behave like my regular posts. In this case, that just means some margins and stuff like that. The rest should be pretty self-explanatory; you'll find the `books-archive` class here as well.

That's really all there is to it. I've managed to add a Books page, as shown in Figure 15-5, to my site, containing each book as a post in a custom post type. Now I can easily update it with new books without having to go through the hassle of editing Pages — just adding a new post to the Books post type will take care of it.

Figure 15-5: The Books page, simple and ready for some TLC

SHOWING OFF THE PRODUCTS

Posts belonging to a custom post type won't show up in the regular stream of updates per default. You can easily make it so, using `query_posts()` or `WP_Query` (which, you might recall, behaves just like `query_posts()` does), but in the case of having a products directory it doesn't make much sense. However you still need to show off your products, which you could do in a number of ways. The following sections provide a few suggestions, which can be combined.

Add a Loop

The most versatile solution for showing off your products is to add a loop outputting the content from the custom post type to your theme. It could be something like this:

```php
<ul>
<?php
        // Let's loop
        $my_query = new
          WP_Query('post_type=books&post_status=publish&posts_per_page=-1');
        while ($my_query->have_posts()) : $my_query->the_post(); ?>
        <li>
            <a href="<?php the_permalink(); ?>" title="<?php
              the_title_attribute();?>">
                    <?php the_title();?>
            </a>
        </li>
<?php endwhile; ?>
</ul>
```

You'll recognize the loop, I'm sure. This one just outputs every post in the post type `books` as a link in a list item (yes, every one; that's why `posts_per_page` is set to `-1` in `WP_Query`).

Want it to be a bit more impressive? Then why not utilize some fancy JavaScript to make a nice slider to show off your products? There are a few featured post plugins that could be used as well, if you can get them to work with a custom post type, and most likely a few plugins that just rely on whatever you put into them. Just like every other loop out there, the only limitation is your own imagination, and your skills with making it look great.

Use Graphics and Links

If you have decent product images or cool promotional material, it is probably a good idea to put them to use to get your visitors to check out your products. The easiest way to gain attention to products on most sites is to just add some linked graphics to whatever widget areas you've got (usually a sidebar), pointing your visitors to the various product pages that way.

In my case, I'm relying on this primarily from posts, but also from widget areas. This solution is most likely best suited for smaller product directories with few updates and additions, meaning that you won't need to expose so many products at the same time. If you have greater needs than this, then the loop option shown previously is probably a better option.

A Simple Menu Entry

Sometimes the best solution is the most obvious one. A menu entry pointing to your products page might not be as visual as a graphic, or as lively as a loop showing off the latest products, but it is efficient and probably something your visitors would expect. Don't forget to link your products page in your menu, if you have one!

BUILDING A LINKS SITE

A links site can be used for many purposes, so the examples in this section are a bit more generic than the previous ones. The idea is to use posts as link items, making them sortable using both categories and tags. However, you're not just going to put a link in the post field, but rather use the title field as the actual link title, and then store the target URL in a custom field. Then you can utilize the excerpt of the content field to display descriptions, details, or whatever may fit your project.

But you need to start at the beginning. These are your premises:

- Every blog post is a link in your link database.
- You use the title field to save the link title (for example, Google).
- You store the destination URL in a custom field called 'URL' (for example www.google.com).
- You categorize your links in any number of categories (for example, Search Engines or Web mail).
- You tag your links with appropriate tags (for example, free, USA, or fonts).
- You use the_excerpt() rather than the_content() for link descriptions, mostly to keep your doors open for the future.

Now you can get started. First, you store the URL in a custom field. To do so, just create a new custom field on the Write post screen in the WordPress admin interface and name it 'URL'. The idea is to put the URL in the value field for each post, and then link the title with it.

Next you need to alter your loop a bit. (For a project like this you'll probably want to design a new theme that fits the bill, but the default theme is used as an example here.)

You use the following code inside the loop:

```
<div <?php post_class(); ?> id="post-<?php the_ID(); ?>">
    <?php
        // The custom field with the URL
        $CustomField = get_post_custom_values('URL'); if (isset($CustomField[0]))
{ ?>
        <h2>
            <a href="<?php echo get_post_meta($post->ID, URL, true); ?>"
              rel="bookmark" title="<?php the_title_attribute(); ?>">
                <?php the_title(); ?>
            </a>
        </h2>
        <div class="entry">
            <?php the_excerpt(); ?>
        </div>
```

```
    <p class="postmetadata">
        Filed in <?php the_category(', ') ?> <?php the_tags('and tagged ', ',
            ', ''); ?> <small><?php the_time('F jS, Y') ?></small>
    </p>
<?php
    // No link
    } else { ?>
    <h2><del><?php the_title(); ?></del></h2>
    <div class="entry">
        <p>Sorry, this link is broken. Please tell an administrator!</p>
    </div>
        <p class="postmetadata">
            It's broken: <?php edit_post_link('Fix it!', '', ' | '); ?> Filed
            in <?php the_category(', ') ?> <?php the_tags('and tagged ', ',
                ', ''); ?> <small><?php the_time('F jS, Y') ?></small>
        </p>
    <?php } ?>
</div>
```

I know it's an ugly hack, but the concept is simple enough. Make sure that there is a URL submitted in the 'URL' custom field. That's what this line does:

```
<?php $CustomField = get_post_custom_values('URL'); if (isset($CustomField[0])) { ?>
```

If it returns true, it'll output the code you want, which contains the linked title and everything.

Next is the actual link title heading, linked to the source obviously. That was the whole point after all.

```
<h2>
    <a href="<?php echo get_post_meta($post->ID, URL, true); ?>" rel="bookmark"
        title="<?php the_title_attribute(); ?>">
            <?php the_title(); ?>
    </a>
</h2>
```

Obviously you're echoing the contents of the 'URL' custom field, which hopefully is a valid URL (there's no check for that, only whether there's something stored in there). The get_post_meta() function first asks for the post ID, then the name of the custom field (which is 'URL'), and then whether to return the content as a string or array (you want the former, hence the true value). And by echoing it, you get it in your little link, and there you go, one linked post title for you! The loop continues, and you do it all over again.

That is, unless you forget to add a URL to the custom field. Then the check mentioned above will skip to the else clause, which just outputs a struck-through post title and a message telling anyone who cares that the URL is broken. There's also an edit link added for good measure; you may want that in the successful results as well.

The rest is pretty basic, with `the_excerpt()` outputting whatever you put in the excerpt field (or the actual content should you have done this wrong), as well as categories, tags, and a date.

That's all there is to it, the basis of using WordPress as a links manager. Sure, you can refine it a bit, but mostly it is cosmetic stuff that you can tackle in your theme.

THE ALTERNATIVE: THE LINK POST FORMAT

Another option would be to use the link post format. This would be a less advanced solution than the previous one perhaps, but might be a better choice depending on what your goals are with the link directory site. The link post format fetches the first link from your post for you to play with.

To use the link post format you must enable it first, in functions.php:

```
add_theme_support( 'post-formats', array( 'link' ) );
```

You can obviously extend that array with more post formats should you want to. The beauty of post formats is that they are easy to check for. You can use the conditional tag `has_post_format()` to check for the link post format, which could be a way for alternative post stylings, of course.

```
if ( has_post_format( 'link' ) {
    echo 'Hey look, this is a link!'
}
```

If you want to use post formats you can update the code in the first example accordingly. For more on post formats, see Chapter 4.

SOME THOUGHTS ABOUT USAGE

Why should you use WordPress to power what at first looks like a simple links directory? The ease of WordPress management as well as the various feeds and sorting capabilities make the platform an excellent choice for this usage. Add the capability to let users submit their own links using plugins or by having them register, and you've got a solid basis to start from. You can even let other sites include the latest links from a certain category or tag using RSS feeds, although you'd probably want to alter the feed output so that the titles in such cases also lead to the destinations specified in the `'URL'` custom fields.

How can you put this to good use? There are obviously tons of possibilities. Niche link sites are popular, but you can take it up a notch with plugins. Why not let people vote or comment on the links, for example? That way you can spark user-contributed material and in turn put it to good use with top link lists and similar features. For a closed group this can be a great way to share resources and stories online, and it is a nice enough option for all those link directory scripts out there. After all, few platforms offer the ease of WordPress, and with the ever-present option of building new features into the site with the ease of theming and addition of plugins, there is no telling where you may end up taking a site like this.

Or you can just use it to share and save links you like, categorizing them and tagging for good measure. That's what `delicious.com` does, after all, so you can certainly put it to good use yourself.

MIXING LINKS POSTS WITH TRADITIONAL CONTENT

Maybe you want to mix this sort of linked title with your traditional content. You know, the kind of site where the post title leads to the actual post, and not elsewhere? What you're looking at, then, is something of a linking aside. In fact, this is really easy to pull off. You just reuse the code and let the custom fields content check do all the work. Something like the following code would do the trick:

```php
<div <?php post_class() ?> id="post-<?php the_ID(); ?>">
    <?php $CustomField = get_post_custom_values('URL');
    // Is there something in the URL custom field?
    if (isset($CustomField[0])) { ?>
        <div class="linkage">
            <h2>
                <a href="<?php echo get_post_meta($post->ID, URL, true); ?>"
                   rel="bookmark" title="<?php the_title_attribute(); ?>">
                    <?php the_title(); ?>
                </a>
            </h2>
            <div class="entry">
                <?php the_excerpt(); ?>
            </div>
        </div>
    <?php // Nope, nothing there - regular post!
    } else { ?>
        <h2>
            <a href="<?php the_permalink() ?>" rel="bookmark" title="Permanent
                Link to <?php the_title_attribute(); ?>">
                <?php the_title(); ?>
            </a>
        </h2>
        <small><?php the_time('F jS, Y') ?> by <?php the_author() ?></small>
        <div class="entry">
            <?php the_content('Read the rest of this entry &raquo;'); ?>
        </div>
        <p class="postmetadata">
            <?php the_tags('Tags: ', ', ', '<br />'); ?> Posted in <?php
                the_category(', ') ?> | <?php edit_post_link('Edit', '', ' | ');
                ?> <?php comments_popup_link('No Comments &#187;',
                '1 Comment &#187;', '% Comments &#187;'); ?>
        </p>
    <?php } ?>
</div>
```

There are some minor changes compared to the code used in the original example. That's because you want to actually output the posts with linked titles when there is no custom field value in `'URL'`, but when there is you do it the way you did before. This version omits some categories and stuff, and with the `div.linkage` added to make it easier to style (although you can use the `post_class()` styles for most of it).

This code will make every post with content in the `'URL'` custom field have a title linked to that URL, rather than the post itself. It is simple enough to add to any theme.

Obviously this would be a lot cleaner if you used post formats, since you could simply use `has_post_format()` and check for the link post format, as explained earlier.

So you can make a links-driven site using WordPress. How about doing a gallery? Of course.

EXPLORING THE GALLERY

Images and WordPress are a breeze these days — for most types of site, at least. The new media functionality, with the `[gallery]` shortcode makes it easy to add sets of photos. However, what do you do if you're the kind of user who wants to publish hundreds, maybe thousands of photos in the long run, and you want to have a traditional photo gallery on your site? There are photo sharing sites, of course, but sometimes you just want to roll things your way, on your own site. This is quite possible to do using WordPress.

In this example, you rely on posts and categories to create a photo gallery. First, name the photo gallery category Gallery (that makes sense, right?). You can have several categories using the same treatment, but we'll stick to one in this example.

The idea is to have each post as a photoset on its own. So your birthday bash and all the photos you snapped while blowing out candles and opening gifts would go in one post, for example, with a proper title and even tagging. Tags are great for sorting, so you can use those any way you like. If you don't want to mix photo gallery posts with regular posts, but still want to use tagging, you need to create a custom taxonomy for photo tagging. That way you won't get a mix of posts in the various tag archives.

So how would this example work? Figure 15-6 is a simple concept sketch for how the posts relate to the Gallery category,

You have a Gallery category and each post is a photoset. You can go about the actual content handling any way you like. The simplest way would be to just upload the images to the post and include them as a thumbnail gallery, using the `[gallery]` shortcode. However,

Figure 15-6: The Gallery model

you could add a description as well, perhaps as the excerpt, and then use that for browsing, feed subscriptions, and also by outputting it under `the_content()` in the theme file. Or you can just write it under the actual photo gallery; it is fine either way.

The important thing with the posts is that they always have images attached to them when in the Gallery category. When you upload images through the media manager in WordPress when writing or editing a particular post, it will get attached to that post. You need that connection both for the [gallery] shortcode and for thumbnail display on the category archive page, the Gallery section in this case.

One more thing before you get to the code. Make sure that your Media settings are suitable for your design and the Gallery section setup. Consult Chapter 13 for more on this matter, which incidentally also tackles things like styling the [gallery] shortcode and more.

THE CATEGORY TEMPLATE

At this point you have posts as photo sets, each containing at least one (but most likely more) image, and you are displaying them using the [gallery] shortcode. Next you create the Gallery section of the site using a category template file. You can tackle this in several ways, but the easiest way would be to find out the ID of the Gallery category by analyzing the URL field when editing it in the WordPress interface (see Figure 15-7).

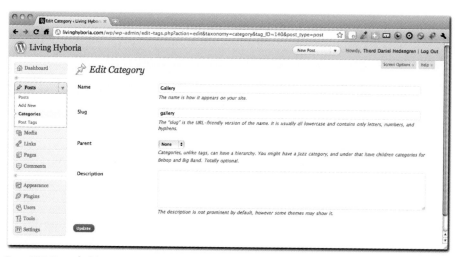

Figure 15-7: How to find the category ID

For this example assume that the Gallery category ID is 140, so your category template file will be named category-140.php.

In a Gallery section you want to display a thumbnail illustrating each photo set (which are the posts, remember?), and there are two ways to go about this. For control, you can just pick one of the thumbnails and set it as a custom field, showing that when listing the photo sets. However, that is another thing you'd have to fiddle with, so instead just pick one of the attached photos and use as illustrative thumbnail that leads into the photo set.

How you want to show off your photo sets is up to you. The code that follows is the most basic solution, just taking a traditional loop and changing how the post is displayed. Further on in this chapter we'll do some cooler stuff. Again, you may want to consult Chapter 13 for some thoughts on basic image setup before you start styling away.

```php
<?php get_header(); ?>

    <div id="content" class="widecolumn">

    <h1 class="listhead">Welcome to the <strong>Gallery</strong></h1>

    <?php if (have_posts()) : while (have_posts()) : the_post(); ?>

            <!-- Thumbnail listing -->
            <div style="padding-left:5px;">
            <?php
                $args = array(
                    'numberposts' => 1,
                    'post_type' => 'attachment',
                    'status' => 'publish',
                    'post_mime_type' => 'image',
                    'post_parent' => $post->ID
                );
                $images = &get_children($args);
                foreach ( (array) $images as $attachment_id => $attachment ) { ?>
                <div id="post-<?php the_ID(); ?>" <?php post_class('gallerypost');
    ?>>

                    <a href="<?php the_permalink() ?>" rel="bookmark"
                        title="<?php the_title_attribute(); ?>">
                        <?php echo wp_get_attachment_image($attachment_id,
                            'thumbnail', ''); ?>
                    </a>
                </div>
            <?php } ?>
            </div>
            <!-- /ends -->

        <?php endwhile; ?>

            <div class="nav widecolumn">
                <div class="left">
                    <?php next_posts_link('Previous image sets') ?>
                </div>
```

```
            <div class="right">
                <?php previous_posts_link('More recent image sets') ?>
            </div>
        </div>

    <?php else : endif; ?>

    </div>

<?php get_sidebar(); ?>
<?php get_footer(); ?>
```

What's happening here is that you rely on `get_children()` to dig out the attachments from the posts. Because the loop gives you a bunch of posts in the first place, you can rely on that to show what category you're in, for example. This is the interesting part:

```php
<?php
    $args = array(
        'numberposts' => 1,
        'post_type' => 'attachment',
        'status' => 'publish',
        'post_mime_type' => 'image',
        'post_parent' => $post->ID
    );
    $images = &get_children($args);
    foreach ( (array) $images as $attachment_id => $attachment ) { ?>
    <div id="post-<?php the_ID(); ?>" <?php post_class('gallerypost'); ?>>
        <a href="<?php the_permalink() ?>" rel="bookmark" title="<?php
          the_title_attribute(); ?>">
            <?php echo wp_get_attachment_image($attachment_id, 'thumbnail', '');
            ?>
        </a>
    </div>
<?php } ?>
```

The arguments passed to `get_children()` tell it to just get one image per loop, set with the `'numberposts'` value, since you don't want to output all attachments on a per-post basis, but only show one image, and a thumbnail at that. You just want attachments, you want them to be published, you're forcing them to be images via the `'post_mime_type'` since videos won't fit here for example, and finally you want the actual post to be the parent. All this is stored in `$args` via the array.

All this is loaded into `get_children()` and then associated with `$images`, which you use in the array in the `foreach` below. That one will only run once in this case, since you just want one image per attachment to associate with the actual post.

It's all downhill from there, with a `div` passing a special class through `post_class()` to make the styling a little easier. The `wp_get_attachment_image()` echoes the image belonging to the attachment ID you got from the `foreach` above, and then outputs the thumbnail version. The last parameter that isn't passed is for outputting media icons, which you don't want. So what you get is the thumbnail, linked to the post (see Figure 15-8).

Figure 15-8: Thumbnail view

Image courtesy of http://livinghyboria.com

You need some styling to make this look half decent. This is what I used on the Living Hyboria site (`http://livinghyboria.com`) from which I took this code snippet:

```
div.gallerypost { float:left; margin: 0 0 10px 10px; padding: 10px;
   background: #e8e8e8; }
      div.gallerypost:hover { background: #800; }
      div.gallerypost img.attachment-thumbnail { width: 120px; height: 120px; }
```

Remember that you may want to change the number of posts displayed if you're just outputting a bunch of thumbnails. Your default 10 posts per page will probably look a little bleak, so you may be better off going with something like 40, using `query_posts()` just before the loop:

```php
<?php
   query_posts($query_string . '&posts_per_page=40');
   if (have_posts()) : while (have_posts()) : the_post();
?>
```

Say you want to add a short description to each photo set (again, that's a post) and list the whole thing with the thumbnail to the left, and the description to the right. The following example makes the thumbnail clickable, as well as the title, which is shown above the description. The code even includes the tags, because I like tagging. The code resides in the same template as the previous example, so the altered code within the loop is shown here:

```php
<div id="post-<?php the_ID(); ?>" <?php post_class('gallerylisting'); ?>>
<?php
    $args = array(
        'numberposts' => 1,
        'post_type' => 'attachment',
        'status' => 'publish',
        'post_mime_type' => 'image',
        'post_parent' => $post->ID
    );
    $images = &get_children($args);
    foreach ( (array) $images as $attachment_id => $attachment ) { ?>
        <div class="gallerylisting-thumb">
            <a href="<?php the_permalink() ?>" rel="bookmark"
                title="<?php the_title_attribute(); ?>">
                    <?php echo wp_get_attachment_image($attachment_id, 'thumbnail',
                        ''); ?>
            </a>
        </div>
        <div class="gallerylisting-desc">
            <h2>
                <a href="<?php the_permalink() ?>" rel="bookmark" title="<?php
                    the_title_attribute(); ?>">
                        <?php the_title(); ?>
                </a>
            </h2>
            <?php the_excerpt(); ?>
            <div class="postmeta"><span class="tags">
                <?php the_tags('Tagged with ',', ',''); ?>
            </span></div>
        </div>
<?php } ?>
</div>
```

In this code, you're outputting the thumbnail in the same way as you did before. You're also getting the_title() and linking it, and the description is fetched using the_excerpt(), which means that you can offer that to people subscribing to a Gallery RSS feed, for example. This solution, illustrated in Figure 15-9, gives a better overview than just spitting out a thumbnail in a grid on a per-photoset basis.

ABOUT THE PHOTOSETS

Each post is a photoset in this setup, containing all the images displayed in thumbnail gallery view using the [gallery] shortcode. Because images uploaded to a particular post are treated as attachments, you can browse to the attachment page (if you choose to link from the [gallery] shortcode output that way) and see the individual image, with a permalink and all.

Figure 15-9: Simple thumbnail and description listing

Image courtesy of http://livinghyboria.com

You will probably have to style the single post view to properly fit your photosets. There are several ways to do this, and perhaps the `post_class()` output will be enough. If you want to output, say, `the_excerpt()` under the gallery, you have to add that. You can do so easily by adding a conditional tag that checks if it is that particular category; if it returns `true` it will output `the_excerpt()`, otherwise it won't.

```php
<?php if (is_category('gallery')) {
    the_excerpt();
} ?>
```

You can also add a template file for attachments (attachment.php, or image.php if you want to dig down deep) and style that accordingly. That would make it a lot easier to add back and forth links, as well as a link back to the original photoset. This is covered in more detail in Chapter 13, so consult that for more on working with actual images.

Another factor to consider is whether each image should offer the commenting functionality. Since each attachment is really a post with a different classification, this functionality will work. It also means that numerous plugins will work, including grading plugins, so why not let people add a grade to your images? There are a lot of possibilities here.

One of those possibilities is to bypass the attachment page entirely, by using an alternate way of displaying images. This usually means a lightbox effect. That too is discussed in Chapter 13, so turn there, and to Chapter 9 for plugins that help you implement the display technique.

No matter how you decide to display the photosets and the actual photos, you're probably wise to style them a little bit differently than any ordinary posts you may have. It is always a good thing when the visitor knows where they are on a site.

OTHER USES

The preceding examples focused on adding a gallery section to just about any site that publishes a lot of images. It can be your personal blog or a newspaper site covering an event; galleries have their place whenever there are a lot of images involved. Since WordPress supports including galleries across posts as well, with a tiny little addition to the [gallery] shortcode, it is relatively easy to first create a photoset post in the Gallery category, and then include that particular gallery using the [gallery] shortcode and the post identifier. All you have to do is pass the post ID to the [gallery] shortcode, like this: [gallery id="952"]. That would output a thumbnail gallery just as if you just passing [gallery] on the post with the particular ID.

There is absolutely nothing that stops a site from expanding on the gallery functionality, involving more categories and, as mentioned at the start in this section, custom taxonomies for more sorting options. In fact, adding a separate taxonomy for tagging photos can be a really good idea if you're not too keen on mixing regular content results with photos. Chapter 6 tells you all you need to know about creating your own taxonomies.

Finally, there's the possibility that the galleries you publish are in fact the main content of your site. There is certainly no shortage of design galleries out there, featuring great CSS-based designs, or WordPress themes (or whatever, really). You can build that kind of site on these premises, and even add a voting element thanks to the numerous available plugins. Since attachments are posts, just about anything you can do with a post can be accessed when viewing an image in attachment view. Naturally, it won't work as well when using lightbox overlays or similar tools.

If you were to build an image gallery you'd probably bypass the whole custom code part for a specific category, and instead make it the default way to output posts. A blog/news part of such a site would be the anomaly, so that would get the custom treatment rather than the other way around. You can categorize or tag any way you like, and put the_excerpt() to good use just as you did in the description example among the gallery template file code snippets. It would, in fact, be really easy to take this concept to the front page should you want to display a thumbnail.

WHAT ABOUT THE FEATURED IMAGES?

Depending on what kind of site you're building, you might want to use featured images to represent the gallery instead of just pulling a thumbnail as in the preceding example. In fact, if galleries are the only thing you publish that might even be the better solution since it is easier to maintain control over what shows up. However, most sites have a plethora of content and chances are that you don't want to limit the featured images to the galleries. Then pulling a thumbnail is a great solution.

THE GALLERY POST FORMAT

Another thing worth keeping in mind is the Gallery post format. If you enable it (see Chapter 6) you can not only style your gallery posts even more thanks to the new class outputted by `post_class()`, you can also check for it using conditional tags (`has_post_format()` springs to mind). This is definitely worth considering, especially if your site is relatively streamlined, where everything really belongs to the same main category content-wise, and all you really want to do is style it according to what's in the post. Post formats are a great way to get control over the content without splitting it up in an too many categories. Use them wisely.

SHORT AND SWEET: OTHER USES FOR WORDPRESS

You can do just about anything with WordPress if you put your mind to it. Here are some final sparks to keep those gears grinding.

EVENT PAGE AND CALENDAR

Because it is so easy to roll out a WordPress website, it has become a pretty popular platform for building event websites. You can easily sort out things like speakers and workshops with custom post types, while keeping the informational pages as Pages, and the blog is obviously just your regular posts. This kind of setup is really easy to work with, making it a popular choice.

The big decision with an event site comes with the schedule and the sign up functionality. A schedule could be managed by a hosted calendar service, but there are also several calendar plugins available that might fit your needs. As for the signup, there are numerous Web services that offer all-in-one solutions, from signup to payment, which is handy. For even more functionality, take look at plugins like wp-eCommerce and the various shopping carts available; they have been used for everything from WordCamps to smaller happenings and might suit you better.

INTRANETS AND COLLABORATION

WordPress is easy to work with as an author, as you no doubt know. That makes it well suited for intranets where teams need to communicate across the organization as well as with each other. Whether it is just an informal blog to keep everyone within the company in the loop, or a major collaborative source of information during projects, the ease of use that WordPress offers makes it a great choice. To get the full power of larger intranets, you might need to push WordPress a bit further with additional plugins and other tools to make it speak to all the other systems on the intranet.

If you need a more collaborative group blog, take a look at the P2 theme (`http://wordpress.org/extend/themes/p2`), a Twitter-like theme where the users can post both short and long updates from the front-end. Some companies rely on this type of setup for internal communication, either within a closed intranet or by using a plugin to keep everything private.

While WordPress isn't a wiki, there are some plugins that can add that type of functionality as well. Whether WordPress is the best fit for your intranet all depends on your needs; for blog-like communication it is obviously a no-brainer, but for other uses you should assess the needs of the company and take it from there.

COMMUNITIES AND FORUMS

With the advent of the BuddyPress plugin (http://buddypress.org), WordPress has become a viable option for communities. Thanks to BuddyPress it is now easier than ever to create a members-driven website, to get users to communicate in groups, and even extend WordPress to blog hosting and forums should you choose. What's even better is that just about any WordPress site can be extended with the BuddyPress functionality thanks to the BuddyPress template pack (http://wordpress.org/extend/plugins/bp-template-pack/), a plugin that helps you BuddyPress-ify your theme.

For forums, BuddyPress ships with a version of bbPress (http://bbpress.org). The future of bbPress is a bit uncertain, but chances are that by the time you read this it is not a stand-alone forum system anymore, but a plugin for WordPress. That is certainly an interesting thought. There are other forum plugins as well, but you should definitely look into how well they handle traffic and heavy load. Should those solutions not fit your needs, you can always turn to external forum systems such as Vanilla (http://vanillaforums.org/), which integrates nicely with the WordPress user database should you want to.

There is no doubt that a lot is going on with the WordPress platform when it comes to extended membership functionality (there are a ton of plugins just for membership) and community features.

DATABASES

Everything changed with custom post types. The fact that you can add several new top layers of content management with a few lines of code makes WordPress extremely versatile. That also means that you can build extensive databases with whatever information you choose with WordPress in the middle, possibly just acting as a user interface. Add the fact that you've got RSS feeds for just about everything in WordPress, and you've got a platform that can distribute its updates to other systems easily enough.

It's daring to say so, but custom post types really make the possibilities seem almost endless. We've come a long way from posts and Pages, haven't we?

STATIC SITES

There are still static websites out there, sites that don't feature news or frequent updates. Why should you use WordPress to power such a site? Isn't it easier to just hack the HTML files and be done with it? A bit, perhaps, but if you're doing this static site for a friend or client, then it can certainly save you a lot of headache if you build it upon WordPress. Maybe it is all Pages, no posts or categories or custom stuff, just a handful of simple pages telling the visitor whatever message it is that the site wants to deliver. If you use WordPress for this, then anyone with half a brain can update these pages. No need to call you just because that corner shop has new holiday hours, or to bother you with adding another simple page about the new office in the town down the road.

Simple static sites powered by WordPress might take a little bit longer to develop, but they can save you a lot of annoying edits in the long run. Perhaps that's not what you want if you bill your clients by the hour, but do them (and yourself) the favor of delivering the best possible product from the start. You'll feel better about it, I'm sure.

YOU CAN BUILD ANYTHING YOU WANT

Well, maybe not anything — even WordPress has limits — but just about. WordPress is an extremely versatile platform and most content-based sites online will work perfectly well with minimal customization work to the system. Thanks to the flexibility of themes and the extensibility offered by plugins, you can really do just about anything with WordPress. The whole idea behind this chapter is to get you thinking along those lines. Whenever I start thinking about a new project, be it a personal site or something for a client, I turn and twist the concept in my head to figure out how to make it happen in as short a time as possible. More often than not, WordPress is the solution to achieving this.

While you may not be able to build everything with WordPress, you'll find that most of your ideas are realizable with this lovely platform.

Index